How to Read Literature Like a Professor

ALSO BY THOMAS C. FOSTER

Twenty-Five Books That Shaped America

How to Read Novels Like a Professor

How to Read Literature Like a Professor

*A Lively and Entertaining Guide
to Reading Between the Lines*

Thomas C. Foster

HARPER LUXE

An Imprint of HarperCollinsPublishers

The excerpts from James Joyce's "The Dead" are reprinted from *Dubliners,* The Modern Library, 1969.

Katherine Mansfield's "The Garden Party" is reprinted from *The Garden Party and Other Stories,* Alfred A. Knopf, 1922.

The excerpt from Elizabeth Bishop's "The Fish" is reprinted by permission of Farrar, Straus and Giroux, Inc.

The excerpt from T. S. Eliot's *The Waste Land* is reprinted by permission of Faber and Faber, Ltd.

First Harper paperback edition published 2003. Revised edition published by Harper Perennial in 2014.

HarperCollins books may be purchased for educational, business, or sales promotional use. For information, please e-mail the Special Markets Department at SPsales@harpercollins.com.

FIRST HARPERLUXE EDITION

HarperLuxe™ is a trademark of HarperCollins Publishers

Library of Congress Cataloging-in-Publication Data is available upon request.

ISBN: 978-0-06-232652-2

14 ID/RRD 10 9 8 7 6 5 4 3 2 1

For my sons, Robert and Nathan

Contents

Preface

The amazing thing about books is how they have lives of their own. Writers think they know their business when they sit down to compose a new work, and I suppose they do, right up to the moment when the last piece of punctuation gets planted on the final sentence. More often than not, that punctuation is a period. It should be a question mark, though, because what occurs from then on is anybody's guess.

The classic example is the writer whose best book goes *thud* upon release. Think Herman Melville or F. Scott Fitzgerald. Melville must have thought, after finding large readerships for earlier novels, that the crazed search for the white whale would be a smash. It wasn't. Nor was Fitzgerald's tale of a romantic dreamer trying to rewrite his past. *The Great Gatsby* is so much subtler, so much more insightful about human nature and its historical moment, than his earlier books that it is almost inconceivable that his huge audience turned away. On the other hand, maybe that is why it turned away. Successfully predicting the coming calamity looks a lot like an excess of gloominess—until the disaster arrives. Humankind, observed Fitzgerald's contemporary T. S. Eliot, cannot bear too much reality. In any case, Fitzgerald lived only long enough to see his books largely out of print, his royalties nonexistent. It would take another generation for the world to discover how great *Gatsby* truly is, three or four times that for *Moby-Dick* to be recognized as a masterpiece.

There are also tales, of course, of unexpected bestsellers that go on and on, as well as flashes in the pan that flare up but then die out without a trace. But it's the Moby-Gatsby kind of story that compels our attention. If you want to know what the world thinks about a writer and her work, check back with us in, oh, two hundred years or so.

Not all stories of publication switchbacks are so stark. We all hope to find an audience—any audience—and we believe we have some idea who that will be. Sometimes we're right, sometimes we're all wet. What follows is a confession of sorts.

The customary acknowledgments and thanks are typically placed at the back of the book. I wish, however, to recognize one special debt of gratitude to a group whose assistance has been monumental. Indeed, without them, this revision would not have been possible. A dozen or so years ago when I was drafting the original, I was pretty clear on the audience for my book. She was a thirty-seven-year-old returning student, probably divorced, probably a nurse forced back to coursework by changes in the licensure rules of the profession. Faced with the prospect of obtaining a bachelor's degree, she chose to follow her heart this time around and pursue a degree in English. She had always been a serious reader, but she had felt that she was missing something in her experience of literature, some deep secret her teachers had known but not imparted to her.

You think I'm kidding, right? I'm not. Teaching at a branch campus of a famous university, I meet her, or her male equivalent, the guy (usually, although there are women as well) laid off from the assembly line at General Motors, again and again. And again. One of the great things about teaching at the University of Michigan–Flint, as opposed to the University of Michigan, is ceaseless contact with adult learners, many of whom hunger for more learning. I also have plenty of the typical-college-student type, but the nontraditional students have taught me a few things. First, never assume anything about background experience. I've had students who have read all of Joyce or Faulkner or Hemingway, and one who had read more Czech novels than I could ever hope to get through, as well as students who had read pretty much only Stephen King or Danielle Steel. There have been Hitchcock fanatics and devotees of Bergman and Fellini, and others who thought *Dallas* was high art. And you can never tell which will be which.

Second, explain yourself. They expect, and are sometimes more vocal about it than their younger classmates, to see how the trick is done. Whether they think I am the high priest or the high charlatan, they want to know how the magic works, how I arrive at my sometimes idiosyncratic readings.

And third, teach precepts, then stand aside. Once I show these older students how I work with texts, I get out of the way. This is not because of the wonders of my approach or my teaching; chiefly, what happens is that I validate something about their own way of reading that gives them permission to run free, and run they do. Younger students do, too, but they are often more inhibited, having spent their whole lives inside classrooms. There's nothing like being out on your own to make you intellectually self-reliant.

Are these older students all geniuses? No, although a few might be. Nor are they all closet intellectuals, although more than a few are—you know, the sort who get nicknamed "Professor" because they're seen reading books on their lunch break. But however smart they may be, they push me and school me even as I do the same to them. So I figured there must be others out there like them. And it was for that group that I wrote this book.

Boy, was I wrong. I was right, too. I have heard from quite a lot of mature readers, some of whom fit the above descriptions, others who had been English majors in college but who had been left with the feeling that something was missing, that some key element of literary study had passed them by. I would receive the occasional e-mail from such readers. Then, about two years in, the nature of those missives changed. I started hearing from English teachers. Not often, but every once in a while. And about six months after that, I started hearing from high school students. The teachers were uniformly glowing in their praise, the students mostly so. With just enough hate mail to make it clear that this wasn't a put-up job. One student said, in one of the more printable messages, "I don't know what the big deal is. Everything in your book I learned in ninth grade." I told her I would like to shake her ninth-grade teacher's hand. And no refunds. It was also at about this time that I heard indirectly that the book was being discussed on a site for Advanced Placement English teachers.

In the years since, I have been blessed to have contact with teachers and students from around the country. There have been all sorts of inquiries, from "What did you mean by X?" to "Can I apply this notion to that book that you didn't discuss?" to "Can you look over my thesis sentence (or my whole paper)?" The first two are great, the latter less so, since it puts me in an awkward ethical position. Even so, it is flattering that students trust a complete stranger enough to ask such questions.

I have also had plenty of direct interaction. I go into several classrooms a year to talk with classes about the book and how they're using it. These visits are a lot of fun and almost always involve a great question or two. Needless to say, the in-person visits are largely limited to places I can drive in a few hours, although I did once go as far afield as Fort Thomas, Kentucky. I have also, thanks to the wonders of the digital age, been able to engage with students electronically. Diane Burrowes, the queen of academic marketing at HarperCollins, stays up nights thinking of new and strange ways to get me, or at least a digital version thereof, into classrooms from New Jersey and Virginia to Flagstaff, Arizona. And of course the development of platforms like Skype has made such visits almost commonplace.

What has struck me most in the ensuing years is the endless inventiveness of secondary English teachers in general and AP teachers in particular. They have figured out ways to use this book that would never have occurred to me if I taught for a thousand years. In one class, each student is assigned as the keeper of a chapter; if Sam is in charge of rain and snow, he makes a poster explaining the significant elements of the chapter, and whenever the reading involves precipitation, Sam is prepared to discuss its implications. I suspect Sam got a raw deal and has to work harder than almost anyone else, but maybe he likes being busy. In another class, students work in groups to make short movies, and every movie must incorporate at least one concept from the book. At the end of the year, they have a mock-Oscar ceremony, complete with tuxedos and statuettes (used sports trophies, I'm told). Now that's just brilliant. What I like best about many of the schemes is the degree of student autonomy built into them. I suspect that one of the appealing elements of the book is that it lacks the apparatus of a textbook, which allows teachers to make of it what they will—and they make many different things of it. In turn, many of them pass that open-endedness along to their students, permitting them to be creative with the text and their own insights.

Is that the key to the book's popularity among teachers? I don't know. I was amazed when I first heard that it was being adopted for courses, my thoughts revolving around the utter absence of academic trappings (things like notes, glosses, and questions at the end of chapters, which, by the way, I've always hated) and the scattershot organization. I grouped the discussions in a way that felt right to me, but that's not the same as making sense for classroom use. Indeed, I am not sure what would make sense in a classroom setting, since I have never, and would never, use the book in a course. How's that for a confession? It is not an excess of modesty, a thing of which I have never been accused, that prevents my using it. The reason is more practical. This book contains most of my literary insights and all my jokes. If I assigned it, I would have nothing left to do. The goal of education, as I see it, is to bring students to the point where they no longer need you—in essence, to put yourself out of a job . . . but that retirement would be a little more sudden than I'd prefer.

So when I heard that teachers were assigning the book as summer reading, I was more than a little astonished. That it has found a home in high schools is testament to the creativity and intelligence of secondary teachers of English. They're working at a time when, we're told, no one reads anymore, yet they somehow manage to inspire a love of reading among their students. They work incredibly hard, grading work by as many as 150 students at a time, a load that just thinking about would make most university professors woozy. They get far too little respect and not nearly enough pay for doing a remarkable job. One of my more waggish colleagues, noting my frequent visits to secondary classes, says that I could have my pick of any high school teaching job in America. He's wrong, of course. I couldn't keep up with the people already there.

To the English teachers who have made *How to Read Literature Like a Professor* a success, I can offer only my profound gratitude. That this book is even in print, much less in the process of being revised, is all your fault. I can't thank each of you individually, but I would like to thank some representative members of the tribe: Joyce Haner (now retired) of Okemos High School (Michigan), for many late-night discussions at, of all places, softball team parties, as well as for being my first welcomer among Michigan teachers; Amy Anderson and Bill Spruytte of Lapeer East High School (Michigan); Stacey Turczyn of Powers Catholic High School in Flint; and Gini Wozny of Academy of the Redwoods in Eureka, California, all of whom sent their—and their students'—recommendations and suggestions for the new edition. Literally dozens of others have offered suggestions in person or via e-mail over the years, and to each of you, many, many thanks. What you do is far more important than any book.

The changes to this edition are modest but, I hope, significant. Most significant, to my troubled mind, is that I was able to remove or correct two or three howling blunders. No, I won't tell you what they were. It's bad enough I've had to live with them, so I certainly won't broadcast my folly. And there are quite a few fit-and-finish issues I was able to resolve, little matters of grammar and orthography—needless repetitions of words or phrases, an unhappy word choice here or there, the usual niggling matters that make it so hard to read one's own work and that make one think, "Surely I could have done better than *that*." But there are also matters of substance. The chapter on sonnet shape was generally deemed not to fit the rest of the volume. It's about form and structure, really, when the rest of the book is about figurative meaning and the way meaning deflects from one object or action or event at the surface level to something else on another. If, like me, you always liked that chapter, fear not. I'm planning a discussion of poetry, quite possibly in e-book form, so that chapter may reappear in a couple of years. The chapters on illness, heart and otherwise, have been shortened and run together; it felt as if the text was straining for length there.

In their place, I added a chapter on characterization and on why being buddies with protagonists is so bad for the health of second fiddles. There's also a new discussion on public versus private symbols. One of the central precepts of the book is that there is a universal grammar of figurative imagery, that in fact images and symbols gain much of their power from repetition and reinterpretation. Naturally, however, writers are always inventing new metaphors and symbols that sometimes recur throughout their work, or that show up once and are never heard from again. In either case, we need a strategy for dealing with these anomalies, so I try to oblige.

I have also included, as a path toward increased analytical confidence, a meditation on taking charge of one's own reading experience, of understanding the reader's importance in the creation of literary meaning.

It's surprising to me how, even as they actively create readings of their own, students and other readers can still maintain an essentially passive view of experiencing texts. It's high time they gave themselves more credit.

Of course, literature is a moving target, and thousands upon thousands of books have been published in the decade or so since the book appeared. While there is no need to overhaul the references and examples from edition to edition, I have used a few illustrations from more recent publications. There have been some terrific developments in poetry, fiction, and creative nonfiction in the last few years, even for those of us who are not enthralled by teenage vampires or Jane Austen's novels beset by monsters and parasitic adaptations. *Mr. Darcy's Second Cousin's Wife Gets a Hangnail.* That sort of thing. Against those trends, however, we can set the appearance of talented newcomers as well as work by established masters in the various genres, writers as diverse and interesting as Zadie Smith, Monica Ali, Jess Walter, Colum McCann, Colm Tóibín, Margaret Atwood, Thomas Pynchon, Emma Donoghue, Lloyd Jones, Adam Foulds, Orhan Pamuk, Téa Obreht, and Audrey Niffenegger. And that's just the fiction writers. There have been startling new finds and painful losses. We sometimes hear of the death of literature or of this or that genre (the novel is a favorite whipping boy), but literature doesn't die, just as it doesn't "progress" or "decay." It expands, it increases. When we feel that it has become stagnant or stale, that usually just means we ourselves are not paying sufficient attention. Whether it's the untold story of a famous writer's wife or the racial newcomers to a changing Britain or America or a boy in a lifeboat with a tiger or a tiger in a Balkan village or a man on a wire between the Twin Towers, new tales, as well as old tales with new wrinkles, continue to be told. Makes you want to keep getting up in the morning just to see what happens next.

While we're on the subject of thanksgiving, I would like to express my gratitude to a critically important population. Every time I meet with students, I am inspired. In the course of my work, naturally I deal with college students, both undergraduate and graduate, on a frequent basis, and those interactions have been rich, full, frustrating, uplifting, disappointing, and sometimes downright miraculous. English majors form a large portion of that group, but thanks to the wonders of general education requirements, I have had a great deal of contact with majors in other fields (biologists are a special favorite), and they inevitably bring different skill sets, different attitudes, and different questions to the table. They make me pay attention.

I have also, for the last ten years or so, had frequent contact with high school students, an experience I wish everyone could have—not merely high-school-age young people, but teenagers in their capacity as students. A great deal has been written and said about this group, most of it negative—they don't read, can't write, don't care about the world around them, don't know anything about history or science or politics or, well, you name it. In other words, the same things that have been said about teenagers since I was one. And for a long time before that. I'm pretty sure that one day we will unearth a clay tablet or a papyrus scroll with those exact sentiments expressed. I'm sure some of it is true, that some of it has always been true. But here's what I know, from my dealings in person and via e-mail, about high school students. They are thoughtful, interested and interesting, curious, rebellious, forward-looking, ambitious, and hardworking. When faced with the choice, many opt for the heavier workload and higher demands of AP classes, even though they could slide through something easier. They are readers. Many read—and some read a huge amount—beyond the syllabus. They write. More than a few aspire to write professionally. When told that it is nearly impossible to make a living as a writer and likely to get even harder, they still aspire to be writers. I know this from all the questions I field and the conversations we have together. And as long as there are young people who are interested in language, in story, in poetry, in writing, there will be literature. It may move into digital realms, it may return to hand-made manuscripts, it may take form in graphic novels or on screens, but it will continue to be created. And read.

A couple of years ago, I gave a talk and reading in Grand Rapids. Students from a local district came to the event to get me to sign books. Not the book that had just been published, but the one they had been assigned the previous year in tenth grade. This book. Now, lest you misunderstand, this event was after the school year, so there was no extra credit on offer. They were there because they loved their English class, which really means they loved the teacher who made the class great, and because the book was written by someone who was (a) in Michigan, (b) coming to their town, and (c) not dead. That last part made me a rarity in their school reading. The books were used. Hard used, lots of underlinings and broken spines and dog-eared covers. A couple seemed to have met a bulldozer. Several of the kids said a variation of the following statement, which I get with some frequency, "My heart sank when I saw that a book on reading was assigned, but it turned out to be pretty cool/not so bad/all right." And they thanked me. *They* thanked me. I nearly wept.

Faced with all that, how could I be anything but grateful?

Introduction
How'd He Do That?

M r. Lindner? That milquetoast?
Right. Mr. Lindner the milquetoast. So what did you think the devil would look like? If he were red with a tail, horns, and cloven hooves, any fool could say no.

The class and I are discussing Lorraine Hansberry's *A Raisin in the Sun* (1959), one of the great plays of the American theater. The incredulous questions have come, as they often do, in response to my innocent suggestion that Mr. Lindner is the devil. The Youngers, an African American family in Chicago, have made a down payment on a house in an all-white neighborhood. Mr. Lindner, a meekly apologetic little man, has been dispatched from the neighborhood association, check in hand, to buy out the family's claim on the house.

At first, Walter Lee Younger, the protagonist, confidently turns down the offer, believing that the family's money (in the form of a life insurance payment after his father's recent death) is secure. Shortly afterward, however, he discovers that two-thirds of that money has been stolen. All of a sudden the previously insulting offer comes to look like his financial salvation.

Bargains with the devil go back a long way in Western culture. In all the versions of the Faust legend, which is the dominant form of this type of story, the hero is offered something he desperately wants—power or knowledge or a fastball that will beat the Yankees—and all he has to give up is his soul. This pattern holds from the Elizabethan Christopher Marlowe's *Dr. Faustus* through the nineteenth-century Johann Wolfgang von Goethe's *Faust* to the twentieth century's Stephen Vincent Benét's "The Devil and Daniel Webster" and *Damn Yankees.* In Hansberry's version, when Mr. Lindner makes his offer, he doesn't demand Walter Lee's soul; in fact, he doesn't even know that he's demanding it. He is, though. Walter Lee can be rescued from the monetary crisis he has brought upon the family; all he has to do is admit that he's not the equal of the white residents who don't want him moving in, that his pride and self-respect, his *identity,* can be bought. If that's not selling your soul, then what is it?

The chief difference between Hansberry's version of the Faustian bargain and others is that Walter Lee ultimately resists the satanic temptation. Previous versions have been either tragic or comic depending on whether the devil successfully collects the soul at the end of the work. Here, the protagonist psychologically makes the deal but then looks at himself and at the true cost and recovers in time to reject the devil's—Mr. Lindner's—offer. The resulting play, for all its tears and anguish, is structurally comic—the tragic downfall threatened but avoided—and Walter Lee grows to heroic stature in wrestling with his own demons as well as the external one, Lindner, and coming through without falling.

A moment occurs in this exchange between professor and student when each of us adopts a look. My look says, "What, you don't get it?" Theirs says, "We don't get it. And we think you're making it up." We're having a communication problem. Basically, we've all read the same story, but we haven't used the same analytical apparatus. If you've ever spent time in a literature classroom as a student or a professor, you know this moment. It may seem at times as if the professor is either inventing interpretations out of thin air or else performing parlor tricks, a sort of analytical sleight of hand.

Actually, neither of these is the case; rather, the professor, as the slightly more experienced reader, has acquired over the years the use of a certain "language of reading," something to which the students are only beginning to be introduced. What I'm talking about is a grammar of literature, a set of conventions and patterns, codes and rules, that we learn to employ in dealing with a piece of writing. Every language has a grammar, a set of rules that govern usage and meaning, and literary language is no different. It's all more or less arbitrary, of course, just like language itself. Take the word "arbitrary" as an example: it doesn't mean anything inherently; rather, at some point in our past we agreed that it would mean what it does, and it does so only in English (those sounds would be so much gibberish in Japanese or Finnish). So too with art: we decided to agree that perspective—the set of tricks artists use to provide the illusion of depth—was a good thing and vital to painting. This occurred during the Renaissance in Europe, but when Western and Oriental art encountered each other in the 1700s, Japanese artists and their audiences were serenely untroubled by the lack of perspective in their painting. No one felt it particularly essential to the experience of pictorial art.

Literature has its grammar, too. You knew that, of course. Even if you didn't know that, you knew from the structure of the preceding paragraph that it was coming. How? The grammar of the essay. You can read, and part of reading is knowing the conventions, recognizing them, and anticipating the results. When someone introduces a topic (the grammar of literature), then digresses to show other topics (language, art, music, dog training—it doesn't matter what examples; as soon as you see a couple of them, you recognize the pattern), you know he's coming back with an application of those examples to the main topic (voilà!). And he did. So now we're all happy, because the convention has been used, observed, noted, anticipated, and fulfilled. What more can you want from a paragraph?

Well, as I was saying before I so rudely digressed, so too in literature. Stories and novels have a very large set of conventions: types of characters, plot rhythms, chapter structures, point-of-view limitations. Poems have a great many of their own, involving form, structure, rhythm, rhyme. Plays, too. And then there are conventions that cross genre lines. Spring is largely universal. So is snow. So is darkness. And sleep. When spring is mentioned in a story, a poem, or a play, a veritable constellation of associations rises in our imaginative sky: youth, promise, new life, young lambs, children skipping . . . on and on. And if we associate even further, that constellation may lead us to more abstract concepts such as rebirth, fertility, renewal.

Okay, let's say you're right and there is a set of conventions, a key to reading literature. How do I get so I can recognize these?

Same way you get to Carnegie Hall. Practice.

When lay readers encounter a fictive text, they focus, as they should, on the story and the characters: who are these people, what are they doing, and what wonderful or terrible things are happening to them? Such readers respond first of all, and sometimes only, to their reading on an emotional level; the work affects them, producing joy or revulsion, laughter or tears, anxiety or elation. In other words, they are emotionally and instinctively involved in the work. This is the response level that virtually every writer who has ever set pen to paper or fingertip to keyboard has hoped for when sending the novel, along with a prayer, to the publisher. When an English professor reads, on the other hand, he will accept the affective response level of the story (we don't mind a good cry when Little Nell dies), but a lot of his attention will be engaged by other elements of the novel. Where did that effect come from? Whom does this character resemble? Where have I seen this situation before? Didn't Dante (or Chaucer, or Merle Haggard) say that? If you learn to ask these questions, to see literary texts through these glasses, you will read and understand literature in a new light, and it'll become more rewarding and fun.

Memory. Symbol. Pattern. These are the three items that, more than any other, separate the professorial reader from the rest of the crowd. English professors, as a class, are cursed with memory. Whenever I read a new work, I spin the mental Rolodex looking for correspondences and corollaries—where have I seen his face, don't I know that theme? I can't *not* do it, although there are plenty of times when that ability is not something I want to exercise. Thirty minutes into Clint Eastwood's *Pale Rider* (1985), for instance, I thought, Okay, this is *Shane* (1953), and from there I didn't watch another frame of the movie without seeing Alan Ladd's face. This does not necessarily improve the experience of popular entertainment.

Professors also read, and think, symbolically. Everything is a symbol of something, it seems, until proven otherwise. We ask, Is this a metaphor? Is that an analogy? What does the thing over there signify? The kind of mind that works its way through undergraduate and then graduate classes in literature and criticism has a predisposition to see things as existing in themselves while simultaneously also representing something else. Grendel, the monster in the medieval epic *Beowulf* (eighth century A.D.), is an actual monster, but he can also symbolize (a) the hostility of the universe to human existence (a hostility that medieval Anglo-Saxons would have felt acutely) and (b) a darkness in human nature that only some higher aspect of ourselves (as symbolized by the title hero) can conquer. This predisposition to understand the world in symbolic terms is reinforced, of course, by years of training that encourages and rewards the symbolic imagination.

A related phenomenon in professorial reading is pattern recognition. Most professional students of literature learn to take in the foreground detail while seeing the patterns that the detail reveals. Like the symbolic imagination, this is a function of being able to distance oneself from the story, to look beyond the purely affective level of plot, drama, characters. Experience has proved to them that life and books fall into similar patterns. Nor is this skill exclusive to English professors. Good mechanics, the kind who used to fix cars before computerized diagnostics, use pattern recognition to diagnose engine troubles: if this and this are happening, then check that. Literature is full of patterns, and your reading experience will be much more rewarding when you can step back from the work, even while you're reading it, and look for those patterns.

When small children, very small children, begin to tell you a story, they put in every detail and every word they recall, with no sense that some features are more important than others. As they grow, they begin to display a greater sense of the plots of their stories—what elements actually add to the significance and which do not. So too with readers. Beginning students are often swamped with the mass of detail; the chief experience of reading *Dr. Zhivago* (1957) may be that they can't keep all the names straight. Wily veterans, on the other hand, will absorb those details, or possibly overlook them, to find the patterns, the routines, the archetypes at work in the background.

Let's look at an example of how the symbolic mind, the pattern observer, the powerful memory combine to offer a reading of a nonliterary situation. Let's say that a male subject you are studying exhibits behavior and makes statements that show him to be hostile toward his father but much warmer and more loving toward, even dependent on, his mother. Okay, that's just one guy, so no big deal. But you see it again in another person. And again. And again. You might start to think this is a pattern of behavior, in which case you would say to yourself, "Now where have I seen this before?" Your memory may dredge up something from experience, not your clinical work but a play you read long ago in your youth about a man who murders his father and marries his mother. Even though the current examples have nothing to do with drama, your symbolic imagination will allow you to connect the earlier instance of this pattern with the real-life examples in front of you at the moment. And your talent for nifty naming will come up with something to call this pattern: the Oedipal complex. As I said, not only English professors use these abilities. Sigmund Freud "reads" his patients the way a literary scholar reads texts, bringing the same sort of imaginative interpretation to understanding his cases that we try to bring to interpreting novels and poems and plays. His identification of the Oedipal complex is one of the great moments in the history of human thought, with as much literary as psychoanalytical significance.

What I hope to do, in the coming pages, is what I do in class: give readers a view of what goes on when professional students of literature do their thing, a broad introduction to the codes and patterns that inform our readings. I want my students not only to agree with me that, indeed, Mr. Lindner is an instance of the demonic tempter offering Walter Lee Younger a Faustian bargain; I want them to be able to reach that conclusion without me. I know they can, with practice, patience, and a bit of instruction. And so can you.

1

Every Trip Is a Quest
(Except When It's Not)

Okay, so here's the deal: let's say, purely hypo-
thetically, you're reading a book about an aver-
age sixteen-year-old kid in the summer of 1968. The
kid—let's call him Kip—who hopes his acne clears up
before he gets drafted, is on his way to the A&P. His
bike is a one-speed with a coaster brake and therefore
deeply humiliating, and riding it to run an errand for
his mother makes it even worse. Along the way he has
a couple of disturbing experiences, including a minorly
unpleasant encounter with a German shepherd,
topped off in the supermarket parking lot where he
sees the girl of his dreams, Karen, laughing and hors-
ing around in Tony Vauxhall's brand-new Barracuda.
Now Kip hates Tony already because he has a name
like Vauxhall and not like Smith, which Kip thinks

is pretty lame as a name to follow Kip, and because the 'Cuda is bright green and goes approximately the speed of light, and also because Tony has never had to work a day in his life. So Karen, who is laughing and having a great time, turns and sees Kip, who has recently asked her out, and she keeps laughing. (She could stop laughing and it wouldn't matter to us, since we're considering this structurally. In the story we're inventing here, though, she keeps laughing.) Kip goes on into the store to buy the loaf of Wonder Bread that his mother told him to pick up, and as he reaches for the bread, he decides right then and there to lie about his age to the Marine recruiter even though it means going to Vietnam, because nothing will ever happen for him in this one-horse burg where the only thing that matters is how much money your old man has. Either that or Kip has a vision of St. Abillard (any saint will do, but our imaginary author picked a comparatively obscure one), whose face appears on one of the red, yellow, or blue balloons. For our purposes, the nature of the decision doesn't matter any more than whether Karen keeps laughing or which color balloon manifests the saint.

What just happened here?

If you were an English professor, and not even a particularly weird English professor, you'd know that you'd just watched a knight have a not very suitable encounter with his nemesis.

In other words, a quest just happened.

But it just looked like a trip to the store for some white bread.

True. But consider the quest. Of what does it consist? A knight, a dangerous road, a Holy Grail (whatever one of those may be), at least one dragon, one evil knight, one princess. Sound about right? That's a list I can live with: a knight (named Kip), a dangerous road (nasty German shepherds), a Holy Grail (one form of which is a loaf of Wonder Bread), at least one dragon (trust me, a '68 'Cuda could definitely breathe fire), one evil knight (Tony), one princess (who can either keep laughing or stop).

Seems like a bit of a stretch.

On the surface, sure. But let's think structurally. The quest consists of five things: (a) a quester, (b) a place to go, (c) a stated reason to go there, (d) challenges and trials en route, and (e) a real reason to go there. Item (a) is easy; a quester is just a person who goes on a quest, whether or not he knows it's a quest. In fact, usually he doesn't know. Items (b) and (c) should be considered together: someone tells our protagonist, our *hero,* who need not look very heroic, to go somewhere and do something. Go in search of the Holy Grail. Go to the store for bread. Go to Vegas and whack a guy. Tasks of varying nobility, to be sure, but structurally all the same. Go there, do that. Note that I said the stated reason for the quest. That's because of item (e).

The real reason for a quest *never* involves the stated reason. In fact, more often than not, the quester fails at the stated task. So why do they go and why do we care? They go because of the stated task, mistakenly believing that it is their real mission. We know, however, that their quest is educational. They don't know enough about the only subject that really matters: themselves. **The real reason for a quest is always self-knowledge.** That's why questers are so often young, inexperienced, immature, sheltered. Forty-five-year-old men either have self-knowledge or they're never going to get it, while your average sixteen-to-seventeen-year-old kid is likely to have a long way to go in the self-knowledge department.

Let's look at a real example. When I teach the late-twentieth-century novel, I always begin with the greatest quest novel of the last century: Thomas Pynchon's *Crying of Lot 49* (1965). Beginning readers can find the novel mystifying, irritating, and highly peculiar. True enough, there is a good bit of cartoonish strangeness in the novel, which can mask the basic quest structure. On the other hand, *Sir Gawain and the Green Knight* (late fourteenth century) and Edmund Spenser's *Faerie Queen* (1596), two of the great quest narratives from early English literature, also have what modern readers must consider cartoonish elements. It's really only a matter of whether we're talking Classics Illustrated or Zap Comics. So here's the setup in *The Crying of Lot 49:*

1) *Our quester:* a young woman, not very happy in her marriage or her life, not too old to learn, not too assertive where men are concerned.

2) *A place to go:* in order to carry out her duties, she must drive to Southern California from her home near San Francisco. Eventually she will travel back and forth between the two, and between her past (a husband with a disintegrating personality and a fondness for LSD, an insane ex-Nazi psychotherapist) and her future (highly unclear).

3) *A stated reason to go there:* she has been made executor of the will of her former lover, a fabulously wealthy and eccentric businessman and stamp collector.

4) *Challenges and trials:* our heroine meets lots of really strange, scary, and occasionally truly

dangerous people. She goes on a nightlong excursion through the world of the outcasts and the dispossessed of San Francisco; enters her therapist's office to talk him out of his psychotic shooting rampage (the dangerous enclosure known in the study of traditional quest romances as "Chapel Perilous"); involves herself in what may be a centuries-old postal conspiracy.

5) *The real reason to go:* did I mention that her name is Oedipa? Oedipa Maas, actually. She's named for the great tragic character from Sophocles' drama *Oedipus the King* (ca. 425 B.C.), whose real calamity is that he doesn't know who he is. In Pynchon's novel the heroine's resources, really her crutches—and they all happen to be male—are stripped away one by one, shown to be false or unreliable, until she reaches the point where she either must break down, reduced to a little fetal ball, or stand straight and rely on herself. And to do that, she first must find the self on whom she can rely. Which she does, after considerable struggle. Gives up on men, Tupperware parties, easy answers. Plunges ahead into the great mystery of the ending. Acquires, dare we say, self-knowledge? Of course we dare.

Still . . .

You don't believe me. Then why does the stated goal fade away? We hear less and less about the will and the estate as the story goes on, and even the surrogate goal, the mystery of the postal conspiracy, remains unresolved. At the end of the novel, she's about to witness an auction of some rare forged stamps, and the answer to the mystery may or may not appear during the auction. We doubt it, though, given what's gone before. Mostly, we don't even care. Now we know, as she does, that she can carry on, that discovering that men can't be counted on doesn't mean the world ends, that she's a whole person.

So there, in fifty words or more, is why professors of literature typically think *The Crying of Lot 49* is a terrific little book. It does look a bit weird at first glance, experimental and superhip (for 1965), but once you get the hang of it, you see that it follows the conventions of a quest tale. So does *Huck Finn. The Lord of the Rings. North by Northwest. Star Wars.* And most other stories of someone going somewhere and doing something, especially if the going and the doing wasn't his idea in the first place.

A word of warning: if I sometimes speak here and in the chapters to come as if a certain statement is always true, a certain condition always obtains, I apologize.

"Always" and "never" are not words that have much meaning in literary study. For one thing, as soon as something seems to always be true, some wise guy will come along and write something to prove that it's not. If literature seems to be too comfortably patriarchal, a novelist like the late Angela Carter or a poet like the contemporary Eavan Boland will come along and upend things just to remind readers and writers of the falseness of our established assumptions. If readers start to pigeonhole African-American writing, as was beginning to happen in the 1960s and 1970s, a trickster like Ishmael Reed will come along who refuses to fit in any pigeonhole we could create. Let's consider journeys. Sometimes the quest fails or is not taken up by the protagonist. Moreover, is every trip really a quest? It depends. Some days I just drive to work—no adventures, no growth. I'm sure that the same is true in writing. Sometimes plot requires that a writer get a character from home to work and back again. That said, when a character hits the road, we should start to pay attention, just to see if, you know, something's going on there.

Once you figure out quests, the rest is easy.

2

Nice to Eat with You: Acts of Communion

Perhaps you've heard the anecdote about Sigmund Freud. One day one of his students, or assistants, or some such hanger-on, was teasing him about his fondness for cigars, referring to their obvious phallic nature. The great man responded simply that "sometimes a cigar is just a cigar." I don't really care if the story is true or not. Actually, I think I prefer that it be apocryphal, since made-up anecdotes have their own kind of truth. Still, it is equally true that just as cigars may be just cigars, so sometimes they are not.

Same with meals in life and, of course, in literature. Sometimes a meal is just a meal, and eating with others is simply eating with others. More often than not, though, it's not. Once or twice a semester at least, I will stop discussion of the story or play under consideration to intone (and I invariably intone in bold): **whenever people eat or drink together, it's communion**. For some reasons, this is often met with a slightly scandalized look, communion having for many readers one and only one meaning. While that meaning is very important, it is not the only one. Nor, for that matter, does Christianity have a lock on the practice. Nearly every religion has some liturgical or social ritual involving the coming together of the faithful to share sustenance. So I have to explain that just as intercourse has meanings other than sexual, or at least did at one time, so not all communions are holy. In fact, literary versions of communion can interpret the word in quite a variety of ways.

Here's the thing to remember about communions of all kinds: in the real world, breaking bread together is an act of sharing and peace, since if you're breaking bread you're not breaking heads. One generally invites one's friends to dinner, unless one is trying to get on the good side of enemies or employers. We're quite particular about those with whom we break bread. We may not, for instance, accept a dinner invitation from someone we don't care for. The act of taking food into our bodies is so personal that we really only want to do it with people we're very comfortable with. As with any convention, this one can be violated. A tribal leader or Mafia don, say, may invite his enemies to lunch and then have them killed. In most areas, however, such behavior is considered very bad form. Generally, eating with another is a way of saying, "I'm with you, I like you, we form a community together." And that is a form of communion.

So too in literature. And in literature, there is another reason: writing a meal scene is so difficult, and so inherently uninteresting, that there really needs to be some compelling reason to include one in the story. And that reason has to do with how characters are getting along. Or not getting along. Come on, food is food. What can you say about fried chicken that you haven't already heard, said, seen, thought? And eating is eating, with some slight variations of table manners. To put characters, then, in this mundane, overused, fairly boring situation, something more has to be happening than simply beef, forks, and goblets.

So what kind of communion? And what kind of result can it achieve? Any kind you can think of.

Let's consider an example that will never be confused with religious communion, the eating scene in Henry Fielding's *Tom Jones* (1749), which, as one of my students once remarked, "sure doesn't look like church." Specifically, Tom and his lady friend, Mrs. Waters, dine at an inn, chomping, gnawing, sucking on bones, licking fingers; a more leering, slurping, groaning, and, in short, sexual meal has never been consumed. While it doesn't feel particularly *important* thematically and, moreover, it's as far from traditional notions of communion as we can get, it nevertheless constitutes a shared experience. What else is the eating about in that scene except devouring the other's body? Think of it as a consuming desire. Or two of them. And in the case of the movie version of *Tom Jones* starring Albert Finney (1963), there's another reason. Tony Richardson, the director, couldn't openly show sex as, well, sex. There were still taboos in film in the early sixties. So what he does is show something else as sex. And it's probably dirtier than all but two or three sex scenes ever filmed. When those two finish swilling ale and slurping on drumsticks and sucking fingers and generally wallowing and moaning, the *audience* wants to lie back and smoke. But what is this expression of desire except a kind of communion, very private, admittedly, and decidedly not holy? I want to be with you, you want to be with me, let us share the experience. And that's the point: communion doesn't need to be holy. Or even decent.

How about a slightly more sedate example? The late Raymond Carver wrote a story, "Cathedral" (1981), about a guy with real hang-ups: included among the many things the narrator is bigoted against are people with disabilities, minorities, those different from himself, and all parts of his wife's past in which he does not share. Now the only reason to give a character a serious hang-up is to give him the chance to get over it. He may fail, but he gets the chance. It's the Code of the West. When our unnamed narrator reveals to us from the first moment that a blind man, a friend of his wife's, is coming to visit, we're not surprised that he doesn't like the prospect at all. We know immediately that our man has to overcome disliking everyone who is different. And by the end he does, when he and the blind man sit together to draw a cathedral so the blind man can get a sense of what one looks like. To do that, they have to touch, hold hands even, and there's no way the narrator would have been able to do that at the start of the story. Carver's problem, then, is how to get from the nasty, prejudiced, narrow-minded person of the opening page to the point where he can actually have a blind man's hand on his own at the ending. The answer is food.

Every coach I ever had would say, when we faced a superior opposing team, that they put on their pants one leg at a time, just like everybody else. What those coaches could have said, in all accuracy, is that those supermen shovel in the pasta just like the rest of us.

Or in Carver's story, cube steak. When the narrator watches the blind man eating—competent, busy, hungry, and, well, normal—he begins to gain a new respect for him. The three of them, husband, wife, and visitor, ravenously consume the cube steak, potatoes, and vegetables, and in the course of that experience our narrator finds his antipathy toward the blind man beginning to break down. He discovers he has something in *common* with this stranger—eating as a fundamental element of life—that there is a bond between them.

What about the dope they smoke afterward?

Passing a joint doesn't quite resemble the wafer and the chalice, does it? But thinking symbolically, where's the difference, really? Please note, I am not suggesting that illicit drugs are required to break down social barriers. On the other hand, here is a substance they take into their bodies in a shared, almost ritualistic experience. Once again, the act says, "I'm with you, I share this moment with you, I feel a bond of community with you." It may be a moment of even greater trust. In any case, the alcohol at supper and the marijuana after combine to relax the narrator so he can receive the full force of his insight, so he can share in the drawing of a cathedral (which, incidentally, is a place of communion).

———————

What about when they don't? What if dinner turns ugly or doesn't happen at all?

A different outcome, but the same logic, I think. If a well-run meal or snack portends good things for community and understanding, then the failed meal stands as a bad sign. It happens all the time on television shows. Two people are at dinner and a third comes up, quite unwished for, and one or more of the first two refuse to eat. They place their napkins on their plates, or say something about losing their appetite, or simply get up and walk away. Immediately we know what they think about the interloper. Think of all those movies where a soldier shares his C rations with a comrade, or a boy his sandwich with a stray dog; from the overwhelming message of loyalty, kinship, and generosity, you get a sense of how strong a value we place on the comradeship of the table. What if we see two people having dinner, then, but one of them is plotting, or bringing about the demise of the other? In that case, our revulsion at the act of murder is reinforced by our sense that a very important propriety, namely that one should not do evil to one's dinner companions, is being violated.

Or consider Anne Tyler's *Dinner at the Homesick Restaurant* (1982). The mother tries and tries to have a family dinner, and every time she fails. Someone can't make it, someone gets called away, some minor disaster befalls the table. Not until her death can her children assemble around a table at the restaurant and achieve dinner; at that point, of course, the body and blood they symbolically share are hers. Her life—and her death—become part of their common experience.

For the full effect of dining together, consider James Joyce's story "The Dead" (1914). This wonderful story is centered around a dinner party on the Feast of the Epiphany, the twelfth day of Christmas. All kinds of disparate drives and desires enact themselves during the dancing and dinner, and hostilities and alliances are revealed. The main character, Gabriel Conroy, must learn that he is not superior to everyone else; during the course of the evening he receives a series of small shocks to his ego that collectively demonstrate that he is very much part of the more general social fabric. The table and dishes of food themselves are lavishly described as Joyce lures us into the atmosphere:

> A fat brown goose lay at one end of the table and at the other end, on a bed of creased paper strewn with sprigs of parsley, lay a great ham, stripped of its outer skin and peppered over with crust crumbs, a neat paper frill round its shin and beside this was

a round of spiced beef. Between these rival ends ran parallel lines of side-dishes: two little minsters of jelly, red and yellow; a shallow dish full of blocks of blancmange and red jam, a large green leaf-shaped dish with a stalk-shaped handle, on which lay bunches of purple raisins and peeled almonds, a companion dish on which lay a solid rectangle of Smyrna figs, a dish of custard topped with grated nutmeg, a small bowl full of chocolates and sweets wrapped in gold and silver papers and a glass vase in which stood some tall celery stalks. In the centre of the table there stood, as sentries to a fruit-stand which upheld a pyramid of oranges and American apples, two squat old-fashioned decanters of cut glass, one containing port and the other dark sherry. On the closed square piano a pudding in a huge yellow dish lay in waiting and behind it were three squads of bottles of stout and ale and minerals, drawn up according to the colours of their uniforms, the first two black, with brown and red labels, the third and smallest squad white, with transverse green sashes.

No writer ever took such care about food and drink, so marshaled his forces to create a military effect of armies drawn up as if for battle: ranks, files, "rival ends," sentries, squads, sashes. Such a paragraph would not be created without having some purpose, some ulterior motive. Now, Joyce being Joyce, he has about five different purposes, one not being enough for genius. His main goal, though, is to draw us into that moment, to pull our chairs up to that table so that we are utterly convinced of the reality of the meal. At the same time, he wants to convey the sense of tension and conflict that has been running through the evening— there are a host of us-against-them and you-against-me moments earlier and even during the meal—and this tension will stand at odds with the sharing of this sumptuous and, given the holiday, unifying meal. He does this for a very simple, very profound reason: we need to be part of that communion. It would be easy for us simply to laugh at Freddy Malins, the resident drunkard, and his dotty mother, to shrug off the table talk about operas and singers we've never heard of, merely to snicker at the flirtations among the younger people, to discount the tension Gabriel feels over the speech of gratitude he's obliged to make at meal's end. But we can't maintain our distance because the elaborate setting of this scene makes us feel as if we're seated at that table. So we notice, a little before Gabriel does, since he's lost in his own reality, that we're all in this together, that in fact we share something.

The thing we share is our death. Everyone in that room, from old and frail Aunt Julia to the youngest music student, will die. Not tonight, but someday. Once you recognize that fact (and we've been given a head start by the title, whereas Gabriel doesn't know his evening has a title), it's smooth sledding. Next to our mortality, which comes to great and small equally, all the differences in our lives are mere surface details. When the snow comes at the end of the story, in a beautiful and moving passage, it covers, equally, "all the living and the dead." Of course it does, we think, the snow is just like death. We're already prepared, having shared in the communion meal Joyce has laid out for us, a communion not of death, but of what comes before. Of life.

3

Nice to Eat You:
Acts of Vampires

What a difference a preposition makes! If you take the "with" out of "Nice to eat with you," it begins to mean something quite different. Less wholesome. More creepy. It just goes to show that not all eating that happens in literature is friendly. Not only that, it doesn't even always look like eating. Beyond here there be monsters.

Vampires in literature, you say. Big deal. I've read *Dracula*. And Anne Rice.

Good for you. Everyone deserves a good scare. But actual vampires are only the beginning; not only that, they're not even necessarily the most alarming type. After all, you can at least recognize them. Let's start with Dracula himself, and we'll eventually see why this is true. You know how in all those Dracula movies, or almost all, the count always has this weird attractiveness to him? Sometimes he's downright sexy. Always, he's alluring, dangerous, mysterious, and he tends to focus on beautiful, unmarried (which in the social vision of nineteenth-century England meant virginal) women. And when he gets them, he grows younger, more alive (if we can say this of the undead), more virile even. Meanwhile, his victims become like him and begin to seek out their own victims. Van Helsing, the count's ultimate nemesis, and his lot, then, are really protecting young people, and especially young women, from this menace when they hunt him down. Most of this, in one form or another, can be found in Bram Stoker's novel (1897), although it gets more hysterical in the movie versions. Now let's think about this for a moment. A nasty old man, attractive but evil, violates young women, leaves his mark on them, steals their innocence—and coincidentally their "usefulness" (if you think "marriageability," you'll be about right) to young men—and leaves them helpless followers in his sin. I think we'd be reasonable to conclude that the whole Count Dracula saga has an agenda to it beyond merely scaring us out of our wits, although scaring readers out of their wits is a noble enterprise and one that Stoker's novel accomplishes very nicely. In fact, we might conclude it has something to do with sex.

Well, of course it has to do with sex. Evil has had to do with sex since the serpent seduced Eve. What was the upshot there? Body shame and unwholesome lust, seduction, temptation, danger, among other ills.

So vampirism isn't about vampires?

Oh, it is. It is. But it's also about things other than literal vampirism: selfishness, exploitation, a refusal to respect the autonomy of other people, just for starters. We'll return to this list a bit later on.

This principle also applies to other scary favorites, such as ghosts and doppelgängers (ghost doubles or evil twins). We can take it almost as an act of faith that ghosts are about something besides themselves. That may not be true in naive ghost stories, but most literary ghosts—the kind that occur in stories of lasting interest—have to do with things beyond themselves. Think of the ghost of Hamlet's father when he takes to appearing on the castle ramparts at midnight. He's not there simply to haunt his son; he's there to point out something drastically wrong in Denmark's royal household. Or consider Marley's ghost in *A Christmas Carol* (1843), who is really a walking, clanking, moaning lesson in ethics for Scrooge. In fact, Dickens's ghosts are always up to something besides scaring the audience. Or take Dr. Jekyll's other half. The hideous Edward Hyde exists to demonstrate to readers that even a respectable man has a dark side; like many Victorians, Robert Louis Stevenson believed in the dual nature of humans, and in more than one work he finds ways of showing that duality quite literally. In *The Strange Case of Dr. Jekyll and Mr. Hyde* (1886) he has Dr. J. drink a potion and become his evil half, while in his now largely ignored short novel *The Master of Ballantrae* (1889), he uses twins locked in fatal conflict to convey the same sense. You'll notice, by the way, that many of these examples come from Victorian writers: Stevenson, Dickens, Stoker, J. S. Le Fanu, Henry James. Why? Because there was so much the Victorians couldn't write about directly, chiefly sex and sexuality, they found ways of transforming those taboo subjects and issues into other forms. The Victorians were masters of sublimation. But even today, when there are no limits on subject matter or treatment, writers still use ghosts, vampires, werewolves, and all manner of scary things to symbolize various aspects of our more common reality.

The last decade of the twentieth century and the first decade (and counting) of the twenty-first could be dubbed the teen vampire era. The phenomenon can likely be traced to Anne Rice's *Interview with the Vampire* (1976) and its successors in the *Vampire Chronicles* series (1976–2003). For a number of years

Rice was a one-woman industry, but slowly other names came forward. Vampires even made it to weekly television with the unlikely hit *Buffy the Vampire Slayer*, which debuted in 1997. Things really took off with Stephenie Meyer's *Twilight* (2005) and the series of teen-and-vampire tales it spawned. Meyer's great innovation is to center the stories on a nonvampire teenage girl and young (these things are relative, I guess) vampire who loves her but must fight his bloodlust. Much has been made of the element of the bloodsucking (and therefore sexual) restraint of the novels, notable in a genre where traditionally the main figures have had no self-control at all. What turned out to be unrestrained was the reading appetite of teenagers; Meyer was the top-selling American author in 2008 and 2009. Critics generally cringed, but, clearly, adolescents don't read book reviews.

Try this for a dictum: **ghosts and vampires are never only about ghosts and vampires**.

Here's where it gets a little tricky, though: the ghosts and vampires don't always have to appear in visible forms. Sometimes the really scary bloodsuckers are entirely human. Let's look at another Victorian with experience in ghost and nonghost genres, Henry James. James is known, of course, as a master, perhaps *the* master, of psychological realism; if you want massive novels with sentences as long and convoluted as the Missouri River, James is your man. At the same time, though, he has some shorter works that feature ghosts and demonic possession, and those are fun in their own way, as well as a good deal more accessible. His novella *The Turn of the Screw* (1898) is about a governess who tries, without success, to protect the two children in her care from a particularly nasty ghost who seeks to take possession of them. Either that or it's about an insane governess who fantasizes that a ghost is taking over the children in her care, and in her delusion literally smothers them with protectiveness. Or just possibly it's about an insane governess who is dealing with a particularly nasty ghost who tries to take possession of her wards. Or possibly . . . well, let's just say that the plot calculus is tricky and that much depends on the perspective of the reader. So we have a story in which a ghost features prominently even if we're never sure whether he's really there or not, in which the psychological state of the governess matters greatly, and in which the life of a child, a little boy, is consumed. Between the two of them, the governess and the "specter" destroy him. One might say that the story is about fatherly neglect (the stand-in for the father simply abandons the children to the governess's care) and smothering maternal concern. Those two thematic elements are encoded into the plot of the novella. The particulars of the encoding are carried by the details of the ghost story. It just so happens that James has another famous story, "Daisy Miller" (1878), in which there are no ghosts, no demonic possession, and nothing more mysterious than a midnight trip to the Colosseum in Rome. Daisy is a young American woman who does as she pleases, thus upsetting the rigid social customs of the European society she desperately wants to approve of her. Winterbourne, the man whose attention she desires, while both attracted to and repulsed by her, ultimately proves too fearful of the disapproval of his established expatriate American community to pursue her further. After numerous misadventures, Daisy dies, ostensibly by contracting malaria on her midnight jaunt. But you know what really kills her? Vampires.

No, really. Vampires. I know I told you there weren't any supernatural forces at work here. But you don't need fangs and a cape to be a vampire. The essentials of the vampire story, as we discussed earlier: an older figure representing corrupt, outworn values; a young, preferably virginal female; a stripping away of her youth, energy, virtue; a continuance of the life force of the old male; the death or destruction of the young woman. Okay, let's see now. *Winter*bourne and *Daisy* carry associations of winter—death, cold—and spring—life, flowers, renewal—that ultimately come into conflict (we'll talk about seasonal implications in a later chapter), with winter's frost destroying the delicate young flower. He is considerably older than she, closely associated with the stifling Euro-Anglo-American society. She is fresh and innocent—and here is James's brilliance—so innocent as to appear to be a wanton. He and his aunt and her circle watch Daisy and disapprove, but because of a hunger to disapprove of someone, they never cut her loose entirely. They play with her yearning to become one of them, taxing her energies until she begins to wane. Winterbourne mixes voyeurism, vicarious thrills, and stiff-necked disapproval, all of which culminate when he finds her with a (male) friend at the Colosseum and chooses to ignore her. Daisy says of his behavior, "He cuts me dead!" That should be clear enough for anyone. His, and his clique's, consuming of Daisy is complete; having used up everything that is fresh and vital in her, he leaves her to waste away. Even then she asks after him. But having destroyed and consumed her, he moves on, not sufficiently touched, it seems to me, by the pathetic spectacle he has caused.

So how does all this tie in with vampires? Is James a believer in ghosts and spooks? Does "Daisy Miller" mean he thinks we're all vampires? Probably not.

I believe what happens here and in other stories and novels (*The Sacred Fount* [1901] comes to mind) is that he deems the figure of the consuming spirit or vampiric personality a useful narrative vehicle. We find this figure appearing in different guises, even under nearly opposite circumstances, from one story to another. On the one hand, in *The Turn of the Screw*, he uses the literal vampire or the possessing spook to examine a certain sort of psychosocial imbalance. These days we'd give it a label, a dysfunctional something or other, but James probably only saw it as a problem in our approach to child rearing or a psychic neediness in young women whom society disregards and discards. On the other hand, in "Daisy Miller," he employs the figure of the vampire as an emblem of the way society—polite, ostensibly normal society—battens on and consumes its victims.

Nor is James the only one. The nineteenth century was filled with writers showing the thin line between the ordinary and the monstrous. Edgar Allan Poe. J. S. Le Fanu, whose ghost stories made him the Stephen King of his day. Thomas Hardy, whose poor heroine in *Tess of the D'Urbervilles* (1891) provides table fare for the disparate hungers of the men in her life. Or virtually any novel of the naturalistic movement of the late nineteenth century, where the law of the jungle and survival of the fittest reign. Of course, the twentieth century also provided plenty of instances of social vampirism and cannibalism. Franz Kafka, a latter-day Poe, uses the dynamic in stories like "The Metamorphosis" (1915) and "A Hunger Artist" (1924), where, in a nifty reversal of the traditional vampire narrative, crowds of onlookers watch as the artist's fasting consumes him. Gabriel García Márquez's heroine Innocent Eréndira, in the tale bearing her name (1972), is exploited and put out to prostitution by her heartless grandmother. D. H. Lawrence gave us any number of short stories where characters devour and destroy one another in life-and-death contests of will, novellas like "The Fox" (1923) and even novels like *Women in Love* (1920), in which Gudrun Brangwen and Gerald Crich, although ostensibly in love with one another, each realize that only one of them can survive and so engage in mutually destructive behavior. Iris Murdoch—pick a novel, any novel. Not for nothing did she call one of her books *A Severed Head* (1961), although *The Unicorn* (1963) would work splendidly here, with its wealth of faux gothic creepiness. There are works, of course, where the ghost or vampire is merely a gothic cheap thrill without any particular thematic or symbolic significance, but such works tend to be short-term commodities without much staying power in readers' minds or the public arena. We're haunted only while we're reading. In those works that continue to haunt us, however, the figure of the cannibal, the vampire, the succubus, the spook announces itself again and again where someone grows in strength by weakening someone else.

That's what this figure really comes down to, whether in Elizabethan, Victorian, or more modern incarnations: exploitation in its many forms. Using other people to get what we want. Denying someone else's right to live in the face of our overwhelming demands. Placing our desires, particularly our uglier ones, above the needs of another. That's pretty much what the vampire does, after all. He wakes up in the morning—actually the evening, now that I think about it—and says something like, "In order to remain undead, I must steal the life force of someone whose fate matters less to me than my own." I've always supposed that Wall Street traders utter essentially the same sentence. My guess is that as long as people act toward their fellows in exploitative and selfish ways, the vampire will be with us.

4

Now, Where Have
I Seen Her Before?

O ne of the great things about being a professor
of English is that you get to keep meeting old
friends. For beginning readers, though, every story
may seem new, and the resulting experience of read-
ing is highly disjointed. Think of reading, on one level,
as one of those papers from elementary school where
you connect the dots. I could never see the picture in a
connect-the-dot drawing until I'd put in virtually every
line. Other kids could look at a page full of dots and
say, "Oh, that's an elephant," "That's a locomotive."
Me, I saw dots. I think it's partly predisposition—
some people handle two-dimensional visualization
better than others—but largely a matter of practice:
the more connect-the-dot drawings you do, the more
likely you are to recognize the design early on. Same

with literature. Part of pattern recognition is talent, but a whole lot of it is practice: if you read enough and give what you read enough thought, you begin to see patterns, archetypes, recurrences. And as with those pictures among the dots, it's a matter of learning to look. Not just *to look* but *where* to look, and *how* to look. Literature, as the great Canadian critic Northrop Frye observed, grows out of other literature; we should not be surprised to find, then, that it also looks like other literature. As you read, it may pay to remember this: **there's no such thing as a wholly original work of literature**. Once you know that, you can go looking for old friends and asking the attendant question: "now where have I seen her before?"

One of my favorite novels is Tim O'Brien's *Going After Cacciato* (1978). Lay readers and students generally like it, too, which explains why it has become a perennial strong seller. Although the violence of the Vietnam War scenes may turn some readers off, many find themselves totally engrossed by something they initially figured would just be gross. What readers sometimes don't notice in their involvement with the story (and it is a great story) is that virtually everything in there is cribbed from somewhere else. Lest you conclude with dismay that the novel is somehow plagiarized or less than original, let me add that I find the book wildly original, that everything O'Brien borrows makes perfect sense in the context of the story he's telling, even more so once we understand that he has repurposed materials from older sources to accomplish his own ends. The novel divides into three interwoven parts: one, the actual story of the war experience of the main character, Paul Berlin, up to the point where his fellow soldier Cacciato runs away from the war; two, the imagined trip on which the squad follows Cacciato to Paris; and three, the long night watch on a tower near the South China Sea where Berlin manages these two very impressive mental feats of memory on the one hand and invention on the other. The actual war, because it really happened, he can't do much about. Oh, he gets some facts wrong and some events out of order, but mostly, reality has imposed a certain structure on memory. The trip to Paris, though, is another story. Actually, it's all stories, or all those Paul has read in his young lifetime. He creates events and people out of the novels, stories, histories he knows, his own included, all of which is quite unwitting on his part, the pieces just appearing out of his memory. O'Brien provides us with a wonderful glimpse into the creative process, a view of how stories get written, and a big part of that process is that you can't create stories in a vacuum. Instead the mind flashes bits and pieces of childhood experiences, past reading, every movie the writer/creator has ever seen, last week's argument with a phone solicitor—in short, everything that lurks in the recesses of the mind. Some of this may be unconscious, as it is in the case of O'Brien's protagonist. Generally, though, writers use prior texts quite consciously and purposefully, as O'Brien himself does; unlike Paul Berlin, he is aware that he's drawing from Lewis Carroll or Ernest Hemingway. O'Brien signals the difference between novelist and character in the structuring of the two narrative frames.

About halfway through the novel, O'Brien has his characters fall through a hole in the road. Not only that, one of the characters subsequently says that the way to get out is to fall back up. When it's stated this baldly, you automatically think of Lewis Carroll. Falling through a hole is like *Alice in Wonderland* (1865). Bingo. It's all we need. And the world the squad discovers below the road, the network of Vietcong tunnels (although nothing like the real ones), complete with an officer condemned to stay there for his crimes, is every bit as much an alternative world as the one Alice encounters in her adventure. Once you've established that a book—a man's book at that, a war book—is borrowing a situation from Lewis Carroll's Alice books, anything is possible. So with that in mind, readers must reconsider characters, situations, events in the novel. This one looks like it's from Hemingway, that one like "Hansel and Gretel," these two from things that happened during Paul Berlin's "real" war, and so on down the line. Once you've played around with these elements for a while, a kind of Trivial Pursuit of source material, go for the big one: what about Sarkin Aung Wan?

Sarkin Aung Wan is Paul Berlin's love interest, his fantasy girl. She is Vietnamese and knows about tunnels but is not Vietcong. She's old enough to be attractive, yet not old enough to make sexual demands on the virginal young soldier. She's not a "real" character, since she comes in after the start of Berlin's fantasy. Careful readers will find her "real" model in a young girl with the same hoop earrings when the soldiers frisk villagers in one remembered war scene. Fair enough, but that's just the physical person, not her character. Then who is she? Where does she come from? Think generically. Lose the personal details, consider her as a type, and try to think where you've seen that type before: a brown-skinned young woman guiding a group of white men (mostly white, anyway), speaking the language they don't know, knowing where to go, where to find food. Taking them west. Right.

No, not Pocahontas. She never led anyone anywhere, whatever the popular culture may suggest. Somehow

Pocahontas has received better PR, but we want the other one.

Sacajawea. If I need to be guided across hostile territory, she's the one I want, and she's the one Paul Berlin wants, too. He wants, he needs, a figure who will be sympathetic, understanding, strong in the ways he's not, and most of all successful in bringing him safely to his goal of getting to Paris. O'Brien plays here with the reader's established knowledge of history, culture, and literature. He's hoping that your mind will associate Sarkin Aung Wan consciously or unconsciously with Sacajawea, thereby not only creating her personality and impact but also establishing the nature and depth of Paul Berlin's need. If you require a Sacajawea, you're really lost.

The point isn't really which native woman figures in O'Brien's novel, it's that there is a literary or historical model who found her way into his fiction to give it shape and purpose. He could have used Tolkien rather than Carroll, and while the surface features would have been different, the principle would have remained the same. Although the story would go in different directions with a change of literary model, in either case it gains a kind of resonance from these different levels of narrative that begin to emerge; the story is no longer all on the surface but begins to have depth. What we're trying to do is learn to read this sort of thing like a wily old professor, to learn to spot those familiar images, like being able to see the elephant before we connect the dots.

You say stories grow out of other stories. But Sacajawea was real.

As a matter of fact, she was, but from our point of view, it doesn't really matter. History is story, too. You don't encounter her directly; you've only heard of her through narrative of one sort or another. She is a literary as well as a historical character, as much a piece of the American myth as Huck Finn or Jay Gatsby, and very nearly as unreal. And what all this is about, finally, is myth. Which brings us to the big secret.

Here it is: **there's only one story**. There, I said it and I can't very well take it back. There is only one story. Ever. One. It's always been going on and it's everywhere around us and every story you've ever read or heard or watched is part of it. *The Thousand and One Nights. Beloved.* "Jack and the Beanstalk." *The Epic of Gilgamesh. The Story of O. The Simpsons.*

T. S. Eliot said that when a new work is created, it is set among the monuments, adding to and altering the order. That always sounds to me a bit too much like a graveyard. To me, literature is something much more alive. More like a barrel of eels. When a writer creates a new eel, it wriggles its way into the barrel, muscles a path into the great teeming mass from which it came in the first place. It's a new eel, but it shares its eelness with all those other eels that are in the barrel or have ever been in the barrel. Now, if that simile doesn't put you off reading entirely, you know you're serious.

But the point is this: stories grow out of other stories, poems out of other poems. And they don't have to stick to genre. Poems can learn from plays, songs from novels. Sometimes influence is direct and obvious, as when the twentieth-century American writer T. Coraghessan Boyle writes "The Overcoat II," a postmodern reworking of the nineteenth-century Russian writer Nikolai Gogol's classic story "The Overcoat," or when William Trevor updates James Joyce's "Two Gallants" with "Two More Gallants," or when John Gardner reworks the medieval *Beowulf* into his little postmodern masterpiece *Grendel.* Other times, it's less direct and more subtle. It may be vague, the shape of a novel generally reminding readers of some earlier novel, or a modern-day miser recalling Scrooge. And of course there's the Bible: among its many other functions, it too is part of the one big story. A female character may remind us of Scarlett O'Hara or Ophelia or even, say, Pocahontas. These similarities—and they may be straight or ironic or comic or tragic—begin to reveal themselves to readers after much practice of reading.

All this resembling other literature is all well and good, but what does it mean for our reading?

Excellent question. If we don't see the reference, it means nothing, right? So the worst thing that occurs is that we're still reading the same story as if the literary precursors weren't there. From there, anything that happens is a bonus. A small part of what transpires is what I call the *aha!* factor, the delight we feel at recognizing a familiar component from earlier experience. That moment of pleasure, wonderful as it is, is not enough, so that awareness of similarity leads us forward. What typically takes place is that we recognize elements from some prior text and begin drawing comparisons and parallels that may be fantastic, parodic, tragic, anything. Once that happens, our reading of the text changes from the reading governed by what's overtly on the page. Let's go back to *Cacciato* for a moment. When the squad falls through the hole in the road in language that recalls *Alice in Wonderland,* we quite reasonably expect that the place they fall into will be a wonderland in its own way. Indeed, right from the beginning, this is true. The oxcart and Sarkin Aung Wan's aunties fall faster than she and the soldiers despite the law of gravity, which decrees that falling bodies all move at thirty-two feet per second squared. The episode allows Paul Berlin to see a Vietcong tunnel, which his inherent terror will never allow him to do in real life, and this fantastic tunnel proves both more elaborate and more harrowing than the real ones. The enemy officer who is condemned to spend the remainder of the war down there accepts his sentence with a weird illogic that would do Lewis Carroll proud. The tunnel even has a periscope through which Berlin can look back at a scene from the real war, his past. Obviously the episode could have these features without invoking Carroll, but the wonderland analogy enriches our understanding of what Berlin has created, furthering our sense of the outlandishness of this portion of his fantasy.

This dialogue between old texts and new is always going on at one level or another. Critics speak of this dialogue as *intertextuality*, the ongoing interaction between poems or stories. This intertextual dialogue deepens and enriches the reading experience, bringing multiple layers of meaning to the text, some of which readers may not even consciously notice. The more we become aware of the possibility that our text is speaking to other texts, the more similarities and correspondences we begin to notice, and the more alive the text becomes. We'll come back to this discussion later, but for now we'll simply note that newer works are having a dialogue with older ones, and they often indicate the presence of this conversation by invoking the older texts with anything from oblique references to extensive quotations.

Once writers know that we know how this game is played, the rules can get very tricky. The late Angela Carter, in her novel *Wise Children* (1992), gives us a theatrical family whose fame rests on Shakespearean performance. We more or less expect the appearance of elements from Shakespeare's plays, so we're not surprised when a jilted young woman, Tiffany, walks onto a television show set distraught, muttering, bedraggled—in a word, mad—and then disappears shortly after departing, evidently having drowned. Her performance is every bit as heartbreaking as that of Ophelia, Prince Hamlet's love interest who goes mad and drowns in the most famous play in English. Carter's novel is about magic as well as Shakespeare, though, and the apparent drowning is a classic bit of misdirection. The apparently dead Tiffany shows up later, to the discomfort of her faithless lover. Shrewdly, Carter counts on our registering "Tiffany = Ophelia" so that she can use her instead as a different Shakespearean character, Hero, who in *Much Ado About Nothing* allows her friends to stage her death and funeral in order to teach *her* fiancé a lesson. Carter employs not only materials from earlier texts but also her knowledge of our responses to them in order to double-cross us, to set us up for a certain kind of thinking so that she can play a larger trick in the narrative. No knowledge of Shakespeare is required to believe Tiffany has died or to be astonished at her return, but the more we know of his plays, the more solidly our responses are locked in. Carter's sleight of narrative challenges our expectations and keeps us on our feet, but it also takes what could seem merely a tawdry incident and reminds us, through its Shakespearean parallels, that there is nothing new in young men mistreating the women who love them, and that those without power in relationships have always had to be creative in finding ways to exert some control of their own. Her new novel is telling a very old story, which in turn is part of the one big story.

But what do we do if we don't see all these correspondences?

First of all, don't worry. If a story is no good, being based on Hamlet won't save it. The characters have to work as characters, as themselves. Sarkin Aung Wan needs to be a great character, which she is, before we worry about her resemblance to a famous character of our acquaintance. If the story is good and the characters work but you don't catch allusions and references and parallels, then you've done nothing worse than read a good story with memorable characters. If you begin to pick up on some of these other elements, these parallels and analogies, however, you'll find your understanding of the novel deepens and becomes more meaningful, more complex.

But we haven't read everything.

Neither have I. Nor has anyone, not even Harold Bloom. Beginning readers, of course, are at a slight disadvantage, which is why professors are useful in providing a broader context. But you definitely can get there on your own. When I was a kid, I used to go mushroom hunting with my father. I would never see them, but he'd say, "There's a yellow sponge," or "There are a couple of black spikes." And because I knew they were there, my looking would become more focused and less vague. In a few moments I would begin seeing them myself, not all of them, but some. And once you begin seeing morels, you can't stop. What a literature professor does is very similar: he tells you when you get near mushrooms. Once you know that, though (and you generally are near them), you can hunt for mushrooms on your own.

5

When in Doubt,
It's from Shakespeare . . .

Quick quiz: What do John Cleese, Cole Porter, *Moonlighting,* and *Death Valley Days* have in common? No, they're not part of some Communist plot. All were involved with some version of *The Taming of the Shrew,* by that former glover's apprentice from Stratford-upon-Avon, William Shakespeare. Cleese played Petruchio in the BBC production of the complete Shakespeare plays in the 1970s. Porter wrote the score for *Kiss Me, Kate,* the modern musical-comedy version on Broadway and on film. The *Moonlighting* episode called "Atomic Shakespeare" was one of the funniest and most inventive on a show that was consistently funny and inventive. It was comparatively faithful to the spirit of the original while capturing the essence of the show's regular characters. The truly odd duck here is *Death Valley Days,* which was an anthology show from the 1950s and 1960s sometimes hosted by a future president, Ronald Reagan, and sponsored by Twenty Mule Team Borax. Their retelling was set in the Old West and completely free of Elizabethan English. For a lot of us, that particular show was either our first encounter with the Bard or our first intimation that he could actually be fun, since in public school, you may recall, they only teach his tragedies. These examples represent only the tip of the iceberg for the perennially abused *Shrew:* its plot seems to be permanently available to be moved in time and space, adapted, altered, updated, set to music, reimagined in myriad ways.

If you look at any literary period between the eighteenth and twenty-first centuries, you'll be amazed by the dominance of the Bard. He's everywhere, in every literary form you can think of. And he's never the same: every age and every writer reinvents its own Shakespeare. All this from a man who we're still not sure actually wrote the plays that bear his name.

Try this. In 1982 Paul Mazursky directed an interesting modern version of *The Tempest.* It had an Ariel figure (Susan Sarandon), a comic but monstrous Caliban (Raul Julia), and a Prospero (famed director John Cassavetes), an island, and magic of a sort. The film's title? *Tempest.* Woody Allen reworked *A Midsummer*

Night's Dream as his film *A Midsummer Night's Sex Comedy.* Natch. The BBC series *Masterpiece Theatre* has recast *Othello* as a contemporary story of black police commissioner John Othello, his lovely white wife Dessie, and his friend Ben Jago, deeply resentful at being passed over for promotion. The action will surprise no one familiar with the original. Add that production to a nineteenth-century opera of some note based on the play. *West Side Story* famously reworks *Romeo and Juliet,* which resurfaces again in the 1990s, in a movie featuring contemporary teen culture and automatic pistols. And that's a century or so after Tchaikovsky's ballet based on the same play. *Hamlet* comes out as a new film every couple of years, it seems. Tom Stoppard considers the role and fate of minor characters from *Hamlet* in his play *Rosencrantz and Guildenstern Are Dead.* And that bastion of high culture, *Gilligan's Island,* had an episode where Phil Silvers, famous as TV's Sergeant Bilko and therefore adding to the highbrow content, was putting together a musical *Hamlet,* the highlight of which was Polonius's "Neither a borrower nor a lender be" speech set to the tune of "Habanera" from Bizet's *Carmen.* Now that's art.

Nor is the Shakespeare adaptation phenomenon restricted to the stage and screen. Jane Smiley rethinks *King Lear* in her novel *A Thousand Acres* (1991). Different time, different place, same meditation upon greed, gratitude, miscalculation, and love. Titles? William Faulkner liked *The Sound and the Fury*. Aldous Huxley decided on *Brave New World*. Agatha Christie chose *By the Pricking of My Thumbs*, which statement Ray Bradbury completed with *Something Wicked This Way Comes*. The all-time champion for Shakespeare references, though, must be Angela Carter's final novel, *Wise Children*. The children of the title are twins, illegitimate daughters of the most famous Shakespearean actor of his age, who is the son of the most famous Shakespearean of *his* age. While the twins, Dora and Nora Chance, are song-and-dance artists—as opposed to practitioners of "legitimate" theater—the story Dora tells is full to overflowing with Shakespearean passions and situations. Her grandfather kills his unfaithful wife and himself in a manner strongly reminiscent of *Othello*. As we saw in the previous chapter, a woman seems to drown like Ophelia, only to turn up in a hugely surprising way very late in the book like Hero in *Much Ado About Nothing*. The novel is full of astonishing disappearances and reappearances, characters in disguise, women dressed as men, and the two most spiteful daughters since Regan and

Goneril brought ruin to Lear and his kingdom. Carter envisions a film production of *A Midsummer Night's Dream* more disastrously hilarious than anything the "rude mechanicals" of the original could conceive of, the results recalling the real-life film version from the 1930s.

Those are just a few of the uses to which Shakespeare's plots and situations get put, but if that's all he amounted to, he'd only be a little different from any other immortal writer.

But that's not all.

You know what's great about reading old Will? You keep stumbling across lines you've been hearing and reading all your life. Try these:

> *To thine own self be true*

> *All the world's a stage, / And all the men and women merely players*

> *What's in a name? That which we call a rose / By any other name would smell as sweet*

> *What a rogue and peasant slave am I*

> *Good night, sweet prince, / And flights of angels sing thee to thy rest!*

> *Get thee to a nunnery*

Who steals my purse steals trash

[Life's] a tale / Told by an idiot, full of sound and fury, / Signifying nothing

The better part of valor is discretion

(Exit, pursued by a bear)

A horse! a horse! my kingdom for a horse!

We few, we happy few, we band of brothers

Double, double, toil and trouble; / Fire burn and cauldron bubble

By the pricking of my thumbs, / Something wicked this way comes

The quality of mercy is not strained, / It droppeth as the gentle rain from heaven

O brave new world, / That has such people in't!

Oh, and lest I forget,

To be, or not to be, that is the question.

Ever heard any of those? This week? Today? I heard one of them in a news broadcast the morning I started composing this chapter. In my copy of *Bartlett's Familiar Quotations*, Shakespeare takes up forty-seven pages. I will admit that not every one of the citations is all *that* familiar, but enough of them are. In fact, the hardest part of compiling my list of quotations was stopping. I could have gone on all day expanding the list without getting into anything too obscure. My first guess is that you probably have not read most of the plays from which these quotations are taken; my second guess is that you know the phrases anyway. Not where they're from necessarily, but the quotes themselves (or the popular versions of them).

All right, so the Bard is always with us. What does it mean?

He means something to us as readers in part because he means so much to our writers. So let's consider why writers turn to our man.

It makes them sound smarter?

Smarter than what?

Than quoting Rocky and Bullwinkle, for instance.

Careful, I'm a big fan of Moose and Squirrel. Still, I take your point. There are lots of sources that don't sound as good as Shakespeare. Almost all of them, in fact.

Plus, it indicates that you've read him, right? You've come across this wonderful phrase in the course of your reading, so clearly you're an educated person.

Not inevitably. I could have given you Richard III's famous request for a horse from the time I was nine.

My father was a great fan of that play and loved to recount the desperation of that scene, so I began hearing it in the early grades. He was a factory worker with a high school education and not particularly interested in impressing anybody with his fancy learning. He was pleased, however, to be able to talk about these great stories, these plays he had read and loved. I think that's a big part of the motivation. We love the plays, the great characters, the fabulous speeches, the witty repartee even in times of duress. I hope never to be mortally stabbed, but if I am, I'd sure like to have the self-possession, when asked if it's bad, to answer, "No, 'tis not so deep as a well, nor so wide as a church door; but 'tis enough, 'twill serve," as Mercutio does in *Romeo and Juliet.* I mean, to be dying and clever at the same time, how can you not love that? Rather than saying it proves you're well-read, I think what happens is that writers quote what they've read or heard, and more of them have Shakespeare stuck in their heads than anything else. Except Bugs Bunny, of course.

And it gives what you're saying a kind of authority.

As a sacred text confers authority? Or as something exquisitely said confers authority? Yes, there is definitely a sacred-text quality at work here. When pioneer families went west in their prairie schooners, space was at a premium, so they generally carried only two books: the Bible and Shakespeare. Name another writer to whom high schoolers are subjected in each of four years. If you live in a medium-sized theater market, there is precisely one writer you can count on being in production somewhere in your area every year, and it is neither August Wilson nor Aristophanes. So there is a ubiquity to Shakespeare's work that makes it rather like a sacred text: at some very deep level he is ingrained in our psyches. But he's there because of the beauty of those lines, those scenes, and those plays. There is a kind of authority lent by something being almost universally known, where one has only to utter certain lines and people nod their heads in recognition.

But here's something you might not have thought of. Shakespeare also provides a figure against whom writers can struggle, a source of texts against which other texts can bounce ideas. Writers find themselves engaged in a relationship with older writers; of course, that relationship plays itself out through the texts, the new one emerging in part through earlier texts that exert influence on the writer in one way or another. This relationship contains considerable potential for struggle, which as we mentioned in the previous chapter is called *intertextuality*. Naturally, none of this is exclusive to Shakespeare, who just happens to be such a towering figure that a great many writers find themselves influenced by him. On intertextuality, more later. For now, an example. T. S. Eliot, in "The Lovesong of J. Alfred Prufrock" (1917), has his neurotic, timorous main character say he was never cut out to be Prince Hamlet, that the most he could be is an extra, someone who could come on to fill out the numbers onstage or possibly be sacrificed to plot exigency. By invoking not a generic figure—"I am just not cut out to be a tragic hero," for instance—but the most famous tragic hero, Hamlet, Eliot provides an instantly recognizable situation for his protagonist and adds an element of characterization that says more about his self-image than would a whole page of description. The most poor Prufrock could aspire to would be Bernardo and Marcellus, the guards who first see the ghost of Hamlet's father, or possibly Rosencrantz and Guildenstern, the hapless courtiers used by both sides and ultimately sent unknowing to their own executions. Eliot's poem does more, though, than merely draw from *Hamlet.* It also opens up a conversation with its famous predecessor. This is not an age of tragic grandeur, Prufrock suggests, but an age of hapless ditherers. Yes, but we recall that Hamlet is himself a hapless ditherer, and it's only circumstance that saves him from his own haplessness and confers on him something noble and tragic. This brief interplay between texts happens in only a couple of lines of verse, yet it illuminates both Eliot's poem and Shakespeare's play in ways that may surprise us, just a little, and that never would have been called into existence had Eliot not caused Prufrock to invoke *Hamlet* as a way of addressing his own inadequacy.

It's worth remembering that comparatively few writers slavishly copy bits of Shakespeare's work into their own. More commonly there is this kind of dialogue going on in which the new work, while taking bits from the older, is also having its say. The author may be reworking a message, exploring changes (or continuities) in attitudes from one era to another, recalling parts of an earlier work to highlight features of the newly created one, drawing on associations the reader holds in order to fashion something new and, ironically, original. Irony features fairly prominently in the use not only of Shakespeare but of any prior writer. The new writer has his own agenda, her own slant to put on things.

Try this for slant. One of the powerful voices to come out of resistance to apartheid in South Africa is Athol Fugard, best known for his play *"Master Harold"* . . . *and the Boys* (1982). In creating this play Fugard turns to you-know-who. Your first instinct might be that he would grasp one of the tragedies, *Othello,* say, where race is already at issue. Instead he turns to the history plays, to *Henry IV, Part II,* to the story of a young man who must grow up. In Shakespeare, Prince Hal must put his hard-partying ways behind him, stop his carousing with Falstaff, and become Henry, the king who in *Henry V* is capable of leading an army and inspiring the kind of passion that will allow the English to be victorious at Agincourt. He must learn, in other words, to wear the mantle of adult responsibility. In Fugard's contemporary reworking, Henry is Harold, Hally to the black pals with whom he loafs and plays. Like his famous predecessor, Hally must grow up and become Master Harold, worthy successor to his father in the family business. What does it mean, though, to become a worthy successor in an unworthy enterprise? That is Fugard's question. Harold's mantle is made not only of adult responsibility but of racism and heartless disregard, and he learns to wear it well. As we might expect, *Henry IV, Part II* provides a means of measuring Harold's growth, which is actually a sort of regression into the most repugnant of human impulses. At the same time, though, *"Master Harold"* makes us reexamine the assumptions of right—and rights—that we take for granted in watching the Shakespearean original, notions of privilege and noblesse oblige, assumptions about power and inheritance, ideas of accepted behavior and even of adulthood itself. Is it a mark of growing up that one becomes capable, as Harold does, of spitting in the face of a friend? I think not. Fugard reminds us, of course, even if he does not mention it directly, that the grown-up King Henry must, in *Henry V*, have his old friend Falstaff banished. Do the values endorsed by Shakespeare lead directly to the horrors of apartheid? For Fugard they do, and his play leads us back to a reconsideration of those values and the play that contains them.

That's what writers can do with Shakespeare. Of course, they can do it with other writers as well, and they do, if somewhat less frequently. Why? You know why. The stories are great, the characters compelling, the language fabulous. And we know him. You can allude to Fulke Greville, but you'd have to provide your own footnotes.

So what's in it for readers? As the Fugard example suggests, when we recognize the interplay between these dramas, we become partners with the new dramatist in creating meaning. Fugard relies on our awareness of the Shakespearean text as he constructs his play, and that reliance allows him to say more with fewer direct statements. I often tell my students that reading is an activity of the imagination, and the imagination in question is not the writer's alone. Moreover, our understanding of both works becomes richer and deeper as we hear this dialogue playing out; we see the implications for the new work, while at the same time we reconfigure our thinking, if only slightly, about the earlier one. And the writer we know better than any other, the one whose language and whose plays we "know" even if we haven't read him, is Shakespeare.

So if you're reading a work and something sounds too good to be true, you know where it's from.

The rest, dear friends, is silence.

6

. . . Or the Bible

C onnect these dots: garden, serpent, plagues, flood, parting of waters, loaves, fishes, forty days, betrayal, denial, slavery and escape, fatted calves, milk and honey. Ever read a book with all these things in them?

Guess what? So have your writers. Poets. Playwrights. Screenwriters. Samuel L. Jackson's character in *Pulp Fiction*, in between all the swearwords (or that one swearword all those times) is a Vesuvius of biblical language, one steady burst of apocalyptic rhetoric and imagery. His linguistic behavior suggests that at some time Quentin Tarantino, the writer-director, was in contact with the Good Book, despite all his Bad Language. Why is that James Dean film called *East of Eden*? Because the author of the novel on which the film is based, John Steinbeck, knew his Book of Genesis. To be east of Eden, as we shall see, is to be in a fallen world, which is the only kind we know and certainly the only kind there could be in a James Dean film. Or a Steinbeck novel.

The devil, as the old saying goes, can quote Scripture. So can writers. Even those who aren't religious or don't live within the Judeo-Christian tradition may work something in from Job or Matthew or the Psalms. That may explain all those gardens, serpents, tongues of flame, and voices from whirlwinds.

In Toni Morrison's *Beloved* (1987), four white men ride up to the house in Ohio where the escaped slave Sethe has been living with her small children. In a fit of determination to "save" her children from slavery, she tries to kill them, succeeding only with her two-year-old daughter, known later as Beloved. No one, neither ex-slave nor free white, can believe or understand her action, and that incomprehension saves her life and rescues her remaining children from slavery. Does her violent frenzy make sense? No. It's irrational, excessive, disproportionate. They all agree on that. On the other hand, there's something about it that, to us, makes sense. The characters all see four white men from slave country riding up the road. We see, and Sethe intuits, that what's coming in the front gate is the Apocalypse. When the Four Horsemen come, it's the Last Day, the time for Judgment. Morrison's color scheme isn't quite that of St. John's original—it's hard to come up with a green horse—but we know them, not least because she actually calls them "the four horsemen." Not riders, not men on horses, not equestrians. Horsemen. That's pretty unambiguous. Moreover, one of them stays mounted with a rifle slung across his lap. That looks a lot like the fourth horseman, the one who in Revelation rides the pale (or green) horse and whose name is Death. In *Pale Rider* Clint Eastwood actually has a character speak the relevant passage so we don't miss the point (although the unnamed stranger in an Eastwood western is pretty much always Death), but here Morrison does the same with a three-word phrase and a pose. Unmistakable.

When the Apocalypse comes riding up your lane, what will you do?

And that is why Sethe reacts as she does.

Morrison is American, of course, and raised in the Protestant tradition, but the Bible is nonsectarian. James Joyce, an Irish Catholic, uses biblical parallels with considerable frequency. I often teach his story "Araby" (1914), a lovely little gem about the loss of innocence. Another way of saying "loss of innocence," of course, is "the Fall." Adam and Eve, the garden, the serpent, the forbidden fruit. Every story about the loss of innocence is really about someone's private reenactment of the fall from grace, since we experience it not collectively but individually and subjectively. Here's the setup: a young boy—eleven, twelve, thirteen years old, right in there—who has previously experienced life as safe, uncomplicated, and limited to attending school and playing cowboys and Indians in the Dublin streets with his friends, discovers *girls*. Or specifically, one girl, his friend Mangan's sister. Neither the sister nor our young hero has a name, so his situation is made slightly generic, which is useful. Being in early adolescence, the narrator has no way of dealing with the object of his desire, or even the wherewithal to recognize what he feels as desire. After all, his culture does all it can to keep boys and girls separate and pure, and his reading has described relations between the sexes in only the most general and chaste of terms. He promises to try to buy her something from a bazaar, the Araby of the title, to which she can't go (significantly, because of a religious retreat being put on by her convent school). After many delays and frustrations, he arrives at the bazaar just as it's closing. Most of the stalls are closed, but he finally finds one where a young woman and two young men are flirting in ways that are not very appealing to our young swain, and she can scarcely be bothered to ask what he wants. Daunted, he says he wants nothing, then turns away, his eyes blinded by tears of frustration and humiliation. He suddenly sees that his feelings are no loftier than theirs, that he's been a fool, that he's been running this errand on behalf of an ordinary girl who's probably never given him a single thought.

Wait a minute. Innocence maybe. But the Fall?

Sure. Innocence, then its loss. What more do you need?

Something biblical. A serpent, an apple, at least a garden.

Sorry, no garden, no apple. The bazaar takes place inside. But there are two great jars standing by the booth, Joyce says, like Eastern guards. And those guards are as biblical as it gets: "So he drove out the man; and he placed at the east of the garden of Eden Cherubims, and a flaming sword which turned every way, to keep the way of the tree of life." That would be Genesis 3:24 for those of you keeping score. As we all know, there's nothing like a flaming sword to separate you from something, and in this case, that something is a former innocence, whether of Eden or of childhood. The thing about loss-of-innocence stories, the reason they hit so hard, is that they're so final. You can never go back. That's why the boy's eyes sting with blinding tears—it's that flaming sword.

Maybe a writer doesn't want enriching motifs, characters, themes, or plots, but just needs a title. The Bible is full of possible titles. I mentioned *East of Eden* before. Tim Parks has a novel called *Tongues of Flame.* Faulkner has *Absalom, Absalom!* and *Go Down, Moses.* Okay, that last one's from a spiritual, but it's biblical in its basis. Let's suppose you want to write a novel about hopelessness and infertility and the sense that the future no longer exists. You might turn to Ecclesiastes for a passage that reminds us that every night is followed by a new day, that life is an endless cycle of life, death, and renewal, in which one generation succeeds another until the end of time. You might regard that outlook with a certain irony and borrow a phrase from it to express that irony—how the certainty that the earth and humanity will renew themselves, a certainty that has governed human assumptions since earliest times, has just been shredded by four years in which Western civilization tried with some success to destroy itself. You just might if you were a modernist and had lived through the horror that was the Great War. At least that's what Hemingway did, borrowing his title from that biblical passage: *The Sun Also Rises.* Great book, perfect title.

More common than titles are situations and quotations. Poetry is absolutely full of Scripture. Some of that is perfectly obvious. John Milton took most of his subject matter and a great deal of material for his great works from you-know-where: *Paradise Lost, Paradise Regained, Samson Agonistes.* Moreover, our early literature in English is frequently about, and nearly always informed by, religion. Those questing knights in *Sir Gawain and the Green Knight* and *The Faerie Queen* are searching on behalf of their religion whether they know it or not (and they generally do know). *Beowulf* is largely about the coming of Christianity into the old paganism of northern Germanic society—after being about a hero overcoming a villain. Grendel, the monster, is descended from the line of Cain, we're told. Aren't all villains? Even Chaucer's pilgrims in *The Canterbury Tales* (1384), while neither they nor their tales are inevitably holy, are making an Easter pilgrimage to Canterbury Cathedral, and much of their talk invokes the Bible and religious teaching. John Donne was an Anglican minister, Jonathan Swift the dean of St. Patrick's Cathedral, Dublin, Edward Taylor and Anne Bradstreet American Puritans (Taylor a minister). Ralph Waldo Emerson was a Unitarian minister for a spell, while Gerard Manley Hopkins was a Catholic priest. One can barely read Donne or Malory or Hawthorne or Rossetti without running into quotations, plots, characters, whole stories drawn from the

Bible. Suffice it to say that every writer prior to some-time in the middle of the twentieth century was solidly instructed in religion.

Even today a great many writers have more than a nodding acquaintance with the faith of their ancestors. In the century just ended, there are modern religious and spiritual poets like T. S. Eliot and Geoffrey Hill or Adrienne Rich and Allen Ginsberg, whose work is shot through with biblical language and imagery. The dive-bomber in Eliot's *Four Quartets* (1942) looks very like a dove, offering salvation from the bomber's fire through the redemption of pentecostal fires. He bor-rows the figure of Christ joining the disciples on the road to Emmaus in *The Waste Land* (1922), uses the Christmas story in "Journey of the Magi" (1927), offers a fairly idiosyncratic sort of Lenten consciousness in "Ash-Wednesday" (1930). Hill has wrestled with mat-ters of the spirit in the fallen modern world through-out his career, so it is hardly surprising to find biblical themes and images in works such as "The Pentecost Castle" or *Canaan* (1996). Rich, for her part, addresses the earlier poet Robinson Jeffers in "Yom Kippur, 1984," in which she considers the implications of the Day of Atonement, and matters of Judaism appear in her poetry with some frequency. Ginsberg, who never met a religion he didn't like (he sometimes described himself as a "Buddhist Jew"), employs material from Judaism, Christianity, Buddhism, Hinduism, Islam, and virtually every world faith.

Not all uses of religion are straight, of course. Many modern and postmodern texts are essentially ironic, in which the allusions to biblical sources are used not to heighten continuities between the religious tradition and the contemporary moment but to illustrate a disparity or disruption. Needless to say, such uses of irony can cause trouble. When Salman Rushdie wrote *The Satanic Verses* (1988), he caused his characters to parody (in order to show their wickedness, among other things) certain events and persons from the Koran and the life of the Prophet. He knew not everyone would understand his ironic version of a holy text; what he could not imagine was that he could be so far misunderstood as to induce a fatwa, a sentence of death, to be issued against him. In modern literature, many Christ figures (which I will discuss in more detail in Chapter 14) are somewhat less than Christlike, a disparity that does not inevitably go down well with religious conservatives. Quite often, though, ironic parallels are lighter, more comic in their outcome and not so likely to offend. In Eudora Welty's masterful story "Why I Live at the P.O." (1941), the narrator is engaged in a sibling rivalry with her younger sister, who has come home after leaving under suspicious if not actually disgraceful circumstances. The narrator, Sister, is outraged at having to cook two chickens to feed five people and a small child just because her "spoiled" sister has come home. What Sister can't see, but we can, is that those two fowl are really a fatted calf. It may not be a grand feast by traditional standards, but it is a feast, as called for upon the return of the Prodigal Son, even if the son turns out to be a daughter. Like the brothers in the parable, Sister is irritated and envious that the child who left, and ostensibly used up her "share" of familial goodwill, is instantly welcomed, her sins so quickly forgiven.

Then there are all those names, those Jacobs and Jonahs and Rebeccas and Josephs and Marys and Stephens and at least one Hagar. The naming of a character is a serious piece of business in a novel or play. A name has to sound right for a character—Oil Can Harry, Jay Gatsby, Beetle Bailey—but it also has to carry whatever message the writer want to convey about the character or the story. In *Song of Solomon* (1977), Toni Morrison's main family chooses names by allowing the family Bible to fall open, then pointing without looking at the text; whatever proper noun the finger points to, there's the name. That's how you get a girl child in one generation named Pilate and one in the next named First Corinthians. Morrison uses this naming practice to identify features of the family and the community. What else can you possibly use—the atlas? Is there any city or hamlet or river in the world that tells us what we're told by "Pilate"? In this case, the insight is not into the character so named, for no one could be less like Pontius Pilate than the wise, generous, giving Pilate Dead. Rather, her manner of naming tells us a great deal about the society that would lead a man, Pilate's father, to have absolute faith in the efficacy of a book he cannot read, so much so that he is guided by a principle of blind selection.

Okay, so there are a lot of ways the Bible shows up. But isn't that a problem for anyone who isn't exactly . . .

A Bible scholar? Well, I'm not. But even I can sometimes recognize a biblical allusion. I use something I think of as the "resonance test." If I hear something going on in a text that seems to be beyond the scope of the story's or poem's immediate dimensions, if it resonates outside itself, I start looking for allusions to older and bigger texts. Here's how it works.

At the end of James Baldwin's story "Sonny's Blues" (1957), the narrator sends a drink up to the bandstand as a gesture of solidarity and acceptance to his brilliantly talented but wayward brother, Sonny, who takes a sip and, as he launches into the next song, sets the drink on the piano, where it shimmers "like the very cup of trembling." I lived for a good while not knowing where that phrase came from, although to the extent I thought about it, I was pretty sure. The story is so rich and full, the pain and redemption so compelling, the language so wonderful throughout, I didn't need to dwell on the last line for several readings. Still, there was something happening there—a kind of resonance, a sense that there's something meaningful beyond the simple meaning of the words. Peter Frampton says that E major is the great rock chord; all you have to do to set off pandemonium in a concert is to stand onstage alone and strike a big, fat, full E major. Everybody in the arena knows what that chord promises. That sensation happens in reading, too. When I feel that resonance, that "fat chord" that feels heavy yet sparkles with promise or portent, it almost always means the phrase, or whatever, is borrowed from somewhere else and promises special significance. More often than not, particularly if the borrowing feels different in tone and weight from the rest of the prose, that somewhere is the Bible. Then it's a matter of figuring out where and what it means. It helps that I know that Baldwin was a preacher's son, that his most famous novel is called *Go Tell It on the Mountain* (1952), that the story already displays a strong Cain-and-Abel element when the narrator initially denies his responsibility toward Sonny, so my scriptural hunch was pretty strong. Happily, in the case of "Sonny's Blues," the story is so heavily anthologized that it's almost impossible not to find the answer—the phrase comes from Isaiah 51:17. The passage speaks of the cup of the Lord's fury, and the context has to do with sons who have lost their way, who are afflicted, who may yet succumb to desolation and destruction. The ending of the story is therefore made even more provisional and uncertain by the quote from Isaiah. Sonny may make it or he may not. He may relapse into addiction and trouble with the law. Beyond that, though, there is the broader sense of the residents of Harlem, where the story is set, and by extension of black America, as afflicted, as having drunk from that cup of trembling. There is hope in Baldwin's last paragraph, but it is hope tempered by knowledge of terrible dangers.

Is my reading greatly enhanced by this knowledge? Perhaps not greatly. Something subtle happens there, but no thunder and lightning. The meaning doesn't move in the opposite direction or shift radically; if it did, that would be self-defeating, since so many readers would not get the allusion. I think it's more that the ending picks up a little greater weight from the association with Isaiah, a greater impact, pathos even. Oh, I think, it isn't just a twentieth-century problem, this business of brothers having trouble with each other and of young men stumbling and falling; it's been going on since forever. Most of the great tribulations to which human beings are subject are detailed in Scripture. No jazz, no heroin, no rehab centers, maybe, but trouble very much of the kind Sonny has: the troubled spirit that lies behind the outward modern manifestations of heroin and prison. The weariness and resentment and guilt of the brother, his sense of failure at having broken the promise to his dying mother to protect Sonny—the Bible knows all about that, too.

This depth is what the biblical dimension adds to the story of Sonny and his brother. We no longer see merely the sad and sordid modern story of a jazz musician and his algebra-teaching brother. Instead the story resonates with the richness of distant antecedents, with the power of accumulated myth. The story ceases to be locked in the middle of the twentieth century and becomes timeless and archetypal, speaking of the tensions and difficulties that exist always and everywhere between brothers, with all their caring and pain and guilt and pride and love. And that story never grows old.

7

Hanseldee and Greteldum

B y now I've beaten you severely about the head and shoulders with the notion that all literature grows out of other literature. We're dealing in this case, however, with a pretty loose category, which could include novels, stories, plays, poems, songs, operas, films, television, commercials, and possibly a variety of newer or not-yet-invented electronic media we haven't even seen. So let's try being a writer for a moment. You want to borrow from some source to add a bit of flesh to the bare bones of your story. Who ya gonna call?

Actually, *Ghostbusters* is not a bad answer. In the short run. Will people in a hundred years, though, be conversant with film comedy of the 1980s? Maybe not. But they will get it right now. If you want topical resonance, current film or television may work fine, although the frame of reference as well as the staying power may be a little limited. But let's think in terms of slightly more canonical sources. The "literary canon," by the way, is a master list of works that everyone pretends doesn't exist (the list, not the works) but that we all know matters in some important way. A great deal of argument goes into what—and more important who—is in the canon, which is to say, whose work gets studied in college courses. This being America and not France, there is no academy that actually sets a list of canonical texts. The selection is more de facto. When I was in school, the canon was very white and male. Virginia Woolf, for example, was the only modern British woman writer who made the cut at a lot of schools. Nowadays, she'll likely be joined by Dorothy Richardson, Mina Loy, Stevie Smith, Edith Sitwell, or any number of others. The list of "great writers" or "great works" is fairly fluid. But back to the problem of literary borrowing.

So, among "traditional" works, from whom should you borrow? Homer? Half of the people who will read that name think of the guy who says "D'oh!" Have you read *The Iliad* lately? Do they read Homer in Homer, Michigan? Do they care about Troy in Troy, Ohio? In the eighteenth century, Homer was a sure bet, although you were more likely to read him in translation than in Greek. But not now, not if you want most of your readers to get the reference. (That's not a reason not to cite Homer, by the way, only a caution that not everyone will get the message.) Shakespeare, then? After all, he's been the gold standard for allusion for four hundred years and still is. On the other hand, there's the highbrow issue—he may turn off some readers who feel you're trying too hard. Plus, his quotes are like eligible persons of the other sex: all the good ones are taken. Maybe something from the twentieth century. James Joyce? Definitely a problem—so much complexity. T. S. Eliot? He's all quotes from elsewhere to begin with. One of the problems with the diversification of the canon is that modern writers can't assume a common body of knowledge on the part of their readers. What readers know varies so much more than it once did. So what can the writer use for parallels, analogies, plot structures, references, that most of his readers will know?

Kiddie lit.

Yep. *Alice in Wonderland. Treasure Island.* The Narnia novels. *The Wind in the Willows* and *The Cat in the Hat. Goodnight Moon.* We may not know Shylock, but we all know Sam I Am. Fairy tales, too, although only the major ones. Slavic folktales, those darlings of the Russian formalist critics of the 1920s, don't have a lot of currency in Paducah. But thanks to Disney, they know "Snow White" from Vladivostok to Valdosta, "Sleeping Beauty" from Sligo to Salinas. An added bonus here is the lack of ambiguity in fairy tales. While we may not know quite what to think about Hamlet's treatment of Ophelia or the fate of Laertes, we're pretty darned sure what we think about the evil stepmother or Rumpelstiltskin. We kind of like the idea of Prince Charming or the healing power of tears.

Of all the fairy tales available to the writer, there's one that has more drawing power than any other, at least in the late twentieth century: "Hansel and Gretel." Every age has its own favorite stories, but the story of children lost and far from home has a universal appeal. For the age of anxiety, the age when Blind Faith sang "Can't Find My Way Home," the age of not just Lost Boys but lost generations, "H&G" has to be the preferred story. And it is. The tale shows up in a variety of ways in a host of stories from the sixties on. Robert Coover has a story called "The Gingerbread House" (1969) whose innovation is that the two children aren't called Hansel and Gretel. The story makes use of our knowledge of the original story by employing signs we'll recognize as standing in for the parts we're familiar with: since we already know the story from the arrival at the gingerbread house till the shove into the oven, Coover doesn't mention it. The witch, for example, as the story progresses is metonymically transformed into the black rags she wears, as if we're just catching her out of the corner of our eye (metonymy is the rhetorical device in which a thing is used to name another thing with which it is closely associated, as when "Washington" is used to represent the federal government's position on an issue). We don't see her attack the children directly; rather, she kills the doves that eat the bread crumbs. In some ways, this act is even more menacing; it's as if she is erasing the only memory of the children's way home. When, at the end of the tale, the boy and girl arrive at the gingerbread house, we only get a glimpse of the black rags flapping in the breeze. We're made to reevaluate what we know of this story, of the degree to which we take its elements for granted. By stopping the story where the drama normally kicks in, with the children innocently transgressing against the witch's property, Coover forces us to see how our responses—anxiety, trepidation, excitement—are conditioned by our previous encounters with the original fairy tale. See, he suggests, you don't need the story because you have already internalized it so completely. That's one thing writers can do with readerly knowledge of source texts, in this case fairy tales. They can mess around with the stories and turn them upside down. Angela Carter does that in *The Bloody Chamber* (1979), a collection of stories that tear the roof off old, sexist fairy tales to create subversive, feminist revisions. She upends our expectations about the story of Bluebeard, or Puss-in-Boots, or Little Red Riding Hood to make us see the sexism inherent in those stories and, by extension, in the culture that embraced them.

But that's not the only way to use old stories. Coover and Carter put the emphasis on the old story itself, while most writers are going to dredge up pieces of the old tale to shore up aspects of their own narratives without placing the focus on "Hansel and Gretel" or "Rapunzel." Okay, let's assume you're the writer. You have a young couple, maybe not children, and certainly not the children of the woodsman, and definitely not brother and sister. Let's say you have a pair of young lovers, and for whatever reason they're lost. Maybe their car broke down far from home; maybe there's no forest, but a city, all public housing high-rises. They've taken a wrong turn, suburban types with a BMW, and they're in a part of town that is wilderness as far as they're concerned. So they're lost, no cell phone, and maybe the only option turns out to be a crack house. What you've got in this hypothetical tale is a fairly dramatic setup that's already fraught with possibility. All perfectly modern. No woodcutter. No bread crumbs.

No gingerbread. So why dredge up some moldy old fairy tale? What can it possibly tell us about this modern situation?

Well, what elements do you want to emphasize in your story? What feature of the plight of these young people most resonates for you? It might be the sense of lostness. Children too far from home, in a crisis not of their own making. Maybe the temptation: one child's gingerbread is another's drugs. Maybe it's having to fend for themselves, without their customary support network.

Depending on what you want to accomplish, you may choose some prior tale (in our case, "H&G") and emphasize what you see as corresponding elements in the two tales. It may be pretty simple, like the guy wishing they had a trail of bread crumbs because he missed a turn or two back there and doesn't know this part of town. Or the woman hoping this doesn't turn out to be the witch's house.

Here's the good deal for you as writer: You don't have to use the whole story. Sure, it has X, Y, and B, but not A, C, and Z. So what? We're not trying to re-create the fairy tale here. Rather, we're trying to make use of details or patterns, portions of some prior story (or, once you really start thinking like a professor, "prior text," since everything is a text) to add depth and texture to your story, to bring out a theme, to lend irony to a statement, to play with readers' deeply ingrained knowledge of fairy tales. So use as much or as little as you want. In fact, you may invoke the whole story simply by a single small reference.

Why? Because fairy tales, like Shakespeare, the Bible, mythology, and all other writing and telling, belong to the one big story, and because, since we were old enough to be read to or propped up in front of a television, we've been living on that story, and on its fairy variants. Once you've seen Bugs Bunny or Daffy Duck in a version of one of the classics, you pretty much own it as part of your consciousness. In fact, it will be hard to read the Brothers Grimm and not think Brothers Warner.

Doesn't that work out to be sort of ironic?

Absolutely. That's one of the best side effects of borrowing from any prior text. Irony, in various guises, drives a great deal of fiction and poetry, even when the work isn't overtly ironic or when the irony is subtle. Let's face it, these two clandestine lovers are hardly babes in the woods. But maybe they are. Socially out of their depth in this part of town. Morally misguided, perhaps. Lost and in danger. Ironically, their symbols of power—BMW, Rolex watch, money, expensive clothes—don't help them a bit and actually make them more vulnerable. Finding their way and avoiding the witch may be as hard for them as for the two pint-sized venturers of the original. So they don't have to push anyone into an oven, or leave a trail of crumbs, or break off and eat any of the siding. And they are probably far from innocent. Whenever fairy tales and their simplistic worldview crop up in connection with our complicated and morally ambiguous world, you can almost certainly plan on irony.

In the age of existentialism and thereafter, the story of lost children has been all the rage. Coover. Carter. John Barth. Tim O'Brien. Louise Erdrich. Toni Morrison. Thomas Pynchon. On and on and on. But you don't have to use "Hansel and Gretel" just because it's the flavor of the month. Or even of the last half century. "Cinderella" will always have her uses. "Snow White" works. Anything in fact with an evil queen or stepmother. "Rapunzel" has her applications; even the J. Geils Band mentions her. Something with a Prince Charming? Okay, but tough to live up to the comparison, so be prepared for irony.

I've been talking here as if you're the writer, but you know and I know that we're really readers. So how does this apply? For one thing, it has to do with how you attack a text. When you sit down to read a novel, you want character, story, ideas, the usual business. Then, if you're like me, you'll start looking for glimpses of the familiar: hey, that kind of feels like something I know. Oh wait, that's out of *Alice in Wonderland*. Now *why* would she draw a parallel to the Red Queen here? Is that the hole in the ground? *Why?* Always, *why?*

Here's what I think we do: we want strangeness in our stories, but we want familiarity, too. We want a new novel to be not quite like anything we've read before. At the same time, we look for it to be sufficiently like other things we've read so that we can use those to make sense of it. If it manages both things at once, strangeness and familiarity, it sets up vibrations, harmonies to go with the melody of the main story line. And those harmonies are where a sense of depth, solidity, resonance comes from. Those harmonies may come from the Bible, from Shakespeare, from Dante or Milton, but also from humbler, more familiar texts.

So next time you go to your local bookstore and carry home a novel, don't forget your Brothers Grimm.

8

It's Greek to Me

In these last three chapters we've talked about three sorts of myth: Shakespearean, biblical, and folk/fairy tale. The connection of religion and myth sometimes causes trouble in class when someone takes myth to mean "untrue" and finds it hard to unite that meaning with deeply held religious beliefs. That's not what I mean by "myth," though. Rather, what I'm suggesting is the shaping and sustaining power of story and symbol. Whether one believes that the story of Adam and Eve is true, literally or figuratively, matters, but not in this context. Here, in this activity of reading and understanding literature, we're chiefly concerned with how that story functions as material for literary creators, the way in which it can inform a story or poem, and how it is perceived by the reader. All three of these mythologies work as sources of material, of correspondences, of depth for the modern writer (and every writer is modern—even John Dryden was not archaic when he was writing), and provided they're recognizable to the reader, they enrich and enhance the reading experience. Of the three, biblical myth probably covers the greatest range of human situations, encompassing all ages of life including the next life, all relationships whether personal or governmental, and all phases of the individual's experience, physical, sexual, psychological, spiritual. Still, both the worlds of Shakespeare and of fairy and folk tales provide fairly complete coverage as well.

What we mean in speaking of "myth" in general is story, the ability of story to explain ourselves to ourselves in ways that physics, philosophy, mathematics, chemistry—all very highly useful and informative in their own right—can't. That explanation takes the shape of stories that are deeply ingrained in our group memory, that shape our culture and are in turn shaped by it, that constitute a way of seeing by which we read the world and, ultimately, ourselves. Let's say it this way: **myth is a body of story that matters.**

Every community has its own body of story that matters. Nineteenth-century composer Richard Wagner went back to the Germanic myths for the material for his operas, and whether the results are good or bad in either historic or musical terms, the impulse to work with his tribal myths is completely understandable. The late twentieth century witnessed a great surge of Native American writing, much of which went back to tribal myth for material, for imagery, for theme, as in the case of Leslie Marmon Silko's "Yellow Woman," Louise Erdrich's Kashpaw/Nanapush novels, and Gerald Vizenor's peculiar *Bearheart: The Heirship Chronicles.* When Toni Morrison introduces human flight into *Song of Solomon,* many readers, white readers especially, take her to be referring to Icarus, whereas what she really has in mind, she has said, is the myth of the flying Africans, a story that matters to her community, her tribe. On one level, there's not much difference between Silko's project and Wagner's; he too is simply going back to the myths of his tribe. We sometimes forget that people in an age of top hats and stiff collars had tribes, but we do so at our peril. In all these cases, what the artist is doing is reaching back for stories that matter to him and his community—for myth.

In European and Euro-American cultures, of course, there's another source of myth. Let me rephrase that: MYTH. When most of us think "myth," we mean the northern shores of the Mediterranean between two and three thousand years ago. We mean Greece and Rome. Greek and Roman myth is so much a part of the fabric of our consciousness, of our unconscious really, that we scarcely notice. You doubt me? In the town where I live, the college teams are known as the Spartans. Our high school? The Trojans. In my state we have a Troy (one of whose high schools is Athens—and they say there are no comedians in education), an Ithaca, a Sparta, a Romulus, a Remus, and a Rome. These communities are scattered around the state and date from different periods of settlement. Now if a town in the center of Michigan, a fair distance from anything that can be called Aegean or Ionian (although it's not very far from the town of Ionia), can be named Ithaca, it suggests that Greek myth has had pretty good staying power.

Let's go back to Toni Morrison for a moment. I'm always slightly amazed that Icarus gets all the ink. It was his father, Daedalus, who crafted the wings, who knew how to get off Crete and safely reach the mainland, and who in fact flew to safety. Icarus, the kid, the daredevil, failed to follow his father's advice and plunged to his death. His fall remains a source of enduring fascination for us and for our literature and art. In it we see so much: the parental attempt to save the child and the grief at having failed, the cure that

proves as deadly as the ailment, the youthful exuber-
ance that leads to self-destruction, the clash between
sober, adult wisdom and adolescent recklessness, and
of course the terror involved in that headlong descent
into the sea. Absolutely none of this has anything to
do with Morrison and her flying Africans, so it's little
wonder that she's a bit mystified by this response of
her readers. But it's a story and a pattern that is so
deeply burrowed into our consciousness that readers
may almost automatically consider it whenever flying
or falling is invoked. Clearly it doesn't fit the situation
in *Song of Solomon*. But it does apply in other works.
In 1558 Pieter Brueghel painted a wonderful picture,
Landscape with Fall of Icarus. In the foreground we
see a plowman and his ox, just beyond him a shepherd
and his flock, and at sea a merchant ship sailing plac-
idly along; this is a scene of utter ordinariness and tran-
quillity. Only in the lower right corner of the painting
is there anything even remotely suggestive of trouble:
a pair of legs askew as they disappear into the water.
That's our boy. He really doesn't have much of a pres-
ence in the frame, but his presence makes all the differ-
ence. Without the pathos of the doomed boy, we have a
picture of farming and merchant shipping with no nar-
rative or thematic power. I teach, with some regularity,
two great poems based on that painting, W. H. Auden's

"Musée des Beaux Arts" (1940) and William Carlos Williams's "Landscape with Fall of Icarus" (1962). They're wonderful poems, very different from each other in tone, style, and form, but in essential agreement about how the world goes on even in the face of our private tragedies. Each artist alters what he finds in the painting. Brueghel introduces the plowman and the ship, neither of which appears in the version that comes to us from the Greeks. And Williams and Auden find, in their turn, slightly different elements to emphasize in the painting. Williams's poem stresses the pictorial elements of the painting, trying to capture the scene while sneaking in the thematic elements. Even his arrangement of the poem on the page, narrow and highly vertical, recalls the body plummeting from the sky. Auden's poem, on the other hand, is a meditation on the private nature of suffering and the way in which the larger world takes no interest in our private disasters. It is astonishing and pleasing to discover that the painting can occasion these two very different responses. Beyond them, readers find their own messages in all this. As someone who was a teenager in the sixties, I am reminded by the fate of Icarus of all those kids who bought muscle cars with names like Mustang and Firebird and Charger and Barracuda. All the driver education and solid parental advice in the world can't overcome the allure of that kind of power, and sadly, in too many cases those young drivers shared the fate of Icarus. My students, somewhat younger than I am, will inevitably draw other parallels. Still, it all goes back to the myth: the boy, the wings, the unscheduled dive.

So that's one way classical myth can work: overt subject matter for poems and paintings and operas and novels. What else can myth do?

Here's a thought. Let's say you wanted to write an epic poem about a community of poor fishermen in the Caribbean. If this was a place you came from, and you knew these people like you know your own family, you'd want to depict the jealousies and resentments and adventure and danger, as well as capturing their dignity and their life in a way that conveys all that has escaped the notice of tourists and white property owners. You could, I suppose, try being really, *really* earnest, portraying the characters as very serious and sober, making them noble by virtue of their goodness. But I bet that wouldn't work. What you'd wind up with instead would probably be very stiff and artificial, and artificiality is never noble. Besides, these folks aren't saints. They make a lot of mistakes: they're petty, envious, lustful, occasionally greedy as well as courageous, elegant, powerful, knowledgeable, profound. And you want noble, after all, not Tonto—there's no Lone Ranger here.

Alternatively, you might try grafting their story onto some older story of rivalry and violence, a story where even the victor is ultimately doomed, a story where, despite occasional personal shortcomings, the characters have an unmistakable nobility. You could give your characters names like Helen, Philoctetes, Hector, and Achille. At least that's what Nobel Prize winner Derek Walcott does in his *Omeros* (1990). Those names are drawn, of course, from *The Iliad,* although Walcott uses elements—parallels, persons, and situations—of both it and *The Odyssey* in his epic.

The question we will inevitably ask is, Why?

Why should someone in the late twentieth century draw on a story that was passed along orally from the twelfth through the eighth century B.C. and not written down until maybe two or three hundred years later? Why should someone try to compare modern fishermen with these legendary heroes, many of whom were descended from gods? Well for starters, Homer's legendary heroes *were* farmers and fishermen. Besides, aren't we all descended from gods? Walcott reminds us by this parallel of the potential for greatness that resides in all of us, no matter how humble our worldly circumstances.

That's one answer. The other is that the situations match up more closely than we might expect. The plot of *The Iliad* is not particularly divine or global. Those who have never read it assume mistakenly that it is the story of the Trojan War. It is not. It is the story of a single, rather lengthy action: the wrath of Achilles (a mere fifty-three days out of ten years). Achilles becomes angry with his leader, Agamemnon, withdraws his support from the Greeks, only rejoining the battle when the consequences of his action have destroyed his best friend, Patroclus. At this point he turns his wrath against the Trojans and in particular their greatest hero, Hector, whom he eventually kills. His reason for such anger? Agamemnon has taken his war prize. Trivial? It gets worse. The prize is a woman. Agamemnon, forced by divine order and by public sentiment to return his concubine to her father, retaliates against the person who most publicly sided against him, Achilles, by taking his concubine, Briseis. Is that petty enough? Is that noble? No Helen, no judgment of Paris, no Trojan horse. At its core, it's the story of a man who goes berserk because his stolen war bride is confiscated, acted out against a background of wholesale slaughter, the whole of which is taking place because another man, Menelaus (brother of Agamemnon) has had *his* wife stolen by Paris, half brother of Hector. That's how Hector winds up having to carry the hopes for salvation of all Troy on his shoulders.

And yet somehow, through the centuries, this story dominated by the theft of two women has come to epitomize ideals of heroism and loyalty, sacrifice and loss. Hector is more stubbornly heroic in his doomed enterprise than anyone you've ever seen. Achilles' grief at the loss of his beloved friend is truly heartbreaking. The big duels—between Hector and Ajax, between Diomedes and Paris, between Hector and Patroclus, between Hector and Achilles—are genuinely exciting and suspenseful, their outcomes sources of grand celebration and dismay. No wonder so many modern writers have often borrowed from and emulated Homer.

And when did that begin?

Almost immediately. Virgil, who died in 19 B.C., patterned his Aeneas on the Homeric heroes. If Achilles did it or Odysseus went there, so does Aeneas. Why? It's what heroes do. Aeneas goes to the underworld. Why? Odysseus went there. He kills a giant from the enemy camp in a final climactic battle. Why? Achilles did. And so on. The whole thing is less derivative than it sounds and not without humor and irony. Aeneas and his followers are survivors of Troy, so here we have this Trojan hero acting out the patterns set down by his enemies. Moreover, when these Trojans sail past Ithaca, home to Odysseus, they jeer and curse the agent of their destruction. On the whole, though, Virgil has him undertake these actions because Homer had already defined what it means to be a hero.

Back to Walcott. Almost exactly two thousand years after Virgil, Walcott has his heroes perform actions that we can recognize as symbolic reenactments of those in Homer. Sometimes it's a bit of a stretch, since we can't have a lot of battlefield duels out in the fishing boats. Nor can he call his Helen "the face that launched a thousand dinghies." Lacks grandeur, that phrase. What he can do, though, is place them in situations where their nobility and their courage are put to the test, while reminding us that they are acting out some of the most basic, most primal patterns known to humans, exactly as Homer did all those centuries before. The need to protect one's family: Hector. The need to maintain one's dignity: Achilles. The determination to remain faithful and to have faith: Penelope. The struggle to return home: Odysseus. Homer gives us four great struggles of the human being: with nature, with the divine, with other humans, and with ourselves. What is there, after all, against which we need to prove ourselves but those four things?

In our modern world, of course, parallels may be *ironized*, that is, turned on their head for purposes of irony. How many of us would see the comedy of three escaped convicts as parallel to the wanderings of Odysseus? Still, that's what brothers Joel and Ethan Coen give us in their 2000 film *O Brother, Where Art Thou?* It's about trying to get home, isn't it? Or this, the most famous example: a single day in Dublin in 1904, on which a young man decides on his future and an older man wanders the city, eventually returning home to his wife in the small hours of the next morning. The book has only one overt clue that this all might have something to do with Homer, its one-word title: *Ulysses* (1922). As we now know, James Joyce envisioned every one of the eighteen episodes of the novel as a parallel to some incident or situation in *The Odyssey*. There's an episode in a newspaper office, for instance, which parallels Odysseus's visit to Aeolus, the god of the winds, but the parallel may seem pretty tenuous. To be sure, newspapermen are a windy group and there are a lot of rhetorical flourishes in the episode, to say nothing of the fact that a gust of wind does zip through at one point. Still, we can see it as resembling the Homeric original only if we understand that resemblance in terms of a funhouse mirror, full of distortion and goofy correspondences—if we understand it, in other words, as an ironic parallel. The fact that it's ironic makes the parallel—and the Aeolus episode—such fun. Joyce is less interested than Walcott in investing his characters with classical nobility, although finally they do take on something of that quality. After watching poor old Leopold Bloom stroll around Dublin all day and half the night, running into no end of trouble and recalling great heartbreak in his life, we may well come to feel he is noble in his own way. His nobility, however, is not that of Odysseus.

Greek and Roman myth, of course, is more than Homer. The transformations of Ovid's *Metamorphoses* show up in all sorts of later works, not least in Franz Kafka's story of a man who wakes up one morning to find he's changed into an enormous beetle. He called it "The Metamorphosis." Indiana Jones may look like pure Hollywood, but the intrepid searcher after fabulous treasure goes back to Apollonius and *The Argonautica*, the story of Jason and the Argonauts. Something a bit homier? Sophocles' plays of Oedipus and his doomed clan show up over and over again in all sorts of variations. There is, in fact, no form of dysfunctional family or no personal disintegration of character for which there is not a Greek or Roman model. Not for nothing do the names of Greek tragic characters figure in Freud's theories. The wronged woman gone violent in her grief and madness? Would you like Aeneas and Dido or Jason and Medea? And as in every good early religion, they had an explanation for natural phenomena, from the change of seasons (Demeter and Persephone and Hades) to why the nightingale sounds the way it does (Philomena and Tereus). Happily for us, most of it got written down, often in several versions, so that we have access to this wonderful body of story. And because writers and readers share knowledge of a big portion of this body of story, this mythology, when writers use it, we readers recognize it, sometimes to its full extent, sometimes only dimly or only because we know the Looney Tunes version. That recognition makes our experience of literature richer, deeper, more meaningful, so that our own modern stories also matter, also share in the power of myth.

Among the more interesting recent developments in writing for younger readers is the *Percy Jackson and the Olympians* series by Rick Riordan. The quintet of novels begins with *The Lightning Thief* (2005). Percy is a misfit kid who finds out he's the son of Poseidon and is accused of stealing Zeus's weapon of choice, the lightning bolt. Then he finds out his pal is a satyr, fights a minotaur, and befriends a daughter of Athena, and all Hades breaks loose. As a demigod, Percy has issues with normality (things like ADHD and dyslexia), but he's the real deal on the hero front, as he gets a chance to prove over and over. His divine bloodlines help, as do his mythic buddies. It's one thing, you know, to be the offspring of a former star pupil at your wizarding prep school, but to have the sea god as your dad, well . . .

Oh, did I forget to say? That title of Walcott's, *Omeros*? In the local dialect, it means Homer. Naturally.

9

It's More Than Just Rain or Snow

It was a dark and stormy night. What, you've heard that one? Right, Snoopy. And Charles Schulz had Snoopy write it because it was a cliché, and had been one for a very long time, way back when your favorite beagle decided to become a writer. This one we know: Edward Bulwer-Lytton, celebrated Victorian popular novelist, actually did write, "It was a dark and stormy night." In fact, he began a novel with it, and not a very good novel, either. And now you know everything you need to know about dark and stormy nights. Except for one thing.

Why?

You wondered that, too, didn't you? Why would a writer want the wind howling and the rain bucketing down, want the manor house or the cottage or the weary traveler lashed and battered?

You may say that every story needs a setting and that weather is part of the setting. That is true, by the way, but it isn't the whole deal. There's much more to it. Here's what I think: weather is never just weather. **It's never just rain.** And that goes for snow, sun, warmth, cold, and probably sleet, although the incidence of sleet in my reading is too rare to generalize.

So what's special about rain? Ever since we crawled up on the land, the water, it seems to us, has been trying to reclaim us. Periodically floods come and try to drag us back into the water, pulling down our improvements while they're at it. You know the story of Noah: lots of rain, major flood, ark, cubits, dove, olive branch, rainbow. I think that biblical tale must have been the most comforting of all to ancient humans. The rainbow, by which God told Noah that no matter how angry he got, he would never try to wipe us out completely, must have come as a great relief.

We in the Judeo-Christian-Islamic world have a fair chunk of mythology invested in rain and its most major by-product. Clearly rain features in other mythologies as well, but for now let this be our cornerstone. Drowning is one of our deepest fears (being land creatures, after all), and the drowning of everything and everybody just magnifies that fear. Rain prompts ancestral memories of the most profound sort.

So water in great volume speaks to us at a very basic level of our being. And at times Noah is what it signifies. Certainly when D. H. Lawrence has the flood go crashing through the family homestead in *The Virgin and the Gypsy* (1930), he's thinking of Noah's flood, the big eraser that destroys but also allows a brand-new start.

Rain, though, can do a lot more. That dark and stormy evening (and I suspect that before general illumination by streetlight and neon all stormy evenings were pretty darned dark) has worlds of atmosphere and mood. Thomas Hardy, a considerably better Victorian writer than Edward B.-L., has a delightful story called "The Three Strangers" (1883) in which a condemned man (escaped), a hangman, and the escapee's brother all converge on a shepherd's house during a christening party. The hangman doesn't recognize his quarry (nor do the members of the party), but the brother does, and runs away, leading to a manhunt and general hilarity, all of which is taking place on a, well, dark and stormy night. Hardy doesn't call it that, but he has great fun describing, in his ironic and detached tone, the rain lashing down on hapless wayfarers, forcing them to seek shelter where they can; hence the appearance of our three gentlemen callers. Now the Bible is never very far from Hardy's thoughts, but I daresay he has no thought of Noah when he's writing about this storm. So why does he bring rain into it?

First of all, as a plot device. The rain forces these men together in very uncomfortable (for the condemned man and the brother) circumstances. I occasionally disparage plot, but we should never discount its importance in authorial decision-making. Second, atmospherics. Rain can be more mysterious, murkier, more isolating than most other weather conditions. Fog is good, too, of course. Then there is the misery factor. Given the choice between alternatives, Hardy will always go for making his characters more miserable, and rain has a higher wretchedness quotient than almost any other element of our environment. With a little rain and a bit of wind, you can die of hypothermia on the Fourth of July. Needless to say, Hardy loves rain. And finally there is the democratic element. Rain falls on the just and the unjust alike. Condemned man and hangman are thrown into a bond of sorts because rain has forced each of them to seek shelter. Rain can do other things as well, but these are the reasons, it seems to me, that Hardy has chosen a nice, malicious rainstorm for his story.

What other things? For one, it's clean. One of the paradoxes of rain is how clean it is coming down and how much mud it can make when it lands. So if you want a character to be cleansed, symbolically, let him walk through the rain to get somewhere. He can be quite transformed when he gets there. He may also have a cold, but that's another matter. He can be less angry, less confused, more repentant, whatever you want. The stain that was upon him—figuratively—can be removed. On the other hand, if he falls down, he'll be covered in mud and therefore more stained than before. You can have it either way, or both ways if you're really good. The problem with cleansing, though, is the problem with wishes: you have to be careful what you wish for, or for that matter what you want cleansed. Sometimes it backfires. In *Song of Solomon*, Toni Morrison gives her poor jilted lover, Hagar, an encounter with cleansing rain. Having been thrown over by her longtime lover (and cousin—it's very awkward), Milkman, for a more "presentable" love interest (with looks and especially hair nearer the "white" ideal), Hagar spends a desperate day buying clothes and accessories, visiting hair and nail salons, and generally turning herself into a simulacrum of the woman she thinks Milkman wants. After spending all her money and psychic energy in this mad plunge into a fantasy image, she is caught out in a rainstorm that ruins her clothes, her packages, and her coiffure. She is left with her despised, kinky "black" hair and her self-loathing. Rather than washing away some taint, the rain cleanses her of illusions and the false ideal of beauty. The experience, of course, destroys her, and she soon dies of a broken heart and overwatering. So much for the salutary effects of cleansing rains.

On the other hand, rain is also restorative. This is chiefly because of its association with spring, but Noah once again comes into play here. Rain can bring the world back to life, to new growth, to the return of the green world. Of course, novelists being what they are, they generally use this function ironically. In the ending of *A Farewell to Arms* (1929), Hemingway, having killed off Frederic Henry's lover during childbirth, sends the grieving protagonist out of the hospital into, you guessed it, rain. It might be ironic enough to die during childbirth, which is also associated with spring, but the rain, which we might properly expect to be life-giving, further heightens the irony. It's hard to get irony too high for Hemingway. So, too, with Joyce's "The Dead." Near the ending, Gretta Conroy tells her husband about the great love of her life, the long-dead Michael Furey, a consumptive boy who stood outside her window in the rain and died a week later. One might argue that this is simply verisimilitude: if the story is set in the west of Ireland, it almost requires rain. No doubt there is justice in this view. But at the same time, Joyce knowingly plays off our expectations of rain as an agent of new life and restoration because he also knows that we have another, less literary set of associations for rain: the source of chills, colds, pneumonia, death. These come together and clash intriguingly in the image of the boy dying for love: youth, death, replenishment, desolation—they're all rattling around in the figure of poor Michael Furey in the rain. Joyce likes his irony about as high as Hemingway's.

Rain is the principal element of spring. April showers do in fact bring May flowers. Spring is the season not only of renewal but of hope, of new awakenings. Now if you're a modernist poet and therefore given to irony (notice that I've not yet alluded to modernism without having recourse to irony?), you might stand that association on its head and begin your poem with a line like "April is the cruellest month," which is exactly what T. S. Eliot does in *The Waste Land*. In that poem, he plays off our cultural expectations of spring and rain and fertility; better, readers don't even have to ask if he is doing it deliberately, since he very thoughtfully provides notes telling us that he's being deliberate. He even tells us which study of romance he's using: Jessie L. Weston's *From Ritual to Romance* (1920). What Weston talks about in her book is the Fisher King mythology, of which the Arthurian legends are just one part. The central figure in this set of myths—the Fisher

King figure—represents the hero as fixer: something in society is broken, perhaps beyond repair, but a hero emerges to put things right. Since natural and agricultural fertility is so important to our ability to feed and sustain ourselves, much of the material Weston deals with has to do with wastelands and the attempts to restore lost fertility; needless to say, rain figures prominently. Following Weston's lead, Eliot emphasizes the absence of rain from the beginning of his poem. On the other hand, water generally is a mixed medium in his text, the River Thames being polluted and a scene of corruption, complete with a slimy-bellied rat on the bank. Moreover, the rain never quite arrives. We're told at the end that rain is coming, but that's not the same as rain actually hitting the ground around us. So then, it isn't quite happening, and we can't be sure of its effect when it does fall, if it does, but its absence occupies a major space in the poem.

Rain mixes with sun to create rainbows. We mentioned this one before, but it merits further consideration. While we may have minor associations with pots of gold and leprechauns, the main function of the image of the rainbow is to symbolize divine promise, peace between heaven and earth. God promised Noah with the rainbow never again to flood the whole earth. No writer in the West can employ a rainbow without being aware of its signifying aspect, its biblical function. Lawrence called one of his best novels *The Rainbow* (1916); it has, as you would guess, a certain amount of flood imagery, along with all the associations that imagery conveys. When you read about a rainbow, as in Elizabeth Bishop's poem "The Fish" (1947), where she closes with the sudden vision that "everything / was rainbow, rainbow, rainbow," you just know there's some element of this divine pact between human, nature, and God. Of course she lets the fish go. In fact, of any interpretation a reader will ever come up with, the rainbow probably forms the most obvious set of connections. Rainbows are sufficiently uncommon and gaudy that they're pretty hard to miss, and their meaning runs as deep in our culture as anything you care to name. Once you can figure out rainbows, you can do rain and all the rest.

Fog, for instance. It almost always signals some sort of confusion. Dickens uses a miasma, a literal and figurative fog, for the Court of Chancery, the English version of American probate court where estates are sorted out and wills contested, in *Bleak House* (1853). Henry Green uses a heavy fog to gridlock London and strand his wealthy young travelers in a hotel in *Party Going* (1939). In each case, the fog is mental and ethical as well as physical. In almost any case I can think of, authors use fog to suggest that people can't see clearly, that matters under consideration are murky.

And snow? It can mean as much as rain. Different things, though. Snow is clean, stark, severe, warm (as an insulating blanket, paradoxically), inhospitable, inviting, playful, suffocating, filthy (after enough time has elapsed). You can do just about anything you want with snow. In "The Pedersen Kid" (1968), William H. Gass has death arrive on the heels of a monster blizzard. In his poem "The Snow Man" (1923), Wallace Stevens uses snow to indicate inhuman, abstract thought, particularly thought concerned with nothingness, "Nothing that is not there and the nothing that is," as he puts it. Very chilling image, that. And in "The Dead," Joyce takes his hero to a moment of discovery; Gabriel, who sees himself as superior to other people, has undergone an evening in which he is broken down little by little, until he can look out at the snow, which is "general all over Ireland," and suddenly realize that snow, like death, is the great unifier, that it falls, in the beautiful closing image, "upon all the living and the dead."

This will all come up again when we talk about seasons. There are many more possibilities for weather, of course, more than we could cover in a whole book. For now, though, one does well to remember, as one starts reading a poem or story, to check the weather.

10

Never Stand Next to the Hero

As you know by now, from time to time I like to give you life advice. This next bit is the most important lesson I can impart to you, so listen up. If you're approached by some guy to drive his chariot, ask his name. If he says, "Hector," do not consent. Do not stand still. Do not walk away. Run. Very fast. When I teach *The Iliad*, my favorite comic routine is pointing out what happens to Hector's charioteers. The average space between a charioteer being named and being skewered is about five lines. Occasionally, he gets speared before being identified, which seems really unfair. We finally reach the point where I have only to say something like, "Oh, look, a new charioteer," then pause. Everyone knows what comes next. Now, Homer actually has a good bit of intentional comedy in his epic, but I'm pretty sure this is not an instance of that. Rather, it stands as an example—or several examples—of the sort of surrogate fate that befalls heroes. And, alas, the people close to them.

If we except lyric poetry, nearly all literature is character-based. That is, it's about *people.* This is not an observation unique in the history of literary criticism, but it bears remembering from time to time. And for people, characters, to hold our interest as readers or viewers, it is important for them to do things from time to time. Big things: go on quests, marry, divorce, give birth, die, kill, take flight, tame the land, make a mark. Small things: go on walks, dine, take in a movie, play in the park, have a drink, fly a kite, find a penny on the ground. Sometimes the small things become big. Sometimes the big things are smaller than they seem at first. No matter how large or small the actions, though, the most important thing that characters can do is change—grow, develop, learn, mature, call it what you will. As we know from our own lives, change can be difficult, painful, arduous, possibly dangerous. Sometimes even fatal.

Just not to the main character.

One of the most complex instances of this surrogacy phenomenon is also one of the oldest. If ever there was a flawed hero, he is Achilles. *The Iliad,* contrary to popular imagination, is not the story of the Trojan War. Rather, it relates the events of a very small period of time, something like fifty-three days out of the war's ten years. You see, even epics work best if they are about not widespread events but single actions and their consequences—the hero returning home, the rescuer coming to the aid of a community plagued by a monster, the fall from grace of the original two humans. This epic is especially pure: the actions of a single man and their impact on thousands. When I say this part in class, I speak in italics: this work is about *the wrath of Achilles.*

The Big Man becomes angry when Agamemnon, the leader of the Greek forces, steals Achilles's war bride. From there, everything that happens stems from his inordinate anger toward Agamemnon and all those who follow him (essentially, everyone except Achilles's circle). From the tide of battle turning against the Greeks to the final showdown with Hector, it's all about Achilles, even in those numerous books in which he makes no appearance. He's mad and he's going home to Phthia (I've long thought that he doesn't go only because it's unpronounceable), which may strike us as more childish than manly. He doesn't go, but while he stays beside his ships, his heart hardens against the Greeks. Hundreds die; he doesn't care. Agamemnon apologizes and offers to give back everything he took, the girl included. Nearly all of the main heroes—Odysseus, Agamemnon, Diomedes, Eurypylus—are injured; no interest. Clearly, there is only one thing that will prompt him to action. He's not going to like it. His second-in-command, Patroclus, begs him to reenter the war or, failing that, to release the rest of his tribe, the Myrmidons, to return to the fighting, with Patroclus in the lead.

You see where this is heading, right?

Before we get there, however, a bit of context. In addition to being second-in-command, Patroclus has been best friends with Achilles since childhood. There's a long, rather soapy story about how the lesser man came to live in the home of the greater, and how their friendship developed. They are repeatedly depicted in the poem in close proximity to each other, sitting close or leaning against each other. Wait, it gets worse. Patroclus will indeed go into battle, but not as himself. Instead, he wears Achilles' armor. This has the long-term effect of causing Achilles to acquire the fabulous armor made for him by the god Hephaestus. In the short term, it allows Patroclus to frighten the Trojans, who believe for a while that he is the person they most fear; it also provides him the opportunity to be almost as great as his friend. That "almost" is key.

Patroclus visits great mayhem on the Trojans, indeed more than any other Greek thus far. At one point he plunges into the mass of the Trojans three times, each time killing nine enemy warriors. That's quite aside from the named killings he accomplishes. He is so terrific, in fact, that he gets carried away and tries to take the city. The mistake proves fatal. The difference between being Achilles and *almost* being Achilles is the difference between living and dying.

Patroclus's death serves several of Homer's narrative purposes, all of them having to do not with him but with Achilles. Most significantly, the great man must lay aside his anger toward Agamemnon. The problem is that he is essentially an angry person, so the emotion can't be dispelled, only redirected. In killing Patroclus, Hector has unwittingly volunteered to become the new target of that fury. Patroclus is also the only person present at the war for whom Achilles could (and does) genuinely grieve. They're friends from childhood, closer than some brothers. Achilles may rage over having his concubine taken away, but he would never mourn her as he does Patroclus. His ritual debasement—pouring ash and sand over his body and in his hair, weeping copiously, throwing himself on the ground—is one of the great scenes in the epic, every bit the rival of any of the battles. And only one man can make that happen. It's just that Patroclus has no say in the matter.

Nearly tied with that reason for Patroclus's death is the need for new armor, Hector having taken the old as spoils of the fight. But wait, you say—if Patroclus doesn't die, Achilles doesn't need new armor. That's true, but the fact is that wonderful though it may be, his old armor just isn't cool enough for him to be the greatest Greek hero, by which the Greeks understood the greatest hero ever (they were kind of like Americans that way). To make the kind of splash Homer has in mind, Achilles needs not just excellent but divine armor, the stuff only a god can make. And he'll get it, compliments of Hephaestus, the Olympian smith. Tough job, but somebody's got to do it.

And that's the problem with being best pals with a hero. They have needs, or perhaps the narrative has needs on their behalf, but they cannot fulfill those requirements directly, not if the story is to continue. Hey, guess what? That's what friends are for. When Shakespeare needs a line to be crossed that cannot be uncrossed between the Capulets and the Montagues, does he kill Romeo? Of course not. Poor Mercutio, who is really a more engaging fellow than the hero, has to carry that freight. If James Fenimore Cooper in *The Last of the Mohicans* needs to establish the villainous bona fides of Magua and give the protagonist a motive for revenge (not that he generally needs one), does he kill off Natty Bumppo? Not on your life. Rather, he kills young Uncas, the son of Natty's best friend and fellow scout, Chingachgook. In fact, in story and song, book and film, there is generally no more persuasive reason for revenge, outrage, or prompting to action than the killing of the best friend (or his progeny). It really doesn't pay to get too close to hero-types.

But that seems so unfair.

Darned right it's unfair. But you know what? No one cares. Literature has its own logic; it is not life. Not only that, but (and this is key): **characters are not people.** Oh, they may seem like people, skipping and raging and weeping and laughing and all the rest, but they aren't actually people, and we forget that at our peril.

What do you mean, they're not people? If that's true, why should we even care about them?

Excellent question. Or questions. First things first: They're not people because they have never existed. I mean, have you ever met one on the street? Naturally, you wouldn't meet Achilles or Huck Finn or someone from historical literature, but you also won't be meeting any characters out of contemporary literature. Which is mostly a good thing. Harry Potter is not running around loose outside the pages of his books, Voldemort either (see what I mean about a good thing?). Oh, you can meet folks dressed like them sometimes, but not the real deal. Characters may be based on actual persons. Hemingway scholars are fond of reminding us that this character is based on that friend or (more commonly) former friend of the novelist, but being based on that friend is a long way from being him. We do not—and should not—read the character through the filter of the original, if there is one.

I know I have said this before and will say it again, but it bears repeating: if it's not in the text, it doesn't exist. We can only read what is present in a novel, play, or film. If something informed the author's creation of the text but the evidence is not present *in* the text, that's a matter for scholars concerned with motives, not with readers wrestling with meaning. Think of it this way: a vast majority of readers will have no access to that nontextual evidence. How, then, can we expect it to have any bearing on the way we read? The characters are purely textual creations, constructs of words. We know them through descriptions of them as well as through their own words and actions and those of other characters—not through the words (unreported) of the writer's brother-in-law or best enemy on whom the character may be "based." We process those words and actions and decide what to think, with a little help from the author.

Now, your second question: if they're not real people, why should we care about them? Why indeed? Why cheer at Harry Potter's victories? Why weep at Little Nell's death? Why feel anything at all for persons who never existed? Easy. Because we can't help ourselves. Here's the thing about those nonpersons that make us care: **Characters are products of writers' imaginations—and readers' imaginations.** Two powerful forces come together to make a literary character. The writer invents him, using such elements of memory and observation and invention as she needs, and the reader—not readers collectively this time but each individual reader in private—reinvents him, using those same element of *his* memory, *his* observation, and *his* invention. The first, writerly, invention sketches out a figure, while the second, readerly, invention receives that figure and fills in the blank spaces. Sometimes we fill in spaces in ways not authorized by the text without ever noticing that we did so; every experienced reader has gone back to some favorite novel in search of a cherished passage, some crystal-clear personality trait, that is in fact absent from the text. We shape, or rather reshape, characters in order to make sense of them. Reading, as I have said elsewhere, is a full-contact sport; we crash up against the wave of words with all of our intellectual, imaginative, and emotional resources. What results can sometimes be as much our creation as the novelist's or playwright's. Or more. Is it any wonder, then, that we care about what happens to them?

Many of us learned during our formative years that having a shallow, immature, impulsive, reckless friend is hazardous. If we were characters in a novel or film, we probably wouldn't have learned that, or would have with our dying breath; the condition is often fatal to bystanders. Three films—among lots of possible examples—make the point: *Rebel Without a Cause* (1955), *Saturday Night Fever* (1977), and *Top Gun* (1986). In each of these films, a young man with a chip on his shoulder is at war with the world: Jim Stark (James Dean) in *Rebel*, Tony Manero (John Travolta) in *Fever*, and Pete "Maverick" Mitchell (Tom Cruise) in *Top Gun*. Their mix of anger, overconfidence, and alienation makes them difficult to handle and often unpredictable. And each of them is responsible for the death of someone close. Jim Stark's recklessness leads to the death of a rival, Buzz Gunderson, in a foolish automotive challenge game when his car goes off a cliff. Jim's acolyte, young Plato Crawford (Sal Mineo), also dies after coming unhinged at the intensity of the events and rushing the police with a pistol Jim had secretly unloaded in an attempt to keep everyone safe. Tony's antics lead to the death of Bobby C., who falls from the Verrazano-Narrows Bridge. Maverick's risk-taking turns dark when he loses control of his F-16, and his Radio Intercept Operator and best friend, Goose (Anthony Edwards), dies in the resulting crash. There's a lot of death here involving falls from great heights, so that might be something to investigate another day.

Structurally, these three films are very similar: the immature young man must learn the lessons he needs to grow up. But because of the nature of the lessons and the cinematic need for drama, those lessons are learned vicariously. In other words, a major motion picture isn't much if the main character dies well before the end. Instead, his lieutenant (or, occasionally, his rival; sometimes both) must do the dying for him. Then we get drama, death, and guilt: the movie trifecta. There are plenty of other instances of this phenomenon. In Joseph Conrad's *Lord Jim*, Jim's overconfidence leads to the death of the local chieftain's son, Dain Waris, whom he treats like a brother. For this transgression, Jim willingly submits to being shot through the heart by the chieftain, Doramin, reminding us that Conrad is, at root, a tragedian.

In David Lean's masterpiece, the film *Lawrence of Arabia*, T. E. Lawrence's (Peter O'Toole, who also played Lord Jim) two young disciples die horribly (quicksand, accident with dynamite) while trying to emulate him, chiefly so that he can learn firsthand that his war is not a game.

These mishaps for seconds-in-command can take many shapes. I've focused on the tragic side here, but they can also be comic or mixed. Huck Finn gets into scrapes, but the bad things happen to the escaped slave Jim, who shares the raft. All kinds of perils threaten Charlie Chaplin's Little Tramp in his various silent films, but the board across the face or the anvil on the head (okay, I don't think there are actually any of *those*) almost always befalls whatever hapless colleague or pursuer happens to be standing beside him. The pie in the face only occasionally hits the comic lead; more commonly, he ducks to pick up a nickel and it hits the wealthy woman or bank president behind him.

There are all kinds of sources of this next-man-over mayhem—cosmic spite, bad luck, the need for a whipping boy, you name it—but they nearly all come under the heading of plot exigency. The plot *needs* something to happen in order to move forward, so someone must be sacrificed. That "someone" is rarely the protagonist.

Oh, the unfairness of it all. In truth, it's worse than that.

You see, literary works are not democracies. We hold this truth to be self-evident, that all men and women are created equal. We may, but the country of Novels, Etc., doesn't. In that faraway place, no character is created equal. One or two get all the breaks; the rest exist to get them to the finish line. Here's what E. M. Forster, whose name you see a lot in these pages, had to say on the subject in his book *Aspects of the Novel*: the fictive world (I'm paraphrasing here) is divided up into *round* and *flat* characters. Round characters are what we could call three-dimensional, full of traits and strengths and weaknesses and contradictions, capable of change and growth. Flat characters, not so much. They lack full development in the narrative or drama, so they're more two-dimensional, like cartoon cutouts. Some critics call these two types of literary personnel *dynamic* and *static*, but we'll go with round and flat. And between these two, round characters get all the breaks. What this means is that, conventionally, the point of a work is to follow one or two major figures through to their endpoint for good or ill, to watch how they develop or grow. Or don't. Pretty much everyone else exists as a plot device and is subject to cancellation whenever the plot demands a sacrifice. If to get to the finish line the hero must walk over a sea of bodies, then so be it. He can die at said line, but he's got to get there. See also *Hamlet*.

I'm going to go out on a limb here, take the generous view, and suggest that in real life, everyone is a fully rounded character. I have from time to time had my doubts, but let's go with it. What I mean is that we are all complete beings. We have many different qualities that don't always fit together very smoothly. More important, we're all capable of growth, development, and change. We can get better, although we sometimes fail to do so. To put this another way, we are all, each and every last one of us, the protagonist of our own story. Those stories frequently clash with one another, so other people may not seem as complete, or at least as urgently complete, as ourselves, but that doesn't alter the other person's reality. But that basic truth has nothing to do with literature. In fictive works, some characters are more equal than other characters. A lot more equal.

To get our heads around this notion, we need to go back to that basic point about characters not being people. They are representations, in greater or lesser detail, of human beings. Real people are made out of a whole lot of things—flesh, bone, blood, nerves, stuff like that. Literary people are made out of words. Can't breathe, can't bleed (even if a surprising number appear to), can't eat, can't love. They can be made to seem to do those things, but they don't actually do them. If you met one on the street, you'd be seriously disappointed. If writers made them as whole as we are, you'd be seriously bored. Even round characters are somewhat less than complete beings. They are merely simulacra, illusions meant to suggest fully formed humans. To the extent that we believe in them, that is a credit to the writer. And to us. But this creates a problem for us. The trick is to believe in them, as reader, and to recognize the unreality, as critic. What we're trying to do here is create expert readers, folks we might describe as reader-critics. You know, readers who can simultaneously take pleasure from a work and analyze it. Yeah, yeah, I know all that Wordsworth noise about "we murder to dissect." It's nonsense. I don't know a soul who appreciates and enjoys literature as much as experts who can really take it apart. Why do you think we became experts in the first place? Because we loved reading this stuff. Intelligent readers can keep both these notions in mind at once. Analysis only sounds threatening to pleasure; in practice, no sweat.

So why aren't all characters round?

Very logical question. Good one, too. The answers are mostly practical, rather than aesthetic. Characters are created on something like a need-to-know basis. Their utility is all that matters. Writers give them only as much reality as they need to do their jobs. Why?

- First of all, focus. If every character was developed to the same highly articulated degree, then how would we know on whom to focus our attention? That could get really confusing, and one thing we know about readers is that they don't like to be any more confused than necessary.

- Second, intensity of labor. Thinking up a full backstory for every character, no matter how minor, as well as the complete panoply of qualities, interests, shortcomings, phobias, and so on would be exhausting. It's hard enough to deal with them the way they are.

- Third, confusion of purpose. If a character is there to be a villain, finding out he loves his mother or owns a dog may be a distraction from the main point. Unless he kicks it (or her). Flat characters are easier to know in terms of their intent and narrative purpose, and we readers can use all the help we can get.

- Fourth, just consider length. Almost every short story would become a novella, perhaps a novel, in order to get in all that detail. Every novel would become *War and Peace*, and *War and Peace* would simply crush your chest. That's a heavy loss of conciseness with no corresponding gain in information. As we saw in the first point, that expansion of information would also be a loss. And I think we can agree that literary works are as long as we wish them to be already.

I've made this flat/round thing sound binary, but it is really more of a continuum. There are wholly flat characters, to be sure. But there are also those who fall somewhere closer to the rounded end of the graph, were we to make one. We find out, for instance, that Claudius, Hamlet's uncle and the villain of the play, is capable of remorse over his actions. Hamlet sees him at prayer; what he doesn't know but we discover is that Claudius is so blackened that he finds himself incapable of praying. Best friend Horatio is loyalty itself, but even he has doubts about the prince from time to time. So if we were to make a scale with, say Rosencrantz and Guildenstern or the gravediggers at one end and Hamlet at the other, we wouldn't see something like a barbell with a long flat line connecting two bundles gathered at either end. Somewhere along that line would appear (in something like this order from flatter on toward rounder) Polonius, Laertes, Horatio, Ophelia, Gertrude, Claudius, Hamlet. In case you're wondering, the ghost of Hamlet's father is pretty flat. Yorick doesn't count. In order to be a character, you have to be more than a skull.

Novelists and playwrights have considered these matters over the years, as we see in their essays and sometimes in their works. Numerous pieces of advice from Forster, John Gardner, Henry James, David Lodge, and others have addressed the question of minor characters. Dickens tries to make up for the lack of attention that his minor figures receive by making them memorable, by giving them some astonishing tic or tagline, as with Mrs. Micawber's "I never will desert Mr. Micawber." No one ever asks her to, making her repeated use of the line more eye-catching. Indeed, when we recall characters from Dickens, it is chiefly the rogue's gallery of secondary figures who spring to mind: Magwitch, Miss Havisham, Jaggers, Bill Sikes, Mr. Micawber, Barkis and Peggotty, Uriah Heep.

During the postmodern era, questions about the inner lives of minor characters have made their way to the page and stage. I mentioned Stoppard's *Rosencrantz and Guildenstern Are Dead* (1966) earlier. Its main thrust is the question, where do minor characters go when they're not onstage? Stoppard is not speaking of the actors playing those roles but of the characters themselves. For those of you who may be a little rusty on your Hamletology, Rosencrantz and Guildenstern are those two hapless dupes who shepherd Hamlet off to England, there ostensibly (but unknown to them) to be killed. Hamlet, however, is not so dim, and he engineers not only an escape but a scheme in which the two messengers deliver their own death warrants to the English king. They have—what?—maybe five minutes of stage time out of three-plus hours of tragedy. What, Stoppard asks, do they get up to during all that downtime? The play seems a bit of absurdist nonsense, but it's nonsense with a purpose. More recently, Jon Clinch gave us the novel *Finn* (2007), which examines in full the life of one of American literature's most odious specimens, Huck Finn's Pap. If anything, he's even worse when given more space. Then there is the cottage industry that seems determined to cover every aspect of all things Austen, including giving minor characters more room to run amok. This trend may be one of the first for which the twenty-first century will need to apologize.

All of this discussion of major and minor characters goes back a long, long way. Aristotle suggested an intimate connection between the shape of the plot and the nature of the characters involved. His discussion is sometimes reduced to the formulation, "Plot is character revealed in action." There have not been a lot of improvements on that notion over the millennia. What he means is that plot, not actions themselves but the way those actions are structured, grows out of the nature of the characters, which we then discover through their actions. The contemporary formulation is this bit of circular thinking: plot is character in action; character is revealed and shaped by plot. We must recognize that character is essential to fictional and dramatic literature. That includes all kinds of characters. We need flat ones as well as round, static as well as dynamic. In the final analysis, they're all doing the same thing, making the story or novel or play reach its end and making that end seem inevitable. What happens to Gatsby must feel like the only outcome, given who Gatsby is and who Nick is and who Daisy is. And Tom and George Wilson and Myrtle Wilson. It takes a village to murder a character.

What's that? You say this time the hero gets bumped off?

Are you sure about that? Maybe we should have a talk.

Interlude
Does He Mean That?

A long about now you should be asking a question, something like this: *you keep saying that the writer is alluding to this obscure work and using that symbol or following some pattern or other that I never heard of, but does he really intend to do that? Can anyone really have all that going on in his head at one time?*

Now that is an excellent question. I only wish I had an excellent answer, something pithy and substantive, maybe with a little alliteration, but instead I have one that's merely short.

Yes.

The chief deficiency of this answer, aside from its lack of pith, is that it is manifestly untrue. Or at least misleading. The real answer, of course, is that no one knows for certain. Oh, for this writer or that one we can be pretty sure, depending on what they themselves tell us, but in general we make guesses.

Let's look at the easy ones—James Joyce, T. S. Eliot, and what we could call the "Intentionalists"—writers who attempt to control every facet of their creative output and who intend virtually every effect in their works. Many of them are from the modernist period, essentially the era around the two world wars of the twentieth century. In an essay called "*Ulysses*, Order, and Myth (1923)," Eliot extols the virtues of Joyce's newly published masterpiece, and proclaims that, whereas writers of previous generations relied on the "narrative method," modern writers can, following Joyce's example, employ the "mythic method." *Ulysses*, as we know from our earlier discussion, is the very long story of a single day in Dublin, June 16, 1904, its structure modeled on Homer's *Odyssey* (Ulysses being the Latin equivalent of the name of Homer's hero, Odysseus). The structure of the novel utilizes the various episodes of the ancient epic, although ironically—Odysseus's trip to the underworld, for instance, becomes a trip to the cemetery; his encounter with Circe, an enchantress who turns men into swine, becomes a trip to a notorious brothel by the protagonists. Eliot uses his essay on Joyce to defend implicitly his own masterpiece,

The Waste Land, which also builds around ancient myths, in this case fertility myths associated with the Fisher King. Ezra Pound borrows from Greek, Latin, Chinese, English, Italian, and French poetic traditions in the *Cantos*. D. H. Lawrence writes essays about Egyptian and Mexican myth, Freudian psychoanalysis, issues in the Book of Revelation, and the history of the novel in Europe and America. Do we really believe that novels or poems by any of these writers, or their contemporaries Virginia Woolf, Katherine Mansfield, Ernest Hemingway, and William Faulkner, will be naive? Doesn't seem likely, does it?

Faulkner, for instance, in *Absalom, Absalom!* (1936) makes use of a title from the Bible—Absalom is David's rebellious son who hangs himself—and plot and characters from Greek mythology. The novel is Faulkner's version of Aeschylus's *Oresteia* (458 B.C.), the tragedy of the returning soldiers from Troy and revenge and destruction on a mythic scale. Their Trojan War is the Civil War, of course, and the murder at the gates is of the illegitimate son by his half brother, not of the returning husband (Agamemnon) by his faithless wife (Clytemnestra), although she is invoked in the mulatto slave, Clytie. He gives us Orestes, the avenging son pursued by Furies and ultimately consumed in the flames of the family mansion, in Henry Sutpen, and Electra, the daughter consumed by grief and mourning, in his sister, Judith. Such baroque planning and complex execution don't leave much room for naive, spontaneous composition.

Okay, so much for the modern writers, but what about earlier periods? Prior to 1900, most poets would have received at least rudimentary elements of a classical education—Latin, some Greek, lots of classical poetry and Dante and Shakespeare—certainly more than your average reader today. They could count on their readers, moreover, having considerable training in the tradition. One of the surest ways to be successful in theater in the nineteenth century was to take a touring Shakespeare company through the American West. If folks in their little houses on the prairie could quote the Bard, is it likely that their writers "accidentally" wrote stories that paralleled his?

Since proof is nearly impossible, discussions of the writer's intentions are not especially profitable. Instead let's restrict ourselves to what he did do and, more important, what we readers can discover in his work. What we have to work with is hints and allegations, really, evidence, sometimes only a trace, that points to something lying behind the text. It's useful to keep in mind that any aspiring writer is probably also a hungry, aggressive reader and will have absorbed a tremendous amount of literary history and literary culture. By the time she writes her books, she has access to that tradition in ways that need not be conscious. Nevertheless, whatever parts have infiltrated her consciousness are always available to her. Something else that we should bear in mind has to do with speed of composition. The few pages of this chapter have taken you a few minutes to read; they have taken me, I'm sorry to say, days and days to write. No, I haven't been sitting at my computer the whole time. First I carried the germ around for a while, mulling over how best to approach it, then I sat down and knocked a few items onto the screen, then I began fleshing out the argument. Then I got stuck, so I made lunch or baked some bread or helped my kid work on his car, but I carried the problem of this chapter around with me the whole time. I sat down at the keyboard again and started in again but got distracted and worked on something else. Eventually I got where we are now. Even assuming equal levels of knowledge about the subject, who probably has had the most ideas—you in five minutes of reading or me in five days of stumbling around? All I'm really saying is that we readers sometimes forget how long literary composition can take and how very much lateral thinking can go on in that amount of time.

And lateral thinking is what we're really discussing: the way writers can keep their eye on the target, whether it be the plot of the play or the ending of the novel or the argument of the poem, and at the same time bring in a great deal of at least tangentially related material. I used to think it was this great gift "literary geniuses" have, but I'm not so sure anymore. I sometimes teach a creative writing course, and my aspiring fiction writers frequently bring in biblical parallels, classical or Shakespearean allusions, bits of REM songs, fairy tale fragments, anything you can think of. And neither they nor I would claim that anybody in that room is a genius. It's something that starts happening when a reader/writer and a sheet of paper get locked in a room together. And it's a great deal of what makes reading the work—of my students, of recent graduates of the Iowa Writers' Workshop, of Keats and Shelley— interesting and fun.

11

... More Than It's Gonna Hurt You: Concerning Violence

Consider. Sethe is an escaped slave, and her children were all born in slave-owning Kentucky; their escape to Ohio is like the Israelites' escape from Egypt in Exodus. Except that this time Pharaoh shows up on the doorstep threatening to drag them back across the Red Sea. So Sethe decides to save her children from slavery by killing them, succeeding with only one of them.

Later, when that murdered child, the title character of Toni Morrison's *Beloved*, makes her ghostly return, she's more than simply the child lost to violence, sacrificed to the revulsion of the escaped slave toward her former state. Instead she is one of, in the words of the epigraph to the novel, the "sixty million and more" Africans and African-descended slaves who died in captivity and forced marches on the continent or in the middle passage or on the plantations made possible by their captive labor or in attempts to escape a system that should have been unthinkable—as unthinkable as, for instance, a mother seeing no other means of rescuing her child except infanticide. Beloved is in fact representative of the horrors to which a whole race was subjected.

Violence is one of the most personal and even intimate acts between human beings, but it can also be cultural and societal in its implications. It can be symbolic, thematic, biblical, Shakespearean, Romantic, allegorical, transcendent. Violence in real life just *is*. If someone punches you in the nose in a supermarket parking lot, it's simply aggression. It doesn't contain meaning beyond the act itself. Violence in literature, though, while it is literal, is usually also something else. That same punch in the nose may be a metaphor.

Robert Frost has a poem, "Out, Out—" (1916), about a momentary lapse of attention and the terrible act of violence that ensues. A farm boy working with the buzz saw looks up at the call to dinner, and the saw, which has been full of menace as it "snarl[s] and rattle[s]" along, seizes the moment, as if it has a mind

of its own, to take off the boy's hand. Now the first
thing we have to acknowledge about this masterpiece
is that it is absolutely real. Only a person who has been
around the ceaseless danger of farm machinery could
have written the poem, with all its careful attention to
the details of the way death lurks in everyday tasks. If
that's all we get from the poem, fine, the poem will in
one sense have done its job. Yet Frost is insisting on
more in the poem than a cautionary tale of child labor
and power tools. The literal violence encodes a broader
point about the essentially hostile or at least uncaring
relationship we have with the universe. Our lives and
deaths—the boy dies of blood loss and shock—are as
nothing to the universe, of which the best that can be
said is that it is indifferent, though it may be actively
interested in our demise. The title of the poem is taken
from *Macbeth*, "Out, out, brief candle," suggesting the
brevity not merely of a teenager's life but of any human
existence, particularly in cosmic terms. The smallness
and fragility of our lives is met with the cold indiffer-
ence not only of the distant stars and planets, which
we can rightly think of as virtually eternal in contrast
to ourselves, but of the more immediate "outer" world
of the farm itself, of the inhumanity of machinery
which wounds or kills indiscriminately. This is not
John Milton's "Lycidas" (1637), not a classical elegy

in which all nature weeps. This nature shows not the slightest ripple of interest. Frost uses the violence here, then, to emphasize our status as orphans: parentless, frightened, and alone as we face our mortality in a cold and silent universe.

Violence is everywhere in literature. Anna Karenina throws herself under the train, Emma Bovary solves her problem with poison, D. H. Lawrence's characters are always engaging in physical violence toward one another, Joyce's Stephen Dedalus is beaten by soldiers, Faulkner's Colonel Sartoris becomes a greater local legend when he guns down two carpetbaggers in the streets of Jefferson, and Wile E. Coyote holds up his little "Yikes" sign before he plunges into the void as his latest gambit to catch the Road Runner fails. Even writers as noted for the absence of action as Virginia Woolf and Anton Chekhov routinely resort to killing off characters. For all these deaths and maimings to amount to something deeper than the violence of the Road Runner cartoon, the violence has to have some meaning beyond mere mayhem.

Let's think about two categories of violence in literature: the specific injury that authors cause characters to visit on one another or on themselves, and the narrative violence that causes characters harm in general. The first would include the usual range of

behavior—shootings, stabbings, garrotings, drown-
ings, poisonings, bludgeonings, bombings, hit-and-
run accidents, starvations, you name it. By the second,
authorial violence, I mean the death and suffering
authors introduce into their work in the interest of plot
advancement or thematic development and for which
they, not their characters, are responsible. Frost's buzz-
saw accident would be such an example, as would Little
Nell on her deathbed in Dickens's *The Old Curiosity
Shop* (1841) and the death of Mrs. Ramsay in Virginia
Woolf's *To the Lighthouse* (1927).

*Is it fair to compare them? I mean, do death by con-
sumption or heart disease really fall into the same uni-
verse as a stabbing?*

Sure. Different but the same. Different: no guilty
party exists in the narrative (unless you count the
author, who is present everywhere and nowhere).
Same: does it really matter to the dead person? Or this:
writers kill off characters for the same set of reasons—
make action happen, cause plot complications, end plot
complications, put other characters under stress.

And that's not enough reason for violence to exist?

With some exceptions, the most prominent being
mystery novels. Figure at least three corpses for a
two-hundred-page mystery, sometimes many more.
How significant do those deaths feel? Very nearly

meaningless. In fact, aside from the necessities of plot, we scarcely notice the deaths in a detective novel; the author goes out of her way, more often than not, to make the victim sufficiently unpleasant that we scarcely regret his passing, and we may even feel a sort of relief. Now the rest of the novel will be devoted to solving this murder, so clearly it is important on some level. But the death lacks gravitas. There's no weight, no resonance, no sense of something larger at work. What mysteries generally have in common is a lack of density. What they offer in terms of emotional satisfaction—the problem solved, the question answered, the guilty punished, the victim avenged—they lack in weightiness. And I say this as a person who generally loves the genre and who has read hundreds of mysteries.

So where does this alleged weight come from?

Not alleged. Felt. We sense greater weight or depth in works when there is something happening beyond the surface. In mysteries, whatever layering there may be elsewhere, the murders live on the narrative surface. It's in the nature of the genre that since the act itself is buried under layers of misdirection and obfuscation, it cannot support layers of meaning or signification. On the other hand, "literary" fiction and drama and poetry are chiefly about those other layers. In that fictive universe, violence is symbolic action. If we only understand *Beloved* on the surface level, Sethe's act of killing her daughter becomes so repugnant that sympathy for her is nearly impossible. If we lived next to her, for instance, one of us would have to move. But her action carries symbolic significance; we understand it not only as the literal action of a single, momentarily deranged woman but as an action that speaks for the experience of a race at a certain horrific moment in history, as a gesture explained by whip scars on her back that take the form of a tree, as the product of the sort of terrible choice that only characters in our great mythic stories—a Jocasta, a Dido, a Medea—are driven to make. Sethe isn't a mere woman next door but a mythic creature, one of the great tragic heroines.

I suggested earlier that Lawrence's characters manage to commit a phenomenal amount of violence toward each other. Here are just a couple of examples. In *Women in Love* Gudrun Brangwen and Gerald Crich meet after each of them has made separate displays of violent will. In front of the Brangwen sisters, Gerald holds a terrified mare at a grade crossing, spurring her until her flanks bleed. Ursula is outraged and indignant, but Gudrun is so caught up in this display of masculine power (and the language Lawrence uses is very much that of a rape) that she swoons. He later sees her engaging in eurythmics—a pre–Great War version of disco—in front of some dangerous Highland cattle. When Gerald stops her to explain the peril she has created for herself, she slaps him hard. This is, mind, their very first meeting. So he says (more or less), I see you've struck the first blow. Her response? "And I shall strike the last." Very tender. Their relationship pretty much follows from that initial note, with violent clashes of will and ego, violent sex, needy and pathetic visitations, and eventually hatred and resentment. Technically, I suppose, she's right, since she does strike the last blow. The last time we see them, though, her eyes are bulging out as he strangles her, until suddenly he stops, overcome by revulsion, and skis off to his own death in the highest reaches of the Alps. Too weird? Want the other example? In his exquisite novella "The Fox," Lawrence creates one of the oddest triangles in literature. Banford and March are two women running a farm, and the only reason their relationship stops short of being openly lesbian must be because of censorship concerns, Lawrence already having had quite enough works banned by that time. Into this curious ménage a young soldier, Henry Grenfel, wanders, and as he works on the farm, a relationship develops between him and March. When the difficulties of a

three-way set of competing interests become insur-
mountable, Henry chops down a tree which twists,
falls, and crushes poor, difficult Banford. Problem
solved. Of course, the death gives rise to issues which
could scuttle the newly freed relationship, but who can
worry about such details?

Lawrence, being Lawrence, uses these violent epi-
sodes in heavily symbolic ways. His clashes between
Gerald and Gudrun, for instance, have as much to do
with deficiencies in the capitalist social system and
modern values as with personality shortcomings of the
participants. Gerald is both an individual and someone
corrupted by the values of industry (Lawrence iden-
tifies him as a "captain of industry"), while Gudrun
loses much of her initial humanism through associa-
tion with the "corrupt" sort of modern artists. And
the murder by tree in "The Fox" isn't about interper-
sonal hostility, although that antipathy is present in the
story. Rather, Banford's demise figures the sexual ten-
sions and gender-role confusion of modern society as
Lawrence sees it, a world in which the essential quali-
ties of men and women have been lost in the demands of
technology and the excessive emphasis on intellect over
instinct. We know that these tensions exist, because
while Banford (Jill) and March (Ellen or Nellie) some-
times call each other by their Christian names, the

text insists on their surnames without using "Miss," thereby emphasizing their masculine tendencies, while Henry is simply Henry or the young man. Only by radically changing the interpersonal sexual dynamic can something like Lawrentian order be restored. There is also the mythic dimension of this violence. Gerald in *Women in Love* is repeatedly described as a young god, tall and fair and beautiful, while Gudrun is named for a minor Norse goddess. Their clash, then, automatically follows mythic patterns. Similarly, the young soldier comes striding onto the makeshift farm as a fertility god, fairly screaming virility. Lawrence shared with many of his contemporaries a fascination with ancient myths, particularly those of the wasteland and various fertility cults. For fertility to be restored to the little wasteland of the failing farm, the potent male and the fertile female must be paired off, and any blocking element, including any females with competing romantic interests, must be sacrificed.

William Faulkner's violence emanates from a slightly different wellspring, yet the results are not entirely different. I know of creative writing teachers who feel Faulkner is the single greatest danger to budding fiction writers. So alluring is his penchant for violence that the imitation Faulknerian story will have

a rape, three cases of incest, a stabbing, two shoot-
ings, and a suicide by drowning, all in two thousand
words. And indeed, there is a great deal of violence
of all sorts in his fictional Yoknapatawpha County. In
the story "Barn Burning" (1939), young Sarty Snopes
watches as his father, a serial arsonist, hires out to a
wealthy plantation owner, Major de Spain, only to
attempt to burn the major's barn in a fit of class re-
sentment. When Sarty (whose full name is Colonel
Sartoris Snopes) attempts to intercede, Major de Spain
rides down Ab, the father, and Sarty's elder brother,
and the last we hear of them is a series of shots from
the major's pistol, leaving Sarty sobbing in the dust.
The arson and the shootings here are, of course, lit-
eral and need to be understood in that light before
we go looking for any further significance. But with
Faulkner, the violence is also historically conditioned.
Class warfare, racism and the inheritance of slavery (at
one point Ab says that slave sweat must not have made
the de Spain mansion white enough and that therefore
white sweat—his—is evidently called for), impotent
rage at having lost the Civil War, all figure in the vio-
lence of a Faulkner story. In *Go Down, Moses* (1942),
Ike McCaslin discovers while reading through planta-
tion ledgers that his grandfather had sired a daughter
by one of his slaves, Eunice, and then, not scrupling

at incest or recognizing the humanity in his slaves that would make his act incest, got that daughter, Tomasina, pregnant. Eunice's response was to kill herself. That act is personal and literal, but it is also a powerful metaphor of the horrors of slavery and the outcomes when people's capacity for self-determination is stripped away utterly. The slave woman has no say in how her body or her daughter's has been used, nor is any avenue open for her to express her outrage; the only escape permitted to her is death. Slavery allows its victims no decision-making power over any aspect of their lives, including the decision to live. The lone exception, the only power they have, is that they may choose to die. And so she does. Even then, old Carothers McCaslin's only comment is to ask whoever heard of a black person drowning herself, clearly astonished that such a response is possible in a slave. That Eunice's suicide takes place in a novel that draws its title from a spiritual, in which Moses is asked to "go down" into Egypt to "set my people free," is no accident. If Moses should fail to appear, it may fall to the captive race to take what actions they can to liberate themselves. Faulknerian violence quite often expresses such historical conditions at the same time that it draws on mythic or biblical parallels. Not for nothing does he call one novel *Absalom, Absalom!*, in which a rebellious, difficult son repudiates his birthright and destroys himself. *Light in August* (1932) features a character named Joe Christmas who suffers emasculation at the novel's end; while neither his behavior nor his particular wound is very obviously Christlike, his life and death have to do with the possibility of redemption. Of course, things change when irony comes in, but that's another matter.

Thus far we've been speaking of character-on-character violence. So what about violence without agency, where writers simply dispose of their characters? Well, it depends. Accidents do happen in real life, of course. So do illnesses. But when they happen in literature they're not really accidents. They're accidents only on the inside of the novel—on the outside they're planned, plotted, and executed by somebody, with malice aforethought. And we know who that somebody is. I can think of two novels from the 1980s that involve characters floating down to earth after a jetliner explosion. Fay Weldon, in *The Hearts and Lives of Men* (1988), and Salman Rushdie, in *The Satanic Verses*, may have slightly different purposes in introducing such massive violence into their story lines and then having some characters survive. We can be fairly sure, however, that they do mean something— several somethings—by the graceful falls to earth that their characters undergo. The little girl in Weldon's novel occupies what amounts to a state of grace in an otherwise corrupt adult world; the easy descent of the airliner's tail section proves a lovely, gentle corollary to this quality in the child. Rushdie's two characters, on the other hand, experience their descent as a fall not from innocence to experience but from an already corrupt life into an existence as demons. So, too, with illness. We'll talk later about what heart disease means in a story, or tuberculosis or cancer or AIDS. The question always is, what does misfortune really tell us?

It's nearly impossible to generalize about the meanings of violence, except that there are typically more than one, and its range of possibilities is far larger than with something like rain or snow. Authors rarely introduce violence straightforwardly, to perform only its one appointed task, so we ask questions. What does this type of misfortune represent thematically? What famous or mythic death does this one resemble? Why this sort of violence and not some other? The answers may have to do with psychological dilemmas, with spiritual crises, with historical or social or political concerns. Almost never, though, are they cut-and-paste, but they do exist, and if you put your mind to it, you can usually come up with some possibilities. Violence is everywhere in literature. We'd lose most of Shakespeare without it, and Homer and Ovid and Marlowe (both Christopher and Philip), much of Milton, Lawrence, Twain, Dickens, Frost, Tolkien, Fitzgerald, Hemingway, Saul Bellow, and on and on. I guess Jane Austen wouldn't be too much affected, but relying on her would leave our reading a little thin. It seems, then, that there's no option for us but to accept it and figure out what it means.

12

Is That a Symbol?

Of course it is.

That's one of the most common questions in class, followed by the answer I generally give. Is that a symbol? Sure, why not. It's the next question where things get hairy: what does it mean, what does it stand for? When someone asks about meaning, I usually come back with something clever, like "Well, what do you think?" Everyone thinks I'm either being a wise guy or ducking responsibility, but neither is the case. Seriously, what do *you* think it stands for, because that's probably what it does. At least for you.

Here's the problem with symbols: people expect them to mean something. Not just any something, but one something in particular. Exactly. Maximum. You know what? It doesn't work like that. Oh, sure, there are some symbols that work straightforwardly: a white flag means, I give up, don't shoot. Or it means, We come in peace. See? Even in a fairly clear-cut case we can't pin down a single meaning, although they're pretty close. So some symbols do have a relatively limited range of meanings, but in general a symbol can't be reduced to standing for only one thing.

If they *can*, it's not symbolism, it's allegory. Here's how allegory works: things stand for other things on a one-for-one basis. Back in 1678, John Bunyan wrote an allegory called *The Pilgrim's Progress*. In it, the main character, Christian, is trying to journey to the Celestial City, while along the way he encounters such distractions as the Slough of Despond, the Primrose Path, Vanity Fair, and the Valley of the Shadow of Death. Other characters have names like Faithful, Evangelist, and the Giant Despair. Their names indicate their qualities, and in the case of Despair, his size as well. Allegories have one mission to accomplish—convey a certain message, in this case, the quest of the devout Christian to reach heaven. If there is ambiguity or a lack of clarity regarding that one-to-one correspondence between the emblem—the figurative construct—and the thing it represents, then the allegory fails because the message is blurred. Such simplicity of purpose has its advantages. George Orwell's *Animal Farm* (1945) is popular among many readers precisely because it's relatively easy to figure out what it all means. Orwell is desperate for us to get *the* point, not *a* point. Revolutions inevitably fail, he tells us, because those who come to power are corrupted by it and reject the values and principles they initially embraced.

Symbols, though, generally don't work so neatly. The thing referred to is likely not reducible to a single statement but will more probably involve a range of possible meanings and interpretations.

Consider the problem of the cave. In his masterful novel *A Passage to India* (1924), E. M. Forster has as his central incident a possible assault in a cave. All through the first half of the work the Marabar Caves hover over the story; they keep being referred to, they're out there, remarkable in some ill-defined way, mysterious. Our independent and progressive heroine, Adela Quested (does that name strike you as symbolic at all?), wishes to see them, so Dr. Aziz, an educated Indian physician, arranges an outing. The caves turn out to be not quite as advertised: isolated in a barren wasteland, unadorned, strange, uncanny. Mrs. Moore, Adela's mother-in-law-to-be, has a very nasty experience in the first of the caves, when she suddenly feels oppressively crowded and physically threatened by the others who have joined her. Adela notices that all sound is reduced to a hollow booming noise, so that a voice or a footfall or the striking of a match results in this booming negation. Mrs. Moore, understandably, has had enough of caves, so Adela does a bit of poking around on her own. In one of the caves she suddenly becomes alarmed, believing that, well, *something* is going on. When next we see her she has fled the scene, running and falling down the hillside to collapse into the arms of the racist English community she so vehemently criticized before. Badly bruised and scraped and poked by cactus spines, she is in shock and utterly convinced that she was assaulted in the cave and that Aziz must have been her assailant.

Was that cave symbolic? You bet.

Of what?

That, I fear, is another matter. We want it to mean something, don't we? More than that, we want it to mean some *thing*, one thing for all of us and for all time. That would be easy, convenient, manageable for us. But that handiness would result in a net loss: the novel would cease to be what it is, a network of meanings and significations that permits a nearly limitless range of possible interpretations. The meaning of the cave isn't lying on the surface of the novel. Rather, it waits somewhere deeper, and part of what it requires of us is to bring something of ourselves to the encounter.

If we want to figure out what a symbol might mean, we have to use a variety of tools on it: questions, experience, preexisting knowledge. What else is Forster doing with caves? What are other outcomes in the text, or uses of caves in general that we can recall? What else can we bring to bear on this cave that might yield up meaning? So here we go.

Caves in general. First, consider our past. Our earliest ancestors, or those who had weather issues, lived in caves. Some of them left us some pretty nifty drawings, while others left behind piles of bones and spots charred from that great discovery, fire. But the point here might be (no guarantees, of course) that the cave, on some level, suggests a connection to the most basic and primitive elements in our natures. At the far end of the spectrum, we might be reminded of Plato, who in the "Parable of the Cave" section of *The Republic* (fourth century B.C.) gives us an image of the cave as consciousness and perception. Each of these predecessors might provide possible meanings for our situation. The security and shelter suggested by some Neolithic memory of caves probably won't work here, but something along the lines of Plato's cave interior may: perhaps this cave experience has something to do with Adela getting in touch with the deepest levels of her consciousness and perhaps being frightened by what she finds there.

Now, Forster's use of the caves. The locals cannot explain or describe the caves. Aziz, a grand promoter of them, must finally admit he knows nothing of them, having never visited the site, while Professor Godbole, who has seen them, describes their effect only in terms of what does not cause it. To each of the characters' questions—are they picturesque? are they historically significant?—he offers a cryptic "No." To his Western audience, and even to Aziz, this set of responses is not helpful. Godbole's message might be that the caves must be experienced before they can be understood or that every person's caves are different. Such a position might be borne out by the example of Mrs. Moore's unpleasant encounter in a different cave. Throughout the early portions of the novel, she has been impatient with other people and resentful of having them—their views, their assumptions, their physical presence— forced on her. One of the ironies of her Indian experi- ence is that in a landscape so vast, the psychological space is so small; she came all this way and can't get away from life, England, people, death closing in on her. When she gets inside the cave, a crush of people threatens her; the jostling and brushing seem overtly hostile in the dark enclosure. Something unidentified but unpleasant—she can't tell if it belongs to a bat or an infant, but it's organic and not nice—rubs across her mouth. Her heartbeat becomes oppressive and she can't breathe, so she flees the cave as quickly as she can and takes a good while to calm down. In her case, the cave seems to force her into contact with her deepest personal fears and anxieties: other people, ungovernable sensations, children and fecundity. There is also the suggestion that India itself threatens her, since all the people aside from Adela and herself in the cave are Indians. While she has tried to be Indian, to be comfortable and understanding of the "natives" in ways other members of the ruling British have not been, she can hardly be said to have mastered the Indian experience. So it may be that what she runs into in the darkness is the fraudulence of her attempt to "be Indian."

On the other hand, maybe she doesn't have an encounter with Something at all. Perhaps what she meets in the cave is instead Nothingness, albeit some years before Jean-Paul Sartre, Albert Camus, and the existentialists of the 1950s and 1960s articulate the dichotomy between, in Sartre's terms, Being and Nothingness. Could it be that what she finds in the cave isn't death per se but the experience of the Void? I think it quite possible, if by no means certain.

So what does Adela's cave stand for? She has, or seems to have, all of the responses that Mrs. Moore does, although hers are different. As a virgin on the edge of spinsterhood who has been shipped halfway around the world to marry a man she doesn't love, she has some very understandable anxieties about matrimony and sex. In fact, her last conversation before entering the cave is with Aziz regarding his own married life, and her questions are probing and even inappropriate. Perhaps this conversation brings on her hallucination, if that is what it is, or perhaps it provokes Aziz or some third party (their guide, for instance) into whatever he does, if anyone does anything.

For Adela, the horror of her cave experience and its booming echo ride roughshod over her soul until she recants her testimony against Aziz during his trial. Once the mayhem dies down and she is safely away from the Indians who have hated her and the English who now hate her, she announces that the echo has stopped. What does this suggest? The cave may bring on or point up a variety of inauthentic experience (another existential concept)—that is, Adela is confronted by the hypocrisy of her life and her reasons for coming to India or agreeing to marry Ronnie, her fiancé, by her failure to take responsibility for her own existence. Or it may represent a breach of the truth (in a more traditional philosophical tradition) or a confrontation with terrors she has denied and can only exorcise by facing them. Or something else. For Aziz, too, the caves speak through their aftermath—of the perfidy of the English, of the falseness of his subservience, of his need to assert responsibility for his own life. It may be that Adela does panic in the face of Nothingness, only recovering herself when she takes responsibility by recanting in the witness box. Perhaps it's all about nothing more than her own self-doubts, her own psychological or spiritual difficulties. Perhaps it is racial in some way.

The only thing we are sure of about the cave as symbol is that it keeps its secrets. That sounds as if I'm punting, but I'm not. What the cave symbolizes will be determined to a large extent by how the individual reader engages the text. Every reader's experience of every work is unique, largely because each person will emphasize various elements to differing degrees, and those differences will cause certain features of the text to become more or less pronounced. We bring an individual history to our reading, a mix of previous readings, to be sure, but also a history that includes, but is not limited to, educational attainment, gender, race, class, faith, social involvement, and philosophical inclination. These factors will inevitably influence what we understand in our reading, and nowhere is this individuality clearer than in the matter of symbolism.

The problem of symbolic meaning is further compounded when we look at a number of writers emphasizing various, distinct elements for a given symbol. As an example, let's consider three rivers. Mark Twain gives us the Mississippi, Hart Crane the Hudson-East-Mississippi/generic-American, and T. S. Eliot the Thames. All three are American writers, all from the Midwest (two from Missouri, no less). Do you suppose there's any chance of their rivers standing for the same thing? In *The Adventures of Huckleberry Finn* (1885), Twain sends Huck and the escaped slave Jim down the Mississippi on a raft. The river is a little bit of everything in the novel. At the beginning it floods, killing livestock and people, including Huck's father. Jim is using the river to escape to freedom, but his "escape" is paradoxical since it carries him deeper and deeper into slave territory. The river is both danger and safety, since the relative isolation from land and detection is offset by the perils of river travel on a makeshift conveyance. On a personal level, the river/raft provides the platform on which Huck, a white boy, can get to know Jim not as a slave but as a man. And of course the river is really a road, and the raft trip a quest that results in Huck growing to maturity and understanding. He knows himself well enough at the end that he will never return to childhood and Hannibal and bossy women, so he lights out for the Territories.

Now take Hart Crane's poem sequence *The Bridge* (1930), which plays with rivers and bridges throughout. He begins with the East River, spanned by the Brooklyn Bridge. From there the river grows into the Hudson and on into the Mississippi, which for Crane embodies all American rivers. Interesting things begin happening in the poem. The bridge connects the two pieces of land cut off from one another by the river, while it has the effect of bisecting the stream. The river meanwhile does separate the land on a horizontal axis but connects along a vertical axis, making it possible for people at one end to travel to the other. The Mississippi becomes of central symbolic importance for Crane because of its immense length, bringing the northernmost and southernmost parts of the nation together while making it virtually impossible to move from east to west without some means of traversing the river. His meanings are quite different from those of Twain. Together the river and the bridge constitute an image of total connection.

And Eliot? Eliot uses the River Thames prominently in *The Waste Land*, written in the immediate aftermath of World War I and of a more personal breakdown. His river carries the detritus of a dying civilization and features, among other things, a rat trailing along the bank; the river is slimy, dirty, its famous bridge falling down (in nursery rhyme form), abandoned by its nymphs. The river is shorn of grandeur, grace, and divinity. In the poem's past, Queen Elizabeth and the Earl of Leicester carry on their dalliance on the water, but their modern counterparts are merely sordid and seedy. Clearly Eliot's river is symbolic; equally clearly, it symbolizes things having to do with the corruption of modern life and collapse of Western civilization that do not come into play with either Twain or Crane. Of course, Eliot's work is heavily ironic, and as we'll discuss later, everything changes when irony climbs aboard.

You will have noticed in these last pages that I assert meaning for these uses of caves and rivers and symbols with considerable authority, and indeed I have a pretty strong grasp of what they mean—for me. The authority I bring to these readings is that of my own background and experience. I incline, for instance, toward a reading of *The Waste Land* based on its historical context (a historicist reading, if you will) in which the poem cannot be divorced from the recent war and its aftermath, but not everyone comes at the poem from that angle. Others may approach it chiefly in formal terms or on biographical grounds, as a response to violent personal and marital upheaval. These and many other approaches are not only valid but produce readings of considerable insight; in fact, I have learned a great deal not only about the poem but about my own shortcomings from alternative approaches. One of the pleasures of literary scholarship lies in encountering different and even conflicting interpretations, since the great work allows for a considerable range of possible interpretations. Under no circumstances, in other words, should you take my pronouncements on these works as definitive.

The other problem with symbols is that many readers expect them to be objects and images rather than events or actions. Action can also be symbolic. Robert Frost is probably the champion of the symbolic action, although his uses of it are so sly that resolutely literal readers can miss the symbolic level entirely. In his poem "Mowing" (1913), for instance, the activity of mowing a field with a scythe (which, mercifully, you and I will never have to do) is first and foremost just what it is, a description of sweeping a field clean of standing hay one stroke at a time. We also notice, though, that mowing carries weight beyond its immediate context, seeming to stand in for labor generally, or for the solitary business of living one's life, or for something else beyond itself. Similarly, the speaker's account of his recent actions in "After Apple Picking" (1914) suggests a point in life as well as a point in the season, and the memory of picking, from the lingering sense of the swaying ladder and the imprint of the rung on his foot soles to the impression of apples on his retinas, suggests the wear and tear of the activity of living on the psyche. Again, the nonsymbolic thinker can see this as a beautiful evocation of an autumnal moment, which it is and pleasurably so, but there is more than just that going on. It may be a little more obvious with the moment of decision in his "The Road Not Taken" (1916), which is why it is the universal graduation poem, but symbolic action can also be found in poem after poem, from the terrible accident in "Out, Out—" to climbing in "Birches" (1916).

So, what are you to do? You can't simply say, Well, it's a river, so it means x, or apple picking, so it means y. On the other hand, you can say this could sometimes mean x or y or even z, so let's keep that in mind to see which one, if either, happens here. Any past experience of literary rivers or labor may be helpful as well. Then you start breaking down the work at hand into manageable pieces. Associate freely, brainstorm, take notes. Then you can organize your thoughts, grouping them together under headings, rejecting or accepting different ideas or meanings as they seem to apply. Ask questions of the text: what's the writer doing with this image, this object, this act; what possibilities are suggested by the movement of the narrative or the lyric; and most important, what does it *feel* like it's doing? Reading literature is a highly intellectual activity, but it also involves affect and instinct to a large degree. Much of what we think about literature, we feel first. Having instincts, though, doesn't automatically mean they work at their highest level. Dogs are instinctual swimmers, but not every pup hits the water understanding what to do with that instinct. Reading is like that, too. The more you exercise the symbolic imagination, the better and quicker it works. We tend to give writers all the credit, but reading is also an event of the imagination; our creativity, our inventiveness, encounters those of the writer, and in that meeting we puzzle out what she means, what we understand her to mean, what uses we can put her writing to. Imagination isn't fantasy. That is to say, we can't simply invent meaning without the writer, or if we can, we ought not to hold her to it. Rather, a reader's imagination is the act of one creative intelligence engaging another.

So engage that other creative intelligence. Listen to your instincts. Pay attention to what you feel about the text. It probably means something.

13

It's All Political

Nowadays we think of *A Christmas Carol* as a private morality play and a nice Christmas tale to boot, but in 1843 Dickens was actually attacking a widely held political belief, hiding his criticism in the story of a wretched miser who is saved by spiritual visitations. There was a theory afoot at that time, left over from the Puritanism of the previous two centuries and promulgated most forcefully by the British social thinker Thomas Malthus, that in helping the poor or in increasing food production to feed more people we would in fact encourage an increase in the number of the impoverished, who would, among other things, simply procreate faster to take advantage of all that surplus gruel. Dickens caricatures this Malthusian thinking in Scrooge's insistence that he wants nothing to do with the destitute and that if they would rather starve than live in the poorhouse or in debtors' prison, then, by golly, "they had best hurry up and do it and decrease the excess population." Scrooge actually says that. What a guy!

Even if you've never heard of Thomas Malthus, when you read *A Christmas Carol* or see one of the umpteen versions of it onscreen, you can tell something is going on beyond the story. If nasty old Scrooge were one of a kind, just a single selfish, embittered man, if he were the only man in England who needed to learn this lesson, the tale would not resonate with us as it does. It's not generally in the way of parables, which *Carol* is, to treat anomalies. No, Dickens picks Scrooge not because he's unique but because he's representative, because there's something of Scrooge in us and in society. We can have no doubt that the story is meant to change us and through us to change society. Some of Scrooge's pronouncements early in the story are almost verbatim from Malthus or his Victorian descendants. Dickens is a social critic, but he's a sneaky one, remaining so consistently entertaining that we may not notice that a major point of his work is to critique social shortcomings. At the same time, you have to be almost willfully blind to read that story and see only Marley's ghost, three spirits, and

Tiny Tim, to fail to notice that the tale attacks one way of thinking about our social responsibility and valorizes another.

Concerning politics in literary texts, here's what I think:

I hate "political" writing—novels, plays, poems. They don't travel well, don't age well, and generally aren't much good in their own time and place, however sincere they may be. I speak here of literature whose primary intent is to influence the body politic—for instance, those works of socialist realism (one of the great misnomers of all time) of the Soviet era in which the plucky hero figures out a way to increase production and thereby meet the goals of the five-year plan on the collective farm—what I once heard the great Mexican novelist Carlos Fuentes characterize as the love affair between a boy, and girl, and a tractor. Overtly political writing can be one-dimensional, simplistic, reduction-ist, preachy, dull.

The political writing I personally dislike is pro-grammatic, pushing a single cause or concern or party position, or it's tied into a highly topical situa-tion that doesn't transfer well out of its own specific time and place. Ezra Pound's politics, for instance, a mixture of anti-Semitism and authoritarianism that made Italian fascism congenial to him, are repugnant to any thinking person, and to the extent that they find expression in his poetry, they destroy everything they touch. But even if they weren't so hideous, their use in his verse tends to be clumsy and heavy-handed, too obviously programmatic. When he starts droning on in the *Cantos* about the evils brought about by "Usura," for instance, eyes glaze over and minds wander. We in the age of credit cards are just not that hopped up about supposed ills of the culture of lending and borrowing between the world wars. The same thing happens with a lot of those left-wing plays of the 1930s; they may have been fine as rallying cries in their day, but as works of lasting interest, they work for lots of us only as cultural anthropology.

I love "political" writing. Writing that engages the realities of its world—that thinks about human problems, including those in the social and political realm, that addresses the rights of persons and the wrongs of those in power—can be not only interesting but hugely compelling. In this category we get the grimy London of Dickens's late work, the fabulous postmodern novels of Gabriel García Márquez and Toni Morrison, the plays of Henrik Ibsen and George Bernard Shaw, Seamus Heaney's poetry of the Northern Irish Troubles, and the feminist struggles with the poetic tradition of Eavan Boland and Adrienne Rich and Audre Lord.

Nearly all writing is political on some level. D. H. Lawrence's work is profoundly political even when it doesn't look like it, even when he is less overt than in *Women in Love*, where he has a character say of a robin that it looks like a "little Lloyd-George of the air." I'm not quite sure how a robin resembles the then prime minister, but it's clear Lawrence didn't approve, and the character clearly shares her creator's politics. I also know that's not the real political element in that novel. No, his real political contribution is in setting a radical individualism in conflict with established institutions. Lawrence's people keep refusing to behave, to submit to convention, to act in a way that conforms to expectations, even expectations of other nonconformists. In *Women in Love* he pillories the bohemianism of the artsy sets of his day, whether the Bloomsbury circle or the group that Lady Ottoline Morrell, the self-consciously bohemian patroness of the arts, gathered around herself. Their avant-gardism merely constitutes another kind of conventionality for him, a way of being "chic" or "in," whereas his heroic ideal goes its solitary way even though it outrage friend as well as foe and confound lover as well as stranger. That radical individualism is politically charged in Lawrence, just as it is in Walt Whitman (whom he admired greatly) and Ralph Waldo Emerson in their very different ways. Indeed, you could argue that the role of the individual is always politically charged, that matters of autonomy and free will and self-determination always drag in the larger society, if only tangentially. Someone like Thomas Pynchon (although, as Chapter 1 suggests, it's not clear there is anyone *like* Pynchon except Pynchon), who seems on one level to be hiding from the body politic, is profoundly political in his concern over the individual's relationship to "America."

Or here's someone whose stories you may not have thought of as inevitably political: Edgar Allan Poe. His tales "The Masque of the Red Death" (1842) and "The Fall of the House of Usher" (1839) both deal with a stratum of society most of us only get to read about: the nobility. In the former, the prince, in the midst of a terrible plague, gathers his friends and associates for a party, at which he locks them away from the afflicted (and poor) society outside the walls of the palace. The titular scourge finds them anyway and by morning they're all dead. In the latter, the host, Roderick Usher, and his sister Madeline are the last survivors of an old aristocratic family. Living in a decaying mansion surrounded by a forbidding landscape, they are themselves decaying. She has a progressive-wasting disease, while he is prematurely aged and decrepit, his hair nearly gone and his nerves shot. He behaves, moreover, like a madman, and there is more than a slight hint at incestuous closeness between brother and sister. In both of these tales Poe offers criticism of the European class system, which privileges the unworthy and the unhealthy, where the entire atmosphere is corrupt and decaying, where the results are madness and death. The landscape of "Usher" resembles no part of America Poe ever saw. Even the appellation "House of Usher" suggests European monarchy and aristocracy—the Houses of Bourbon or Hanover, for instance—rather than an American place or family. Roderick has buried his sister alive, possibly knowing she wasn't dead, certainly becoming aware of it as time in the story passes. Now why would he do a thing like that? When she escapes, having clawed her way out, she falls into his arms and they collapse to the floor, both dead. The narrator narrowly escapes before the house itself pulls apart and crashes into the "black and lurid tarn" at its base. If all of that doesn't suggest an unhealthy, unholy, and distinctly un-American relationship between brother and sister, then one of us is missing something.

Edgar Allan Poe, superpatriot?

Okay, you're right, that may be going too far. Still, he implicitly believes that what Europe represents is degraded and decaying (and these are not the only examples). Moreover, Poe suggests strongly that this is the inevitable and even just outcome of a corrupt social organization. And that, dear friends, is political.

Ready for another example? How about "Rip Van Winkle"? I'm sure you have doubts. Tell me what you remember.

Okay. Rip Van Winkle, who's lazy and not a great provider for his family, goes hunting. Actually, he's really just getting away from his nagging wife. He meets some odd characters playing ninepins, with whom he drinks a little bit and falls asleep. When he wakes up his dog is gone and his gun has rusted and fallen apart. He has white hair and a beard a mile long and very stiff joints. He makes his way back to town and finds out he's been asleep for twenty years and his wife is dead and everything has changed, including the signs at the hotel. And that's pretty much the story.

Pretty much. Nothing very political in that, right? Except that we need to consider two questions:

1) What does it mean that Dame Van Winkle is dead?

2) How does that connect with the change of Georges on the hotel sign?

During the twenty years he's been away, the American Revolution has happened, the picture of British King George has been transformed by the proprietors into that of our George (Washington), although with the same face. There's a liberty cap atop the flagpole, which carries a new flag, and the tyrant (Dame Van Winkle) is dead. Rip nearly gets attacked when he says he's loyal to the old George, but once that gets straightened out, he finds out he's free and he likes it.

So everything's better?

Definitely not. Irving is writing in 1819 and is observant enough to know that liberty brought with it some problems. Things have become a little run-down. The hotel has some broken windows and needs a facelift, and the town and its people are generally a little more ragged than they were before the war. But there's a kind of energy that drives them, a certainty that their lives are their own and nobody by golly is going to boss them around. They speak their minds and do what they want. And tyranny and absolute rule are dead. In other words, this slightly scruffy assemblage of people is on the way to defining for itself what it means to be American and free. So not everything is better, but the things that really matter—freedom, self-determination—they *are* better.

How can I be so sure that Irving means to imply all that? Part of his protective coloration is as this rather naive, rustic spinner of tales, but that's not him; it's pure disguise. Washington Irving was a man of great sophistication who studied law, was admitted to the bar, served in Spain as a diplomat, wrote histories as well as fiction, traveled widely. Does that sound like a man who didn't understand what his narrative signified? His ostensible narrator, Diedrich Knickerbocker, is a jolly companion who spins out these tales of his Dutch ancestors without seeing all the implications. Irving saw them, though. He knew, moreover, that with Rip and "The Legend of Sleepy Hollow" (1819) he was creating an American consciousness in literature, a thing that hadn't existed prior to his time. Like Poe, he sets himself up in opposition to European literary tradition, offering instead a body of work that could only come from an American and that features and celebrates freedom from its former colonial power.

So is every literary work political?

I can't go that far. Some of my more political colleagues may tell you yes, that every work is either part of the social problem or part of the solution (they'll give it to you with rather more subtlety than that, but that's the gist). I do think, though, that most works must engage with their own specific period in ways that can be called political. Let's say this: writers tend to be men and women who are interested in the world around them. That world contains many things, and on the level of society, part of what it contains is the political reality of the time—power structures, relations among classes, issues of justice and rights, interactions between the sexes and among various racial and ethnic constituencies. That's why political and social considerations often find their way onto the page in some guise, even when the result doesn't look terribly "political."

An example. When Sophocles is a very old man, he finally writes the middle third of his Theban trilogy of plays, *Oedipus at Colonus* (406 B.C.), in which the old and frail Oedipus arrives at Colonus and receives the protection of the Athenian king, Theseus. Theseus is everything we might want in a ruler: strong, wise, gentle, tough when necessary, determined, coolheaded, compassionate, loyal, honest. Theseus protects Oedipus from potential harm and guides him to the sacred spot where the old man is fated to die. Is that political? I think so. You see, Sophocles is writing this not only at the end of his life but at the end of the fifth century B.C., which is to say at the end of the period of Athenian greatness. The city-state is threatened from the outside by Spartan aggression and from the inside by leaders who, whatever their virtues, sure aren't Theseus. What he's saying is, in effect, we could really use a leader like Theseus again; maybe *he* could get us out of this mess and keep Athens from total ruin. Then outsiders (Creon in the play, the Spartans in reality) wouldn't be trying to overrun us. Then we'd still be strong and just and wise. Does Sophocles actually say any of these things? No, of course not. He's old, not senile. You say these things openly, they give you hemlock or something. He doesn't have to say them, though; everyone who sees the play can draw his own conclusions: look at Theseus, look at whatever leader you have near to hand, look at Theseus again—hmmm (or words to that effect). See? Political.

All this matters. Knowing a little something about the social and political milieu out of which a writer creates can only help us understand her work, not because that milieu controls her thinking but because that is the world she engages when she sits down to write. When Virginia Woolf writes about women of her time only being permitted a certain range of activities, we do her and ourselves a great disservice by not seeing the social criticism involved. For instance, in *Mrs. Dalloway* (1925), Lady Bruton invites Richard Dalloway, a member of Parliament, and Hugh Whitbread, who has a position at court, to luncheon. Her purpose is to dictate to them material she wants to see introduced into legislation and sent as a letter to the *Times*, all the while protesting that she's merely a woman who doesn't understand these matters as a man would. What Woolf shows us is a very capable, if not entirely lovable, woman using the fairly limited Richard and the completely doltish Hugh to make her point in a society that would not take the point seriously if it was seen as coming directly from her. In the years after the Great War, the scene reminds us, ideas were judged on the basis of the class and gender of the person putting them forward. Woolf handles all of this so subtly that we may not think of it as political, but it is.

It always—or almost always—is.

14

Yes, She's a Christ Figure, Too

This may surprise some of you, but we live in a Christian culture. What I mean is that since the preponderance of cultural influences has come down to us from European early settlers, and since those early settlers inflicted their values on the "benighted" cultures they encountered ("benighted," from the Old English, meaning "anyone darker than myself"), those inflicted values have gained ascendancy. This is not to say that all citizens of this great republic are Christians, any more than that they are all great republicans. I once heard a well-known Jewish professor of composition speak about walking into her very first final examination in college only to be confronted with this question: "discuss the Christian imagery in *Billy Budd*." It simply never occurred to her professor back in the

1950s that Christian imagery might be alien territory for some students.

Institutions of higher learning can no longer blithely assume that everyone in class is a Christian, and if they do, it's at their own risk. Still, no matter what your religious beliefs, to get the most out of your reading of European and American literatures, knowing something about the Old and New Testaments is essential. Similarly, if you undertake to read literature from an Islamic or a Buddhist or a Hindu culture, you're going to need knowledge of other religious traditions. Culture is so influenced by its dominant religious systems that whether a writer adheres to the beliefs or not, the values and principles of those religions will inevitably inform the literary work. Often those values will not be religious in nature but may show themselves in connection with the individual's role within society, or humankind's relation to nature, or the involvement of women in public life, although, as we have seen, just as often religion shows up in the form of allusions and analogues. When I read an Indian novel, for example, I'm often aware, if only dimly, of how much I'm missing due to my ignorance of the various religious traditions of the subcontinent. Since I'd like to get more out of my reading, I've worked to reduce that ignorance, but I still have a way to go.

Okay, so not everyone is a Christian around these parts, nor do those who would say they are necessarily have more than a nodding familiarity with the New Testament, aside from John 3:16, which is always beside the goalposts at football games. But in all probability they do know one thing: they know why it's called Christianity. Okay, so it's not the most profound insight ever, but it matters. A lot. Northrop Frye, one of the great literary critics, said in the 1950s that biblical typology—the comparative study of types between the Old and New Testaments and, by extension, out into literature—was a dead language, and things haven't improved since then. While we may not be all that well versed in types and archetypes from the Bible, we generally recognize, whatever our religious affiliation, some of the features that make Christ who he is.

Whether you do or not, this list may be helpful:

1) crucified, wounds in the hands, feet, side, and head

2) in agony

3) self-sacrificing

4) good with children

5) good with loaves, fishes, water, wine

6) thirty-three years of age when last seen

7) employed as carpenter

8) known to use humble modes of transportation, feet or donkeys preferred

9) believed to have walked on water

10) often portrayed with arms outstretched

11) known to have spent time alone in the wilderness

12) believed to have had a confrontation with the devil, possibly tempted

13) last seen in the company of thieves

14) creator of many aphorisms and parables

15) buried, but arose on the third day

16) had disciples, twelve at first, although not all equally devoted

17) very forgiving

18) came to redeem an unworthy world

You may not subscribe to this list, may find it too glib, but if you want to read like a literature professor, you need to put aside your belief system, at least for the period during which you read, so you can see what the writer is trying to say. As you're reading that story or poem, religious knowledge is helpful, although religious belief, if too tightly held, can be a problem. We want to be able to identify features in stories and see how they are being used; in other words, we want to be analytical.

Say we're reading a book, a novel. Short novel, say. And let's say this short novel has a man in it, a man no longer young, in fact old, as well as very poor and engaged in a humble profession. Not carpentry, say, but fishing. Jesus had some dealings with fishermen, too, and is often connected symbolically with fish, so that's a point of similarity. And the old fisherman hasn't had much good luck for a long time, so no one believes in him. In general there's a lot of doubt and nonbelief in our story. But one young boy believes in him; sadly, though, the boy isn't allowed to accompany the fisherman any- more, because everyone, the boy's parents included, think the old man is bad luck. There's a second point of similarity: *he's good with children.* Or at least one child. And he has one *disciple.* And this old man is very good and pure, so that's another point. Because the world he lives in is rather sullied and unworthy, fallen even.

During his solitary fishing trip, the old man hooks into a big fish that takes him far out beyond his known limits, to where the sea becomes *a wilderness*. He's all alone, and he's put through *great physical suffering*, during which even he begins to doubt himself. His *hands* are ripped up by the struggle, he thinks he's broken something in his *side*. But he bucks himself up with *aphorisms* like "A man is not made for defeat. A man can be destroyed but not defeated"—inspiring things like that. Somehow he can endure this whole episode, which lasts *three days* and which finally makes it seem to those on land that he's dead. His great fish is ruined by sharks, but he manages to drag this huge ruined skeleton back to port. His return is like *a resurrection*. He has to walk up a hill from the water to his shack, and he carries his mast, which looks like *a man carrying a cross* from a certain point of view. *Then he lies on his bed, exhausted by his struggles, his arms thrown out in the position of crucifixion, showing his damaged, raw hands.* And the next morning, when people see the great fish, even the doubters begin to believe in him again. He brings *a kind of hope, a kind of redemption*, to this fallen world, and . . . yes?

Didn't Hemingway write a book like that?

Yes, *The Old Man and the Sea* (1952), a nearly perfect literary parable, so clear, with symbols so available, that the Christian imagery is accessible to even beginning readers. But let's give old Hemingway some credit here; the narrative is more subtle than I've just made it sound. And the struggle is so vivid and concrete that one can get a lot out of it—triumph over adversity, the value of hope and faith, the attainment of grace—without placing undue weight on the old man, Santiago, as a Christ figure.

So must all Christ figures be as unambiguous as this? No, they don't have to hit all the marks. Don't have to be male. Don't have to be Christian. Don't even have to be good. (See the stories of Flannery O'Connor for example after example.) There, however, we're starting to get into irony, and that's a whole different area where I don't want to go just yet. Yet. But if a character is a certain age, exhibits certain behaviors, provides for certain outcomes, or suffers in certain ways, your literary antennae should begin to twitch. How should we know, though? Here's a handy list, not all-inclusive, but a start:

YOU MIGHT BE A CHRIST FIGURE IF YOU ARE . . .
(CHECK ANY THAT APPLY):

__ *thirty-three years old*

__ *unmarried, preferably celibate*

__ *wounded or marked in the hands, feet, or side*
     (crown of thorns extra credit)

__ *sacrificing yourself in some way for others (your life is best, and your sacrifice doesn't have to be willing)*

__ *in some sort of wilderness, tempted there, accosted by the devil*

Oh, you get the point. Consult previous list.

Are there things you don't have to do? Certainly. Consider Santiago again. Wait, you say, shouldn't he be thirty-three? And the answer is, sometimes that's good. But a Christ figure doesn't need to resemble Christ in every way; otherwise he wouldn't be a Christ figure, he'd be, well, Christ. The literal elements—changing water into wine, unless in some clumsy way such as pouring out someone's water and filling his glass with wine; stretching loaves and fishes to feed five thousand; preaching (although some do); suffering actual crucifixion; literally following in his footsteps—aren't really required. It's the symbolic level we're interested in.

Which brings us to another issue we've touched upon in other chapters. Fiction and poetry and drama are not necessarily playgrounds for the overly literal. Many times I'll point out that a character is Christlike because he does X and Y, and you might come back with, "But Christ did A and Z and his X wasn't like that, and besides, this character listens to AC/DC." Okay, so the heavy-metal sound isn't in the hymnal. And this character would be very hard pressed to take over Savior duty. No literary Christ figure can ever be as pure, as perfect, as divine as Jesus Christ. Here as elsewhere, one does well to remember that writing literature is an exercise of the imagination. And so is reading it. We have to bring our imaginations to bear on a story if we are to see all its possibilities; otherwise it's just about somebody who did something. Whatever we take away from stories in the way of significance, symbolism, theme, meaning, pretty much anything except character and plot, we discover because our imagination engages with that of the author. Pretty amazing when you consider that the author may have been dead for a thousand years, yet we can still have this kind of exchange, this dialogue, with her. At the same time, this doesn't indicate the story can mean anything we want it to, since that would be a case of our imagination not bothering with that of the author and just inventing whatever it wants to see in the text. That's not reading, that's writing. But that's another matter, and one we'll discuss elsewhere.

On the flip side, if someone in class asks if it's possible that the character under discussion might be a Christ figure, citing three or four similarities, I'll say something like, "Works for me." The bottom line, I usually tell the class, is that Christ figures are where you find them, and as you find them. If the indicators are there, then there is some basis for drawing the conclusion.

Consider the case of June Kashpaw, who is less a character in Louise Erdrich's *Love Medicine* than a plot device: she dies, her son inherits the money, which he turns into a car, and the car eventually falls into the hands of her illegitimate (and unacknowledged) son. You know, my mother, the car. But she's also much more than that. Although June barely appears in the novel, she is the first character we meet. I will be the first to admit that she lacks a good deal in the Christlike department. She's an alcoholic, a woman who has been reduced to, essentially, prostitution to get by, and an almost entirely selfish person, which coincidentally means that she was a lousy mother, although that's neither here nor there when we are comparing her to Jesus. Her death, in fact, comes from one of those sexual encounters, when she stumbles away from the pickup truck where she's just had sex with a mud engineer for an oil company and tries to walk back to the reservation (an impossibly far distance in any event) through a terrible blizzard.

Clearly, unpromising material. But don't give up on her just yet. This is all happening at Easter, and June's associations are multiple. When they meet in a bar, the man peels her a colored egg, and then another. He says of the first that it matches her "turtleneck," which she informs him is called a "shell." She feels fragile, like the egg, yet she also has a sort of out-of-body experience, as if her pure self is untouchable, incapable of being corrupted by this very fallen world. Later, when she falls out of his pickup, she arranges her clothing and begins walking toward home. Even the blizzard can't stop her as she walks over the snow "like water and came home."

But wait, as the commercials tell us, there's more. June experiences a resurrection of sorts in the form of that car, a blue Firebird that her son, King, buys with her insurance money. The car eventually passes to Lipsha Morrissey, the illegitimate son, in a rigged card game orchestrated by Lipsha's father, Gerry Nanapush. That June is associated with the car is established repeatedly, not least when King, in a fit of rage, violently attacks the vehicle. Much later, in Erdrich's 1993 novel *The Bingo Palace*, June's ghost comes by in the ghost of "her" car to take Gerry, who is nothing like a ghost, away into another blizzard. Pretty interesting stuff, especially when we consider that the Firebird suggests the Phoenix, the bird that regenerates itself by bursting into flame and rising from its own ashes.

June also has her own disciples, of an ironic sort. At the family gathering a few months after her death, several of the women gossip about her, telling her story in a sort of mythic fashion. She is by no means a figure of veneration to them, yet they cannot stop talking about her. And Lipsha, naive and longing for connection, turns her, along with Gerry, into figures to be nearly worshipped. Blind to all her faults, he even declares that her abandoning him to be raised by his grandmother Kashpaw was an act of compassion, given how badly the acknowledged son turned out. June becomes not merely a tragic figure, one who ruined herself and, from the perspective of her Kashpaw in-laws, her husband (although Gordie Kashpaw seems perfectly capable of self-destruction without outside agency), but a figure of myth whose story organizes and informs the lives of those she leaves behind. Most significantly, the gospel of June ultimately saves Lipsha and gives him a sense of belonging.

So, Christ figure? She won't work for everyone, and indeed readers of a more religious bent may find the suggestion offensive. I would remind doubters, however, that her death comes in a chapter titled "The World's Greatest Fisherman," which counts for something. She's about the best we can hope for in an ironic age. Christ figures can suggest many things, not all of which are remotely Christlike. As is often the case, it's effects we're after, not details, when we look for these parallels.

Why, you might ask, are there Christ figures? As with most other cases we've looked at where the work engages some prior text, the short answer is that probably the writer wants to make a certain point. Perhaps the parallel deepens our sense of the character's sacrifice if we see it as somehow similar to the greatest sacrifice we know of. Maybe it has to do with redemption, or hope, or miracle. Or maybe it is all being treated ironically, to make the character look smaller rather than greater. But count on it, the writer is up to something. How do we know what he's up to? That's another job for imagination.

15

Flights of Fancy

I took just enough physics in school to master one significant fact: human beings cannot fly. Here's a principle that always holds. If it flies, it isn't human. Birds fly. Bats fly. Insects sometimes fly. Certain squirrels and fish sail for a bit and seem to fly. Humans? Thirty-two feet per second squared. Same as bowling balls. If you drop me and a bowling ball off the Tower of Pisa (and please don't) at the same time, the bowling ball won't go splat. Otherwise we're the same.

Airplanes?

No doubt about it, airplanes and blimps and helicopters and autogiros have changed the way we perceive flight, but for almost all of human history, we've been earthbound.

Meaning what?

Meaning that when we see a person suspended in the air, even briefly, he is one or more of the following:

1) a superhero

2) a ski jumper

3) crazy (redundant if also number 2)

4) fictional

5) a circus act, departing a cannon

6) suspended on wires

7) an angel

8) heavily symbolic

Of course, just because we can't fly doesn't mean we don't dream of it. We chafe at laws, particularly when we feel they're unfair or inhibiting or both, as with the law of gravity. The steady winner in magic acts, since most magicians can't afford an elephant for the vanishing act, is levitation. British imperialists in the nineteenth century came back from the Eastern realms with tales of swamis who had mastered the art of hovering above the ground. Our comic book superheroes defy gravity in various ways, whether through flight directly (Superman), tethers (Spider-Man), or gadgets (Batman).

Culturally and literarily, we have toyed with the idea of flight since earliest times. Few stories from Greek mythology capture the imagination like that of Daedalus and Icarus: the ingenious father's attempt to save his son from a tyrant as well as from his own invention (the labyrinth) by coming up with an even more marvelous creation; the solemn parental warning ignored in a burst of youthful exuberance; the fall from a great height; a father's terrible grief and guilt. Flight alone is a wonder; with these other elements, a complete and compelling myth. Other cultures share this fascination. Toni Morrison has spoken of the myth of the flying Africans. The Aztecs saw a particularly important god, Quetzalcoatl, as a snake with feathered wings. Christian popular belief often sees new arrivals in heaven decked out with wings and a harp—emblems of flight and music which are natural properties of the birds but denied humans. Scripturally, flight is one of the temptations of Christ: Satan asks him to demonstrate his divinity by launching himself from the promontory. Perhaps it is that episode that has associated witchcraft with flight through so much of our history, or perhaps it is merely that our misplaced desire for flight has turned to envy.

So what does it mean when literary characters fly? Take, for example, Morrison's *Song of Solomon* and its highly ambiguous airborne ending, with Milkman suspended in mid-leap toward Guitar, each of them knowing only one can survive. Morrison's use of the myth of the flying Africans introduces a specific historical and racial reference that is outside the experience of most readers, but we recognize various implications. Milkman's great-grandfather, Solomon, flew off to Africa but couldn't hold on to his youngest child, Jake, dropping him back to earth and slavery. Flying off, in this instance, suggests casting off the chains of slavery on one level and returning "home" (Africa for Solomon, Virginia for Milkman) on another. In general, flying is freedom, we might say, freedom not only from specific circumstances but from those more general burdens that tie us down. It's escape, the flight of imagination. All of this is very good. Well then, what about Pilate, Milkman's unfortunately named aunt? After she dies, a bird swoops down, grabs the earring box containing a slip of paper with her name on it, and flies away. Milkman suddenly realizes that of all the people he's ever known, Pilate alone had the power of flight, even though she never left the ground. What does it mean to say that someone who remains physically earthbound has been able to fly? It's spiritual, we might conclude. Her soul could soar, which you can't say about anybody else in the novel. She is the character of spirit and love;

her last utterance is a wish that she could have known more people so she could have loved them all. Such a character is not anchored at all. She's flying in a way we don't need to know the underlying myth of the flying Africans to comprehend.

So freedom, escape, return home, largeness of spirit, love. That's a lot for just one work to do with flying. What about others? What about *E.T.*? When those bicycles leave the street in the Steven Spielberg classic, what's the situation? The adults of the community, representing conformity, hostility to anything new, xenophobia, suspicion, a lack of imagination, are bearing down on our young heroes. They've even set up a roadblock. At just the moment when things look worst, the bicycles leave the earth and, with it, the earth-bound grown-ups. Escape? Certainly. Freedom? You bet. Wonder, magic? Absolutely.

It's really pretty straightforward: **flight is freedom.**

It doesn't always work out that way, but the basic principle is pretty sound. Angela Carter's *Nights at the Circus* (1984) offers a comparative rarity, a fictional character who actually possesses wings. Carter's heroine, Fevvers (whose name paradoxically suggests both "feathers" and "tethers"), is a woman whose flying act has made her the toast of circuses and music halls across Europe. It has also set her apart. She is not like other people, cannot comfortably fit into normal human life. Carter's use of flight differs from Morrison's in that it does not emphasize freedom and escape. Like Franz Kafka's Hunger Artist, Fevvers has a gift that places her in a cage: her flights are contained indoors, her world is a stage where even the fourth wall is a barrier, since she is so different from her audience that she cannot freely join them. There are a couple of points that should be made here. First, as I have intimated several times before and will discuss later, **irony trumps everything**. But irony typically depends on an established pattern on which it can work its inversions. All of Carter's irony here, naturally enough, builds on a foundation of expectations having to do with flying and wings. If flying is freedom, and if Fevvers's flying represents a kind of counterfreedom, then we have an inversion that creates significance: she's trapped by the ability most symbolic of freedom. Without our expectations about the meaning of flight, Fevvers is simply an oddity on a stage. The second point has to do with different kinds of freedom: just as Morrison's Pilate can fly without ever leaving the ground, so Fevvers can find freedom even within the limitations of her fishbowl world. Her act frees her to express her sexuality in ways not available to other women in the novel's highly restricted late-Victorian society. She can dress, speak, and act in a manner that would be deeply shocking in other contexts. Her freedom, like her "imprisonment," is paradoxical. Carter uses Fevvers, with her mix of earthy sexuality and avian ability, to comment on the situation of women in English society; it's a strategy that is perfectly normal for Carter, whose novels typically, and comically, undercut assumptions about masculine and feminine roles, holding up our received notions for scrutiny and occasional ridicule. Social criticism is the outcome of this subversive strategy, flight the device by which Carter sets up her ironic notions of freedom and imprisonment.

Characters like Fevvers who possess wings are particularly interesting to us. And why not? How many of your friends and neighbors sport feathers? In truth, stories with winged characters make up a pretty small genre, but those few stories hold a special fascination. Gabriel García Márquez's story "A Very Old Man with Enormous Wings" (1968) features a nameless old man who falls from the sky during a monsoonal rain. His wings are indeed enormous. Some of the poor people in the coastal Colombian town where he lands take him to be an angel, but if he is, he's a very odd one. He's dirty and smelly, and his ragged wings harbor parasites. It is true that shortly after he plops down in the yard of Pelayo and Elisenda, their child recovers from a life-threatening fever, but his other "miracles," if he has anything to do with them, don't work exactly right. One character fails to recover health but nearly wins the lottery, while another, although not cured of leprosy, sprouts sunflowers from his sores. Still, the residents are fascinated by this new arrival, so much so that the peasant couple constructs a cage and puts him on display. Although the old man does nothing remarkable, so many people come and pay the small admission fee that Pelayo and Elisenda become wealthy. We never know what the old man is, and speculation among the townspeople is hilarious as well as occasionally bizarre (his green eyes suggest to one character that he's a Norwegian sailor), but his hapless, shabby appearance and long-suffering silence clearly benefit the family in a nearly miraculous fashion. In the way of those who receive miraculous aid, they are unappreciative and even a little resentful at having to provide for the old man. Eventually the old man regains his strength and, seen only by the wife, flaps away, his ungainly flight recalling a rather disreputable vulture more than any angel. Like Carter, García Márquez plays on our notions of wings and flight to explore the situation's ironic possibilities. In fact, he goes even further in some ways. His winged character is literally caged; moreover, he's dirty and unkempt and bug-ridden, not at all what we expect from potential angels. On one level, the story asks us if we would recognize the Second Coming if it occurred, and perhaps it reminds us that the Messiah was not generally acknowledged when he did come. The angel doesn't look like an angel, just as the King didn't look like a king, certainly not like the sort of military ruler the Hebrews had expected. Does the old man choose not to fly? Has he been reduced in power and appearance purposely? The story never says, and in its silence it poses many questions.

Of course, his mode of arrival poses another question for us.

What about characters who don't quite fly or whose flights are interrupted? Since Icarus, we've had stories of those whose flights end prematurely. In general, this is a bad thing, given what is the opposite of flying. On the other hand, not all crashes end disastrously. At almost the exact same moment (the novels were published within months of each other), Fay Weldon and Salman Rushdie introduced characters—two in each case—falling from great heights, from exploding airliners. In Weldon's *Hearts and Lives of Men* the contested child of an ugly divorce is kidnapped, and she and her kidnapper float down to safety as the rear section of the plane, containing only the two of them, rather improbably disobeys certain laws of aerodynamics to glide gently to earth. Rushdie's two main characters, Gibreel and Saladin, fall bodily to the ground, their landings softened by the snow-covered English beach on which they land. In each case, there is an element of rebirth in their cheating what would typically prove to be certain death. The characters are not inevitably better off in their new lives; Rushdie's two are particularly devilish, while Weldon's little girl loses the immense privilege of her previous existence for a very long time, gaining instead the sort of life Dickens would invent for one of his waifs. Nevertheless, the act of falling from vast heights and surviving is as miraculous, and as symbolically meaningful, as the act of flight itself. As thrilled as we are by the prospect of flying, we are also frightened at the prospect of falling, and anything that seems to defy the inevitability of a plummeting demise sets our imaginations working overtime. The survival of these characters demands that we consider the implications. What does it mean to survive certain death, and how does such survival alter one's relationship to the world? Do the characters' responsibilities to themselves, to life itself, change? Is the survivor even the same person any longer? Rushdie asks outright if birth inevitably involves a fall, while Weldon poses questions that are equally suggestive.

If our consideration of flying were limited to those works where characters literally fly, we'd have a pretty thin discussion. These examples of actual flight, necessary as they are, remain valuable chiefly for the instruction they give us in interpreting figurative flight. There's an Irish novel about a little boy growing up to become a writer. As he matures, he finds that in order to acquire the experience and vision he needs to become a writer, he'll have to leave home. Problem: home is an island. The only way he's going to be able to leave is to cross a body of water, which is the most dramatic and final sort of home-leaving one can take (and he is a young man with a fear of water). Fortunately, he has the right name to help him out: Dedalus. Not a very Irish name for a young man from Dublin, nor is it the first name he tried for young Stephen, but it's the one James Joyce settled on for *A Portrait of the Artist as a Young Man* (1916). Stephen feels hemmed in by the strictures of Irish life, by family and politics and education and religion and narrow-mindedness; as we know by now, the antidote to limitations and shackles is freedom. The latter parts of the novel are filled with images of birds, feathers, and flying, all of which, while not referring to literal flight, evoke thoughts of metaphorical flight, of escape. Stephen has an epiphany, a Joycean religio-aesthetic word for an awakening, of a wading girl, in which moment he experiences the sensation of beauty and harmony and radiance that convinces him he must be an artist. The girl is neither singularly beautiful nor memorable in herself. Rather, the scene is beautiful in its totality, or perhaps it would be more accurate to say in his perception of its totality. In this moment the narration describes her as a bird, from the feathery edges of her drawers to her breast like that of some "dark-plumaged bird." Subsequent to this epiphany, Stephen begins to ruminate on his namesake, the crafter of wings for escape from a different island, whom he comes to think of as "hawklike." Finally he announces that he must fly past the nets he sees as set to trap him into the conventionality and smallness that is every Dubliner's inheritance. His understanding of flight is purely symbolic, yet his need for escape is no less real for that. In order for him to become a creator, his spirit must soar; he must be free.

Indeed, often in literature the freeing of the spirit is seen in terms of flight. In his poetry, William Butler Yeats often contrasts the freedom of birds with the earthbound cares and woes of humans. In his great "The Wild Swans at Coole" (1917), for instance, he watches the beautiful birds rise and wheel, forever young, while he, a middle-aged man, feels the pull of gravity more heavily with each passing year. He makes much of Zeus taking the swan's form to ravish Leda and beget Helen (of Troy) on her, and he sees the archangel's appearance to the Virgin Mary in terms of wings and birds as well.

Similarly, we speak of the soul as taking wing. Seamus Heaney has several poems where the souls of the departed are said to flutter away from the body, and in this he is far from alone. The notion that the disembodied soul is capable of flight is deeply embedded in the Christian tradition, and I suspect in many others as well, although it is not universal. For the ancient Greeks and Romans, such a concept was problematic, since the souls of blessed and damned alike went to an underground realm, but the belief in a celestial heaven leads much of later Western culture to a sense of the soul's lightness. In "Birches" Robert Frost imagines climbing the supple birches up toward heaven, then being lightly set back on the ground, and he declares that both going and coming back would be good (even without wings). When Claudius, Hamlet's villainous uncle, tries to pray, he fails, saying, "My words fly up, my thoughts remain below." The spirit cannot rise up, Shakespeare suggests, when weighed down by the guilt of an unconfessed murder. When Hamlet lies dead at the play's end, his friend Horatio mourns him, saying, "Good night, sweet prince,/And flights of angels sing thee to thy rest!" As we all know by now, if Shakespeare said it, it must be true.

These flights of fancy allow us, as readers, to take off, to let our imaginations take flight. We can sail off with characters, freed of the limitations of our tuition payments and mortgage rates; we can soar into interpretation and speculation.

Happy landings.

16

It's All About Sex . . .

There's an ugly rumor circulating that English professors have dirty minds. It's not true, of course. We're no more dirty-minded than society at large, although that may not be of any great comfort. Well, let me assure you that English professors are not innately prurient. It's just that they can recognize the sexual intentions of writers, who may well have dirty minds. So how did all this smutty thinking find its way into world literature?

Blame it on Freud. He put it there.

More accurately, he found it and showed it to the rest of us. When he published *The Interpretation of Dreams* in 1900, he unlocked the sexual potential of the subconscious. Tall buildings? Male sexuality. Rolling landscapes? Female sexuality. Stairs? Sexual intercourse. Falling down stairs? Oh my. All of this may be regarded these days as so much hokum in the arena of psychoanalysis, but it's like gold in terms of literary analysis. Suddenly we discover that sex doesn't have to look like sex: other objects and activities can stand in for sexual organs and sex acts, which is good, since those organs and acts can only be arranged in so many ways and are not inevitably decorous. So land-scapes can have a sexual component. So can bowls. Fires. Seashores. And 1949 Plymouths, one supposes. Virtually anything, if the writer so decides. Oh yes, Freud taught us well. And some of those he taught are writers. Suddenly, as the twentieth century gets roll-ing, two things are happening. Critics and readers are learning that sexuality may be encoded in their read-ing, while writers are learning that they can encode sexuality into their writing. Headaches, anyone?

Of course, the twentieth century didn't invent sexual symbolism. Consider the Grail legends. A knight, usu-ally a very young one whose "manhood" is barely established, sallies forth bearing his lance, which will certainly do until a phallic symbol comes along. The knight becomes the emblem of pure, if untested, male-ness in search of a chalice, the Holy Grail, which if you think about it is a symbol of female sexuality as under-stood once upon a time: the empty vessel, waiting to be filled. And the reason for seeking to bring together the lance and the chalice? Fertility. (Freud gets help here from Jessie L. Weston, Sir James Frazer, and Carl Jung, all of whom explain a great deal about mythic thinking, fertility myths, and archetypes.) Typically the knight rides out from a community that has fallen on hard times. Crops are failing, rains have stopped, livestock and possibly humans are dying or failing to be born, the kingdom is turning into a wasteland. We need to restore fertility and order, says the aging king, too old now to go in search of fertility symbols. Perhaps he can no longer use his lance, so he sends the young man. It isn't wanton or wild sex, but it's still sex.

Flash-forward a millennium or so. Hang a left at New York and go to Hollywood. There's a moment in *The Maltese Falcon* (1941) when Humphrey Bogart's Sam Spade, at night, is leaning over Mary Astor's Brigid O'Shaughnessy, kissing her by a window, and then the next moment we're looking at the curtains of the window blowing gently in the morning sunlight. No Sam. No Brigid. Young viewers sometimes don't notice those curtains, so they want to know what happened between Sam and Brigid. It may seem a small detail, but it matters greatly that we understand so that we see how much Sam Spade's judgment may be compromised, and how difficult turning her in at the end is going to be. For those who remember a time when the movies not only didn't show people "doing it," they also didn't show people having done it or talking about having done it, those curtains might as well bear the following printed legend: *yes, they did. And they enjoyed it.* For people of that age, one of the sexiest shots in film consists of waves breaking on a beach. When the director cut to the waves on the beach, somebody was getting lucky. These abstractions were necessary under the Hayes Code, which controlled content in Hollywood films from around 1935 until 1965, more or less, throughout the height of the studio system. The Hayes Code said a lot of different things, but the one we're interested in was that you could stack bodies like cordwood if they were dead (although usually without blood), but living bodies couldn't get horizontal together. Husbands and wives were nearly always shown in separate beds. I noticed this once more the other night when I watched Hitchcock's *Notorious* (1946), where Claude Rains and Ingrid Bergman have twin beds. The man has never been born who, finding himself married to Ingrid Bergman, would assent to sleeping in twin beds. Even an evil Nazi like Claude Rains. But in the movies in 1946, that's what happened. So film directors resorted to anything they could think of: waves, curtains, campfires, fireworks, you name

it. And sometimes the results were dirtier than show-
ing the real thing. At the end of Hitchcock's *North by
Northwest* (1959), Cary Grant and Eva Marie Saint find
themselves rescued from the face of Mount Rushmore
when the good guys kill Martin Landau before he can
send our heroes to their deaths. In one of the truly great
cuts, Grant, who is struggling to hold Miss Saint on the
rock face, is suddenly pulling her up into the sleeping
compartment of the train (and referring to her as Mrs.
Thornhill); this shot is followed by an equally famous
one—the last shot of the film—of the train entering a
tunnel. No need to comment on that one.

Okay, you say, but that's film. What about books?

I barely know where to begin. Let's try something
tame first, Ann Beattie's story "Janus" (1985). A
youngish woman, married but not particularly in love
with her husband, has had an affair with another man,
the only tangible result of which is a bowl the lover
bought for her. The woman, Andrea, comes more and
more to identify with the bowl and to obsess over it.
She's a real-estate agent, and she often places the bowl
in a prominent place in clients' houses before she shows
them; she gets up at night to check on it and make sure
it's all right; and most tellingly, she will not permit
her husband to put his keys in her bowl. Do you see
the sexuality embedded in that set of images? How do

keys work? Whose keys are they? Where can he not put them? Whose talisman is the bowl he can't put them in? Consider, for instance, that Hank Williams/ George Thorogood classic, "Move It on Over," and the complaint about his lady changing locks and leaving him with a key that no longer fits. Every American should know enough of the blues to understand exactly what keys and locks signify, and to blush when they're referred to. That pattern of imagery is just part of the much older tradition identified by Freud/Weston/ Frazer/Jung about lances and swords and guns (and keys) as phallic symbols, chalices and grails (and bowls, of course, also) as symbols of female sexual organs. Back to Andrea's bowl: it really is about sex. Specifically, it's about her identity as a woman, an individual, and a sexual being, rather than as an extension of a lover or a husband. She fears being merely an auxiliary of some man's existence, although her autonomy, as symbolized by the bowl, is made problematic by its having been purchased for her by . . . a man. He only buys it, though, after seeing that she really connects with the bowl, so it really is hers in the end.

To talk about sex in literature almost inevitably leads to discussion of D. H. Lawrence. The great thing about Lawrence, from my point of view, is that you can never go wrong bringing sex into the analysis. Partly because sex had been taboo for so long and therefore was a largely untapped resource for the novelist, he worked tirelessly to explore the subject. His work has plenty of mentions of sexual relations, some oblique, some explicit, and in his last novel, *Lady Chatterley's Lover* (1928), the great forbidden reading-fruit of everyone's youth, he pushes right past the limits of censorship of his time. The sexiest scene he ever wrote, though, is not a sex scene. It's wrestling. In *Women in Love*, the two main male characters wrestle one evening, in language in which the sexual charge is ferocious. They've been going on about blood brotherhoods and the closeness of their friendship, so the wrestling is not all that surprising. Lawrence isn't comfortable making them openly homosexual but he wants a relationship—and a physical expression—that is nearly as close as the love-and-sex relationship between man and woman. Ken Russell certainly understood what the scene was about when he filmed the novel back in 1969; I hadn't understood it, being too conditioned not to look for anything homoerotic and, I suppose, too insecure as to what that might say about one of my favorite writers. Once I saw the film, though, I went back and reread the scene, and Russell got it right.

My favorite Lawrence story, bar none, is called "The Rocking-Horse Winner" (1932), about a little boy who wants to please his mother. His father is a failure in business and therefore a great disappointment to the materialist mother. The son, Paul, senses the desperation for money in the house, senses his mother's dissatisfaction, senses the inability of his mother to love him, or anyone, in the face of her own colossal self-absorption. He connects the lack of his mother's love with the lack of money, then discovers that he can pick the winners of upcoming horse races if he rides his rocking horse to the point of exhaustion. Here's what Lawrence has to say:

> He wanted luck, he wanted it, he wanted it. When the two girls were playing dolls in the nursery, he would sit on his big rocking horse, charging madly into space, with a frenzy that made the little girls peer at him uneasily. Wildly the horse careered, the waving dark hair of the boy tossed, the eyes had a strange glare in them. The girls dared not speak to them. . . . He knew the horse could take him to where there was luck, if only he forced it. . . . At last he stopped forcing his horse into the mechanical gallop and slid down.

Say what you will, I think he's talking about masturbation. When I teach this story, I try to lead the students to this idea without insisting on it. Usually there is one hardy and perceptive soul who gets it and asks, with something between a smirk and a cringe, the question I'm hoping for. One or two others nod, as if they sort of thought that but were afraid to think it through. Thirty-five others look like the ceiling is about to fall.

Is it really?

Let's look at the pattern that's set up: child wants to supplant father in his mother's affections, child desperately wants mother's approval and love, child engages in highly secretive behavior involving frenetic, rhythmic activity that culminates in transporting loss of consciousness. What does that sound like to you? This is one of the clearest Oedipal situations ever captured in fiction, and for good reason. Lawrence was part of the first generation to read Freud and so, for the first time, to consciously employ Freudian thinking in literature. The notion of sublimation kicks in here, for both character and writer. Obviously, sexual engagement with the mother is not an option, so Lawrence sends the boy, Paul, in search of the luck his mother desires so terribly. The means of his search is sufficiently creepy that it frightens his presexual sisters and causes consternation among the adults, who feel that he's too big for a rocking horse.

Is it really masturbation? Not literally. That would be icky and not particularly interesting. But symbolically it fulfills the function of masturbation. Think of it as a surrogate for a surrogate for sex. What could be clearer?

Why? Part of the reason for all this disguised sex is that, historically, writers and artists couldn't make much use of the real thing. Lawrence, for instance, had numerous novels suppressed and undertook a monumental battle with the British censors. Same as in film.

Another reason is that scenes in which sex is coded rather than explicit can work at multiple levels and sometimes be more intense than literal depictions. Those multiple levels have traditionally been to protect innocents. Dickens, who could be very suggestive, was aware that his novels were often read around the family breakfast table, and he wanted to protect children from anything luridly sexual, as well as to provide wives with plausible deniability. With a scene of encoded sex, Mother could pretend not to notice that something untoward was going on while Father was enjoying his private smirk. There's a scene in *Our Mutual Friend* (1865) in which the two villains, Mr. Venus and Silas Wegg, are plotting evil. In fact, Silas Wegg is reading some financial news of a very tantalizing nature to the seated Mr. Venus, whose pegleg begins to rise from the floor until, at the moment of greatest excitement, it is pointing straight out in front of him. And then he falls over. Various family members could see this as either slapstick buffoonery or as quite suggestive slapstick buffoonery. In any case, everybody gets a giggle.

Even in our highly permissive age, though, sex often doesn't appear in its own guise. It is displaced into other areas of experience in much the same way it is in our own lives and our own consciousnesses. Ann Beattie's character Andrea doesn't think of her problems as being chiefly sexual or romantic. But they are, as we and her creator can see. So it's unlikely that her sexual issues will present themselves in terms of sexual organs and acts; much more likely they'll look like . . . a bowl and some keys.

17

. . . Except Sex

E ver try to write a sex scene? No, seriously. Tell you what: go try. In the interest of good taste, I'll request that you limit yourself to members of the same species and for clarity that you limit yourself to a mere pair of participants, but aside from that, no restrictions. Let 'em do whatever you want. Then when you come back, in a day, in a week, in a month, you'll have found out what most writers already know: describing two human beings engaging in the most intimate of shared acts is very nearly the least rewarding enterprise a writer can undertake.

Don't feel bad. You never had a chance. What are your options? The possible circumstances that lead two people to sexual congress are virtually limitless, but the act itself? How many options do you have?

You can describe the business clinically as if it were a do-it-yourself manual—insert tab A into slot B—but there are not that many tabs or slots, whether you use the Anglo-Saxon names or their Latinate alternatives. Frankly there just isn't that much variety, with or without the Reddi-Wip, and besides, it's been written in the mass of pornography ad nauseam. You can opt for the soft-core approach, describing parts and movements in a haze of breathy metaphors and heroic adverbs: *he achingly stroked her quivering skiff as it rode the waves of her desire, etc.* This second sort is hard to write without seeming (a) quaint, (b) squeamish, (c) hugely embarrassed, (d) inept. To tell the truth, most writing that deals directly with sex makes you wish for the good old days of the billowing curtain and the gently lapping waves.

I honestly believe that if D. H. Lawrence could see the sorry state of sex scenes that developed within a generation of his death, he would retract *Lady Chatterley's Lover.* The truth is that most of the time when writers deal with sex, they avoid writing about the act itself. There are a lot of scenes that jump from the first button being undone to a postcoital cigarette (metaphorically, that is) or that cut from the unbuttoning to another scene entirely. The further truth is that even when they write about sex, they're really writing about something else.

Drives you crazy, doesn't it? When they're writing about other things, they really mean sex, and when they write about sex, they really mean something else. If they write about sex and mean strictly sex, we have a word for that. Pornography.

In the Victorian age, sex was nearly impossible to find in polite literature, due to rigid censorship both official and self-imposed. Not surprisingly, there was plenty of impolite literature. The era was unsurpassed in its production of pornography. Maybe it was that mountain of dirty writing that used up all the possibilities of writing about sex.

Even in the modernist period, though, there were limits. Hemingway was restricted in his use of curse words. Joyce's *Ulysses* was censored, banned, and confiscated in both the United Kingdom and the United States, in part for its sexual references (lots of sex thought, even if the only sex act shown in it is onanistic). Constance Chatterley and her lover, Mellors, really broke ground in plainly shown and plainspoken sex, although the novel's obscenity trial, effectively ending censorship in the United States, did not take place until 1959.

Strangely, with less than a century of sexual writing as standard practice, there is almost nothing left but cliché.

There's a very famous sex scene in John Fowles's *French Lieutenant's Woman* (1969) between the two main characters, Charles and Sarah. In fact, it's the only sex scene in the novel, which is odd, given the extent to which the novel is about love and sex. Our lovers enter her bedroom in a seedy hotel, he carrying her from the sitting room because she has sprained her ankle. He lays her on the bed and joins her amid frenetic shifting and removal of clothing, which, this book being set in Victorian times, is considerable. Soon the deed is done and he lies spent beside her, at which point the narrator points out that "precisely ninety seconds" have elapsed since he walked from her to look into the bedroom. In that time he walked back, picked her up, carried her to the bed, fumbled and groped, and consummated their love. Now there are several possible constructions we can put on this particular description of the act of love. Perhaps Fowles wants to address, for reasons unknown, the shortcomings of Victorian males in the ardor department. Perhaps he wants to ridicule his poor hero. Perhaps he wants to make some point about male sexual inadequacy or the fallibility of desire. Perhaps he wants to accentuate the comic or ironic incongruity between the brevity of the sexual act and its consequences. Of the first of these, why bother? Besides, he admits in a famous essay on the crafting of the novel that he really has no knowledge of nineteenth-century lovemaking, and in depicting sex between a Victorian man and woman what he's really writing is "science fiction." Of the second, it seems needlessly cruel, particularly when we've recently seen Charles in the arms of a young prostitute, where, rather than making love, he vomits into a pillow. Must he always be beset with performance issues? Of the third, sixty thousand words seems rather a lot with which to surround a tiny treatise on male sexuality. Of the fourth possibility, we know that incongruities, comic or otherwise, fascinate the novelist.

Let's consider another possibility, though. Charles has traveled from Lyme Regis, in the southwest, to London, where he has met with his future father-in-law, Mr. Freeman. Charles is horrified at the ill-judged marriage he has brought upon himself, complete with an offer of a job in business (anathema to a Victorian gentleman). He sees that he does not love the woman he is engaged to nor the conformity which she and her father, as members of the rising middle class, covet. He seems to be on a tether between the poles of his restricted future, with Mr. Freeman and the horrors of a life in commerce at one end in London, and his fiancée, Ernestina, at the other in Lyme Regis. Charles has come back through Exeter, where the seedy hotel is located, in full-panic flight. Sarah, the "fallen" woman (although we find out she probably is not), represents both the forbidden fruit, always tempting, and the way out of the marital disaster that he envisions awaiting him. His fascination with Sarah, which has been building throughout the novel, is a fascination with the unconventional aspects of himself, as well as with the possibilities of freedom and individual autonomy she represents. Sarah is the future, the twentieth century, for which Charles may not be ready. He carries not a woman but an entire constellation of possibilities into the bedroom. What chance does his sexual performance have?

For the most part, even our sexiest writing doesn't have all that much sex in it. Okay, except Henry Miller's novels, which really do have that much sex in them, and it's pretty much about the sex. But even with Miller, the sex is on one level symbolic action claiming for the individual freedom from convention and for the writer freedom from censorship. He's celebrating the removal of restrictions *and* writing hot sex.

But look at Miller's sometime pal Lawrence Durrell. (What is it about people named Lawrence and sex, anyway?) His *Alexandria Quartet*—the novels *Justine, Balthazar, Mountolive,* and *Clea* (1957–60)—is chiefly about the forces of politics and history and the impossibility of the individual escaping those forces, although it registers in readers' minds as heavily slanted toward the sexual. A lot of sex talk, of reports of sex, and of scenes taking place immediately before or immediately after sex. I would maintain this is not from trepidation on the writer's part (it's hard to find any evidence of Durrell being inhibited about much of anything) but from his sense that in novels so overheated by passion, the sexiest thing he can do is show everything but the lovemaking itself. Moreover, the sex that occurs is invariably tied up with something else: cover for espionage, personal sacrifice, psychological neediness, desire for power over someone else. He presents virtually no sexual encounters that can be described as healthy, robust meetings of lovers. Sex in Alexandria is really pretty creepy when all's said and done. And it's all done.

Two of the most notorious novels of that same period of the late 1950s and early 1960s, Anthony Burgess's *A Clockwork Orange* (1962) and Vladimir Nabokov's *Lolita* (1958) are famous for bad sex. Not bad as in unsatisfactory; bad as in evil. The protagonist of Burgess's novel is a fifteen-year-old leader of a gang whose specialties are theft with violence, violence without theft, and rape, to which he refers as "the old in-out in-out." The rapes we "see" do in fact take place in the narrative, but they are strangely distanced from us. For one thing, as many potential readers already know, Alex narrates in a patois he calls Nadsat, a mix of English and slang words, many of them of Slavic origin. The effect of this linguistic mode is to describe things in such alien ways that the acts themselves seem alien as well. For another thing, Alex is so interested in his own delight at stage-managing the violence and rape, and in the terror and cries of the victims, that he almost neglects the sexual particulars. His most straightforward narration of a sexual scene is when he picks up two prepubescent girls; even then, he's more interested in their cries of pain and outrage than in the activity occasioning them. Beyond that, Burgess is interested in depravity, not prurience. He's writing a novel of ideas with an attractive/revolting main character, so his chief concern is not to make the sex and violence interesting, but to make Alex sufficiently revolting—and he succeeds admirably. Some would say too well.

Lolita is a slightly different case. Nabokov has to make his middle-aged protagonist, Humbert Humbert, depraved, certainly, but part of the revulsion we feel at his interest in his underage stepdaughter Lolita lies in the way our sympathy is co-opted by this monster narrating the story. He's so charming we are nearly taken in, but then he reminds us what he is doing to this young girl and we're outraged again. Nabokov being Nabokov, though, there's a kind of "gotcha!" in it: we're disgusted by Humbert, but sufficiently fascinated to keep reading. The sex, then, like the narrative, is a kind of linguistic-philosophical game that ensnares us and implicates us in the crimes we would officially denounce. Nor is there that much sex in the novel. Only a small amount of pederasty is even remotely tolerable. Much of the novel's notoriety, actually, beyond the fact that it has any pederasty, lies in its triple-X imitators. The word "Lolita" almost immediately became a staple in titles of a certain kind of pornographic film: *Teenage Lolitas, Wanton Teenage Lolitas, Really Wanton Teenage Lolitas,* titles like that. Really original dirty-movie titles. There, presumably, the sex is strictly about sex.

What's that? You think it's just a guy thing?

Definitely not. Djuna Barnes, a contemporary of Lawrence and Joyce, investigates the world of sexual desire, fulfillment, and frustration in her dark classic, *Nightwood* (1937). The poet Mina Loy could have made T. S. Eliot faint. Modern women writers—as diverse as Anaïs Nin, Doris Lessing, Joyce Carol Oates, Iris Murdoch, and Edna O'Brien—ever since have investigated ways of writing about sex. I suspect

O'Brien holds the distinction of having more books banned in Ireland than any other Irish novelist. Sex in her books nearly always takes on a political cast as characters explore their sexuality while at the same time throwing off the restrictions of a conservative, repressed, religious society. O'Brien's writing about sex is really writing about liberation, or sometimes the failure of liberation; it's religious or political or artistic subversion.

The queen of sexual subversiveness, though, must be the late Angela Carter. Like O'Brien, Carter can write a very convincing sex scene. And also like her, she almost never lets it be only about sex. Carter nearly always intends to upset the patriarchal apple cart. To call her writing women's liberation is to largely miss her point; Carter attempts to discover paths by which women can attain the standing in the world that male-dominated society has largely denied them, and in so doing she would liberate all of us, men and women alike. In her world, sex can be wildly disruptive. In her last novel, *Wise Children,* when the main character and narrator, Dora Chance, engages in sex, the aim is usually self-expression or exertion of control over her life. As a woman and a minor entertainer, she has comparatively little control, and as an illegitimate orphan whose father refuses to recognize her and her twin,

Nora, she has even less. Taking some form of control once in a while therefore becomes all the more essential. She "borrows" Nora's boyfriend for her sexual initiation (he's none the wiser). Later she makes love to the boy of her dreams at a party during which her father's mansion burns to cinders. And finally, as a septuagenarian, she makes love to her hundred-year-old uncle, again while a very considerable shock is being delivered to her father, who is her uncle's twin. I'm not sure I can decode all the things that scene means, but I'm pretty sure it is not primarily about sex. Or aesthetics. If nothing else, it is a radical assertion of the life force. It can also be attacked from almost every angle on the psychological and sexual-political compasses. Also, right after their lovemaking, her uncle makes his twin nieces mothers for the first time, presenting them with orphaned twins, grand-nephew and -niece. In Carter's experience, human parthenogenesis remains somewhere in the future, so sex is still required to produce babies. Even symbolically.

Now here's the thing about that: you're going to figure it out. You don't need me to tell you that this scene involving sex among the very old means something. Moreover, your guess is as good as mine when it comes to what it means. Maybe better. The image of these two elderly people making violent (the downstairs chandelier sways alarmingly) love in the bed of their father/brother is so rich with possibilities that you almost can't go wrong, and perhaps no one can extract all its possibilities. So go for it.

That's generally true. You just *know* that these scenes mean something more than what's going on in them. It's true in life as well, where sex can be pleasure, sacrifice, submission, rebellion, resignation, supplication, domination, enlightenment, the whole works. Just the other day a student mentioned a sex scene in a novel. "What's up with that?" she asked. "It has to be about something else. It's just so weird and creepy that it has to be about something else. Does it mean . . ." And then she told us exactly what it meant. All I could add was that it's not only true of weird sex. Sometimes even good literary sex is about something else.

Oh, right. You can't really write about modern literary sex and skip over *it*, can you? Here's the thing. Lawrence didn't approve of strong language in private life and was almost prudish in some ways on the subject of promiscuity. Yet very near the end of his life, only in his early forties and dying of tuberculosis, he pens this outrageously frank, open novel, *Lady Chatterley's Lover*, about love and sex between members of two very different classes, between a peer's wife and her husband's gamekeeper, a man who uses all the Anglo-Saxon words for body parts and functions. Lawrence knows he won't write many more novels, he's coughing up his lungs, and he's pouring his life into this dirty story that's so far beyond anything he's already written—and had censored—that he knows, even if he pretends not to, that this thing will never have a wide readership in his lifetime. So now it's my turn.

What's up with that?

18

If She Comes Up, It's Baptism

Q uick question: I'm walking down the road and suddenly I fall into a pond. What happens?

You drown?

Thanks for the vote of confidence.

Or you don't?

That pretty much covers it. Now what does it mean?

Does it really mean anything either way? I mean, if you drown, you drown. If you get out, maybe all it means is you can swim.

Fair enough. For a character in a novel, though, the case is different. What does it mean if he drowns, or if he doesn't? Have you ever noticed how often literary characters get wet? Some drown, some merely get drenched, and some bob to the surface. What difference does it make?

First of all, let's take care of the obvious. You can fall into the water in an instant, from a bridge that gives way, for instance, or you can be pushed, pulled, dragged, tripped, or tipped over. All of which have their own meanings, of course, and can be taken quite literally. Beyond that, drowning or not has profound plot implications, as do the means by which a character does or doesn't drown.

Consider, just for a moment, that a disconcertingly large number of writers meet their ends in water. Virginia Woolf. Percy Bysshe Shelley. Ann Quin. Theodore Roethke. John Berryman. Hart Crane. Some walked in, some jumped, others swam out and didn't come back. Shelley's boat capsized and *Frankenstein*'s author became a very young widow. Iris Murdoch, who drowns enough characters that it seems like a hobby, herself nearly drowned in the sea fairly late in her career. Young Sam Clemens, years away from being Mark Twain, repeatedly had to be fetched out of the Mississippi. So maybe on some level tossing characters into the drink is (a) wish fulfillment, (b) exorcism of primal fear, (c) exploration of the possible, and not just (d) a handy solution to messy plot difficulties.

But back to our soggy character. Is he rescued? Does he swim out? Grab a piece of driftwood? Rise up and walk? Each of those would imply something different on the symbolic level. For instance, rescue might suggest passivity, good fortune, indebtedness. The piece of driftwood raises issues of luck and coincidence, serendipity rather than planning.

Remember the situation that begins Judith Guest's *Ordinary People* (1976)? Most likely. If you're over a certain age, you probably saw the film in a theater (almost everyone did, evidently), and if you're under a certain age you had it assigned, at least, in high school English.

So you know the deal. Two brothers go out sailing on Lake Michigan, a storm comes up, and one of them drowns. And one doesn't. Now the story works because it's the older, stronger son, the swimming star and apple of his mother's eye, the one who never dies except in family tragedies and war stories, who perishes. The younger one, Conrad, the one who would never survive, survives. And he's tortured by his success at living, to the point where he tries to kill himself. Why? He can't be alive. It's impossible. His brother was "stronger" and didn't make it, so weakling Conrad has to be dead, too. Except he's not. And what he has to learn, through his sessions with the psychiatrist, is that he was stronger; he may not have been the athlete his brother was, but in the moment of crisis he had the tenacity or luck to hang on to the boat and not be swept away, and now he'll just have to learn to live with it. This learning-to-live business turns out to be hard, since everyone, from the swimming coach to kids at school to his mother, seems to feel that he's the wrong one to still be here.

At this point you're probably saying, "Yeah, he's alive. So . . . ?"

Exactly. So he's not just alive. He's alive all over again. Not only should he have died out in that storm, we can say that in a sense he did die, that the Conrad we meet in the book is not the same Conrad we would have met before the storm. And I don't just mean in terms of Heraclitus, that you can't step into the same river twice, although that's part of it.

Heraclitus—who lived around 500 B.C.—composed a number of adages, what are called his "apothegms of change," all of which tell us that everything is changing at every moment, that the movement of time causes ceaseless change in the cosmos. The most famous of these sayings is that one cannot step into the same river twice. He uses a river to suggest the constantly shifting nature of time: all the little bits and pieces that were floating by a moment ago are somewhere else now and floating at different rates from each other. But that's not really what I have in mind here about Conrad. True, when he is rescued from the lake and steps back into the stream of his life, everything has shifted and changed, but there's a more violent change in the universe where he's concerned.

Which is what?

He's reborn.

See this in symbolic terms. A young man sails away from his known world, dies out of one existence, and comes back a new person, hence is reborn. Symbolically, that's the same pattern we see in baptism: death and rebirth through the medium of water. He's thrown into the water, where his old identity dies with his older brother. The self who bobs to the surface and clings to the sailboat is a new being. He goes out an insecure, awkward younger brother and comes back an only child, facing a world that knows him as that kid brother, as his old self. The swimming coach can't stop reminding him how much better his brother was. His mother can't relate to him without the filter of his brother. Only the shrink and his father can really deal with him as himself, the shrink because he never knew the brother and his father because he just can. Moreover, it's not just everyone else who has a problem; Conrad himself can't really understand his new position in the world, since he's lost some key elements to placing himself in it. And here's the thing he discovers: being born is painful. And that goes whether you're born or reborn.

Not every character gets to survive the water. Often they don't want to. Louise Erdrich's wonderful *Love Medicine* (1986) may just be the wettest book ever set on dry land. At the end of the novel Lipsha Morrissey, who's as close to a protagonist as the novel comes, observes that once all the northern prairie was an ocean, and we realize that we've been watching the drama play out over the remnants of that sea. His mother, June, walks across the snow of an Easter blizzard "like water" and dies. His uncle Nestor Kashpaw has repeated thoughts of swimming to the bottom of Lake Matchimanito and staying there—an image conflating death and escape. The scene I want to talk about, though, involves Henry Lamartine Jr. and the river. Henry Jr. is a Vietnam veteran suffering from post-traumatic stress disorder. He seems to come out of it a little when his brother Lyman damages their prized car, a red Chevrolet convertible, almost beyond repair. Repair it Henry does, though, and when he's all finished they go on a picnic by the flooded river. They seem to be having a great time, talking and laughing and drinking beer, when Henry Jr. suddenly runs out into the middle of the roiling, flooded stream. He says, rather simply, that his boots are filling with water, and then he's gone. When Lyman realizes he can't save his brother, he feels that in dying, Henry has purchased Lyman's share of the car, so he starts it and rolls it down into the stream to be with Henry. The scene is part personal tragedy, part Viking funeral, part Chippewa trip to the next world, all strange.

What does the scene mean? I've been insisting that in novels things are rarely as simple as they seem on the surface. Henry Jr. doesn't just drown. If that's what it were about, Erdrich would simply have him fall in and hit his head on a rock or something. He *elects* to go in, thereby choosing not only his relation to the world around him but his manner of leaving it. In a sense, Henry has been drowning in life since he came back from the war—he can't adjust, can't form relationships, can't leave his nightmares behind. In a manner of speaking, he's already lost, and the issue for the novelist is how to have him physically depart the scene. There are a lot of deaths in Erdrich's novels that are suicides or, at best, what a British coroner would call "death by misadventure." If we take a straight sociological (or daytime-talk-showological) view, we have to say, "It's terrible how hopeless and depressed their lives are." Which is true, of course. But I don't think that's the point. The characters' deaths are a form of choosing, of exerting control in a society that has taken control from them. Henry Jr. decides how he's going to leave this world, and in so doing offers a symbolic action—he's swept away in the flood.

So there are literary drownings like Henry Jr.'s, and near-drowning baptisms like Conrad's, but a character's baptism can also be less harrowing. In the wonderful *Song of Solomon*, Toni Morrison has Milkman Dead get wet three times. First he steps into a small stream while searching for gold in a cave, then he's given a bath by Sweet, the woman he meets on his trip into his familial past, and then he swims with Sweet in the river. So he gets wet three times. There's a religious or ritual association here—it resembles baptism in some sects, where the believer is immersed thrice, in the name of the Father, Son, and Holy Ghost. Of course, it is worth noting that Milkman is not inevitably more religious, or at least not in any conventional sense, but he's clearly changed. Nicer, more considerate, less of a sexist pig. More responsible. More grown up. High time, too, since he's thirty-two.

So what happens to make him a changed man?

Yes, he gets wet. Now, his getting wet is different from Hagar's disastrous trip in the rain, in that he enters bodies of water. Rain can be restorative and cleansing, so there's a certain overlap, but it generally lacks the specific baptismal associations of submersion. And Milkman does eventually go all the way in.

But if characters reformed every time they got wet, no book would ever have rain. The thing about baptism is, you have to be ready to receive it. And what preps Milkman for this change is a steady process of divestiture. Literally. He leaves parts of his outer shell as he goes on this quest: his Chevrolet breaks down, his shoes give out, his suit is ruined, and his watch is stolen. All the things that mark him as a fine city fellow and his father's son, gone. That's his problem, see? He's no one on his own when he starts out. He's Macon Dead III, son and heir of Macon Dead II and inheritor of all his worst tendencies. In order to become a new person, he has to lose all the outer remnants of his raiment, all the things he has acquired from being the son of his father. Then he's ready to become a new person, to undergo his baptismal immersion. The first time he goes into water, he steps into a little stream he's trying to cross, but since he's just starting out, the experience only begins to cleanse him. He's still after gold, and characters who seek gold aren't ready for change. Later, after much has happened to change him gradually, he is bathed by Sweet, in a cleansing that is both literal and ritual. Of equal importance, he returns the favor and bathes her. Their intent clearly is not religious; if it were, religion would be far more popular than it is. But what the characters intend as erotic ritual can have spiritual implications in the novel. When Milkman swims in the river for his third immersion, though, he knows it's significant *for him:* he whoops, he hollers, he laughs at danger, he's a brand-new person and he feels it. Which is what dying and rebirth is all about.

In her *Beloved,* Morrison makes even greater use of the symbolic implications of baptism and drowning. When Paul D. and the chain gang escape from the prison, they do so during a flood of biblical proportions by diving down under the mud below their cell doors and swimming, as one being, up through the muck and the mud, emerging into new lives. Later (chronologically, although it takes place previously in the narrative), when Beloved makes her appearance, she emerges from water. On this, more in a bit. When Sethe gives birth to Denver, she does so in a canoe, for heaven's sake, and on the Ohio River no less. Now that particular body of water is significant in the novel, separating as it does slaveholding Kentucky from abolitionist Ohio. Ohio may not be much more hospitable to black folks in other ways, but at least they aren't slaves there. So to enter the river on the south side and climb out on the north, or even to cross it, is to emerge from a kind of death into a new life.

So when writers baptize a character they mean death, rebirth, new identity?

Generally, yes. But we need to be a little careful here. Baptism can mean a host of things, of which rebirth is only one. Literal rebirth—surviving a deadly situation—is certainly a part of it, just as symbolic rebirth is the point of the sacrament of baptism, in which taking the new believer completely underwater causes him to die out of his old self and to be reborn in his identity as a follower of Christ. It has always seemed to me that the whole business probably ties in with some cultural memory of Noah's flood, of the whole world drowning and then this small remnant being set down on dry land to restore life to earth, cleansed of the sin and pollution that had marked human life right before the flood. Seen this way, baptism is a sort of reenactment on a very small scale of that drowning and restoration of life. Of course, I'm not a biblical scholar and may therefore be miles off base. Still, it's certainly true that baptism is itself a symbolic act and that there's nothing inherent in the act that makes a person more religious or causes God to take notice. It's not as if this is an activity universally practiced among the world's religions, or even among the big three Western religions.

So in a literary work, does submersion in water always signify baptism?

Well, it isn't *always* anything. "Always" and "never" aren't good words in literary studies. Take rebirth.

Does it represent baptism? If you mean, Is it spiritual, then we can say, sometimes. Sometimes, though, it may just signify birth, a new start, largely stripped of spiritual significance.

Let's take my old standby D. H. Lawrence. (In a passage of Joyce's *Ulysses*, Leopold Bloom thinks that Shakespeare has a quote for every day of the year. He could have added that Lawrence has a symbolic situation for all those days.) In "The Horse Dealer's Daughter" (1922), he has a young woman, Mabel, nearly drown herself, rescued at the last moment by the local doctor. Her family horse farm has been sold off after her father's death, and although she's been little more than a drudge in the family structure, she can't bear to leave and go to the only place, a manor house, that will take her in. So she cleans the gravestone of her long-dead mother (clearly indicating her intent to join Mom) and walks into the nearby pond. When young Dr. Fergusson sees her go under, he races in to save her, nearly dying in the process as she pulls both of them under. He manages with some difficulty to get her above water again, to carry her to safety and generally to care for her, which is clearly a first for both of them. Here's where things get messy, though. The *doctor* brings her forth from her watery bed. She is coated not with clean water but with *slimy, smelly, rather disgusting* fluid. When she awakens, she has been *cleaned up and wrapped in a blanket,* under which she's as *naked* as, well, the day she was born. In fact, it is the day she is born. Or reborn. And if you're going to be born, you may need a doctor in attendance (although he usually doesn't have to dive in with you, to the relief of mothers everywhere), and there's going to be all that amniotic fluid and afterbirth, and after that the cleansing and a receiving blanket and the whole bit.

So what does she do with this brand-new life of hers?

Tell young Fergusson "I love you," a thought which has never occurred to either of them until this moment. And his reborn self thinks it's a satisfactory idea, even though he's never found her attractive until this moment. But she's a brand-new person, and so is he, and these new selves find something in each other the old ones, limited by their associations with the rest of her family, couldn't possibly find. Is it spiritual? That probably depends on what you think about possessing a brand-new self. It's not overtly religious. On the other hand, almost nothing happens in Lawrence that doesn't seem to me to be deeply spiritual, even if it's in fairly mystifying ways.

So when a character drowns, what does that mean?

Oh, they die. Remember me mentioning Iris Murdoch earlier? Given half the chance, she'd drown the Seventh Fleet. If there's water in one of her novels, somebody's going to drown. In *The Unicorn* (1963), she has a character nearly drown in a bog, in order to have a cosmic vision, and then be saved only to have the vision fade before it can do him any good. Later, she has two characters drown in separate but related incidents, or at least one drown and the other fall over a cliff by the sea. And Flannery O'Connor, along the same lines only more peculiar, has a story called "The River" (1955) in which a little boy, having watched baptisms joining people to God on a Sunday, goes back to the river the next day to join God on his own. Yes, he does, sad to say. And Jane Hamilton, in *A Map of the World* (1994), has her main character allow a child to drown through negligence, then she has to deal with the consequences throughout the remainder of the novel. Not to mention John Updike's *Rabbit, Run* (1960), in which Rabbit Angstrom's wife, Janice, drunkenly drowns their child while trying to bathe it. Each of these instances is particular. It's a little like Tolstoy says at the beginning of *Anna Karenina* about families: All happy families are the same, but every unhappy one has its own story. The rebirths/baptisms have a lot of common threads, but every drowning is serving its own purpose: character revelation, thematic development of violence or failure or guilt, plot complication or denouement.

To return to Morrison's character Beloved rising from the water, back from the dead. On the personal level, the river may be the Styx, the river of the dead in the Greek underworld that the spirits crossed to enter Hades. And it certainly functions that way: she has returned from the dead, literally. But the river stands for something else as well. In its small way, it is the middle passage, that watery sojourn that, one way and another, took the lives of millions, as Morrison says in the novel's epigraph. Beloved has died when her mother kills her rather than allow her to be taken back across the river into slavery. The drowning imagery is not merely personal here but cultural and racial. Not every writer can pull that one off, but Morrison can.

Like baptism, drowning has plenty to tell us in a story. So when your character goes underwater, you have to hold your breath. Just, you know, till you see her come back up.

19

Geography Matters . . .

L et's go on vacation. You say okay and then ask your
first question, which is . . . Who's paying? Which
month? Can we get time off? No. None of those.

Where?

That's the one. Mountains or beaches, St. Paul or
St. Croix, canoeing or sailing, the Mall of America or
the National Mall. You know you have to ask because
otherwise I might take you to some little trout stream
twenty-seven miles from a dirt road when you really
want to watch the sun go down from a white sand
beach.

Writers have to ask that question, too, so we read-
ers should consider its implications. In a sense, every
story or poem is a vacation, and every writer has to
ask, every time, Where is this one taking place? For

some, it's not that tough. William Faulkner often said he set the majority of his work on his "little postage stamp of ground," his fictional Yoknapatawpha County, Mississippi. After a few novels, he knew that ground so intimately he didn't even have to think about it anymore. Thomas Hardy did the same thing with his mythic Wessex, the southwest corner of England—Devon and Dorset and Wiltshire. And we feel that those novels and stories couldn't be set anywhere but where they are, that those characters couldn't say the things they say if they were uprooted and planted in, say, Minnesota or Scotland. They'd say different things and perform different acts. Most writers, though, are less tied to one place than Faulkner or Hardy, so they have to give it some thought.

And we readers have to give their decisions some thought as well. What does it mean to the novel that its landscape is high or low, steep or shallow, flat or sunken? Why did this character die on a mountaintop, that one on the savanna? Why is this poem on the prairie? Why does Auden like limestone so much? What, in other words, does geography mean to a work of literature?

Would everything be too much?

Okay, not in every work, but frequently. In fact, more often than you think. Just think about the stories that really stay with you: where would they be without geography. *The Old Man and the Sea* can only take place in the Caribbean, of course, but more particularly in and around Cuba. The place brings with it history, interaction between American and Cuban culture, corruption, poverty, fishing, and of course baseball. Any boy and any older man might, I guess, take a raft trip down a river. It could happen. But a boy, Huck Finn, and an older man, the escaped slave Jim, and their raft could only make the story we know as *The Adventures of Huckleberry Finn* by being on that particular river, the Mississippi, traveling through that particular landscape and those particular communities, at a given moment in history. It matters when they reach Cairo and the Ohio empties into the big river; it matters when they reach the Deep South, because Jim is running away in the worst possible direction. The great threat to a slave was that he might be sold *down* the river, where things got progressively worse the farther south you went, and he's floating straight into the teeth of the monster.

And that's geography?

Sure, what else?

I don't know. Economics? Politics? History?

So what's geography, then?

I usually think of hills, creeks, deserts, beaches, degrees latitude. Stuff like that.

Precisely. Geography: hills, etc. Stuff: economics, politics, history. Why didn't Napoleon conquer Russia? Geography. He ran into two forces he couldn't overcome: a ferocious Russian winter and a people whose toughness and tenacity in defending their homeland matched the merciless elements. And that savagery, like the weather, is a product of the place they come from. It takes a really tough people to overcome not merely one Russian winter but hundreds of them. Anthony Burgess has a novel about the Russian winter defeating the French emperor, *Napoleon Symphony* (1974), in which he brings to life, better than anyone who isn't Tolstoy, that geography and that weather: the vastness of it, the emptiness, the hostility to the invading (and then, retreating) troops, the total absence of any possibility of comfort or safety or solace.

So what's geography? Rivers, hills, valleys, buttes, steppes, glaciers, swamps, mountains, prairies, chasms, seas, islands, people. In poetry and fiction, it may be mostly people. Robert Frost routinely objected to being called a nature poet, since by his count he only had three or four poems without a person in them. Literary geography is typically about humans inhabiting spaces, and at the same time the spaces inhabiting humans. Who can say how much of us comes from our physical surroundings? Writers can, at least in their own works, for their own purposes. When Huck meets the Shepherdsons and the Grangerfords or sees the duke and the dauphin tarred and feathered by the townspeople, he sees geography in action. Geography is setting, but it's also (or can be) psychology, attitude, finance, industry—anything that place can forge in the people who live there.

Geography in literature can also be more. It can be revelatory of virtually any element in the work. Theme? Sure. Symbol? No problem. Plot? Without a doubt.

In Edgar Allan Poe's "The Fall of the House of Usher," the narrator spends the opening pages describing a landscape and a day as bleak as any in literature. We want to get to the titular house, of course, to meet the last, appalling members of the Usher clan, but Poe doesn't want us there before he's prepared us. He treats us to "a singularly dreary tract of country," to "a few rank sedges" and "white trunks of decayed trees," to "the precipitous brink of a black and lurid tarn," so that we're ready for the "bleak walls" of the house with its "vacant eye-like windows" and its "barely perceptible fissure" zigzagging its way down the wall right down to "the sullen waters of the tarn." Never perhaps have landscape and architecture and weather (it's a particularly dingy afternoon) merged as neatly with mood and tone to set a story in motion. We are nervous and dismayed by this description even before anything has happened, so of course when things do begin happening, when we meet Roderick Usher, one of the creepiest characters to ever grace the pages of a story, he can't give us the creeps because we already have them. But he sure can make them worse, and he does. Actually, the scariest thing Poe could do to us is to put a perfectly normal human specimen in that setting, where no one could remain safe. And that's one thing landscape and place—geography—can do for a story.

Geography can also define or even develop character. Take the case of two contemporary novels. In Barbara Kingsolver's *Bean Trees* (1988), the main character and narrator reaches late adolescence in rural Kentucky and realizes she has no options in that world. That condition is more than social; it grows out of the land. Living is hard in tobacco country, where the soil yields poor crops and hardly anyone makes much of a go of things, where the horizon is always short, blocked by mountains. The narrator feels her figurative horizons are also circumscribed by what seem like local certainties: early pregnancy and an unsatisfactory marriage to a man who will probably die young. She decides to get away, driving a 1955 Volkswagen to Tucson. On her way she changes her name from Marietta (or Missy) to Taylor Greer. As you know by now, there's rebirth when there's a renaming, right? Out west she meets new people, encounters a completely alien but inviting landscape, becomes the de facto mother of a three-year-old Native American girl she calls Turtle, and finds herself involved in the shelter movement for Central American refugees. She wouldn't have done any of these things in claustrophobic old Pittman, Kentucky. What she discovers in the West are big horizons, clear air, brilliant sunshine, and open possibilities. She goes, in other words, from a closed to an open environment, and she seizes the opportunities for growth and development. Another character in another novel might find the heat oppressive, the sun destructive, and space vacant, but she wouldn't be Taylor Greer. In Toni Morrison's *Song of Solomon*, Milkman Dead grows up without ever learning who he really is until he leaves his Michigan home and travels back to the family home country in eastern Pennsylvania and Virginia. In the hills and hollows (not unlike the ones Taylor Greer must flee to breathe) he finds a sense of roots, a sense of responsibility and justice, a capacity for atonement, and a generosity of spirit he never knew before. He loses nearly everything of his associated with the modern world in the process—Chevrolet, fine clothes, watch, shoes—but they prove to be the currency with which he buys his real worth. At one point direct contact with the earth (he's sitting on the ground and leaning back against a tree) provides him with an intuition that saves his life. He responds just in time to ward off a murderous attack. He could have done none of those things had he stayed in his familiar geography; only by leaving "home" and traveling to his real home can he find his real self.

It's not too much to say, I think, that geography can be character. Take Tim O'Brien's Vietnam masterpiece, *Going After Cacciato*. The main character, Paul Berlin, admits that the American soldiers don't really know the land, don't understand what they're up against. And it's a forbidding place: dry or wet, but always hot, full of microbe-filled water and leeches the size of snakes, rice paddies and mountains and shell craters. And tunnels. The tunnels turn the land itself into the enemy, since the land hides the Vietcong fighters only to deliver them virtually anywhere, producing surprise attacks and sudden death. The resulting terror gives the land a face of menace in the minds of the young Americans. When one of their number is killed by a sniper, they order the destruction of the nearby village, then sit on a hill and watch as shell after shell, alternating high explosives and incendiary white phosphorus, pulverize the village. A cockroach couldn't survive. Why do they do it? It isn't a military target, only a village. Did the bullet come from the village? Not exactly, although the shooter was either a VC villager or a soldier sheltered by the village. Is he still there? No, the place is deserted when they look for revenge. You could make the claim that they go after the community of people who housed the enemy, and certainly there's an element of that. But the real target is the physical village—as place, as center of mystery and threat, as alien environment, as generic home of potential enemies and uncertain friends. The squad pours its fear and anger at the land into this one small, representative piece of it: if they can't overcome the larger geography, they can at least express their rage against the smaller.

Geography can also, and frequently does, play quite a specific plot role in a literary work. In E. M. Forster's early novels, English tourists find ways of making mischief, usually unwittingly and not always comically, when they travel to the Mediterranean. In *A Room with a View* (1908), for instance, Lucy Honeychurch travels to Florence, where she sheds much of her racially inherited stiffness while losing her heart to George Emerson, the freethinking son of an elderly radical. She finds what looks like scandal only to ultimately discover freedom, and a big part of that freedom stems from the passionate, fiery nature of the Italian city. Much of the comedy in the novel grows out of Lucy's battle to reconcile what she "knows" is right with what she feels to be right for her. Nor is she alone in her struggles: most of the other characters stumble into awkwardness of one sort or another. Forster's later masterpiece, *A Passage to India,* focuses on other types of mayhem growing from English misbehavior as the rulers of India and from very confused feelings that beset recent arrivals on the subcontinent. Even our best intentions, he seems to suggest, can have disastrous consequences in an alien environment. Half a century after Forster's lightweight comedies of folly in Italy, Lawrence Durrell reveals an entire culture of libertines and spies in his beautiful tetralogy, *The Alexandria Quartet.* His northern European characters displaced to Egypt exhibit every sort of kink, sexual and otherwise, from the old sailor with a glass eye and a predilection for young boys to the incestuous Ludwig and Liza Pursewarden to nearly everyone's inability to be faithful to spouse or lover. Darley, the narrator of the first and fourth volumes, tells us that there are at least five genders (although he leaves specifying them to our imaginations) in Alexandria, then shows them to us at full throttle. One might suppose that the heat of an Egyptian summer would induce some lassitude in these already overheated northerners, but there's little evidence of that. Evidently an

Englishman released from perpetual rain and fog is nearly unstoppable.

What separates the sexual behavior of Forster's characters from that of Durrell's, aside from time, is D. H. Lawrence. His works, culminating in the over-wrought and infamous, if not always successful, *Lady Chatterley's Lover*, opened the way for more sexual directness. Like many modern writers, he sent his characters south in search of trouble, but curiously, that trouble was not typically sexual, since he, being quite advanced, could get his people in sexual trouble right in the midst of inhibited Britain. Instead, when his travelers find sunshine in the south, they also encounter curious and sometimes dangerous political and philosophical ideas. Crypto-fascism in Australia in *Kangaroo* (1923). Psychosexual male bonding in *Aaron's Rod* (1922). The return of the old Mexican blood religion in *The Plumed Serpent* (1926). Desire and power in his little novella *The Woman Who Rode Away* (1928). What Lawrence does, really, is employ geography as a metaphor for the psyche—when his characters go south, they are really digging deep into their subconscious, delving into that region of darkest fears and desires. Maybe it takes a kid from a mining town in Nottinghamshire, which Lawrence was, to recognize the allure and peril of the sunny south.

Of course, this is not exclusive to Lawrence. Thomas Mann, a German, sends his elderly writer to Venice to die (in *Death in Venice*, 1912), but not before discovering a nasty streak of pedophilia and narcissism in himself. Joseph Conrad, England's greatest Polish writer, sends his characters into hearts of darkness (as he calls one tale of a trip into Africa) to discover the darkness in their own hearts. In *Lord Jim* (1900), the main character has his romantic dreams shattered during his first experience in the Indian Ocean, and is symbolically buried in Southeast Asia until he rises, redeemed through love and belief in himself, only to be killed. In *Heart of Darkness* (1899), the narrator, Marlow, travels up the Congo River and observes the near-total disintegration of the European psyche in Kurtz, who has been in-country so long that he has become unrecognizable.

Okay, so here's the general rule: whether it's Italy or Greece or Africa or Malaysia or Vietnam, **when writers send characters south, it's so they can run amok.** The effects can be tragic or comic, but they generally follow the same pattern. We might add, if we're being generous, that they run amok *because they are having direct, raw encounters with the subconscious.* Conrad's visionaries, Lawrence's searchers, Hemingway's hunters, Kerouac's hipsters, Paul Bowles's down-and-outers and seekers, Forster's tourists, Durrell's libertines—all head south, in more senses than one. But do they fall under the influence of warmer climes, or do those welcoming latitudes express something that's already been trying to make its way out? The answer to that question is as variable as the writer—and the reader.

Now most of this has had to do with fairly specific places, but types of places also come into play. Theodore Roethke has a wonderful poem, "In Praise of Prairie" (1941), about, well, prairies. Do you know how few poems there are of any quality about prairies? No, his isn't quite the only one. It's not a landscape that's inevitably viewed as "poetic." Yet somehow Roethke, the greatest poet ever to come from Saginaw, Michigan, finds beauty in that perfectly horizontal surface, where horizons run away from the eye and a drainage ditch is a chasm. Beyond this one poem, though, the *experience* of being a flatlander informs his work in obvious ways, as in his poems about this uniquely American/ Canadian open, flat agricultural space, in the sequence *The Far Field* (1964), for instance, but in less subtle ways as well. His voice has a naive sincerity in it, a quiet, even tone, and his vision is of a vast nature. Flat ground is as important to Roethke's psyche, and therefore to his poetry, as the steep terrain of the English Lake District famously was to William Wordsworth.

As readers, we need to consider Roethke's midwestern-ness as a major element in the making and shaping of his poems..

Seamus Heaney, who in "Bogland" (1969) actually offers a rejoinder to Roethke in which he acknowledges that Northern Ireland has to get by without prairies, probably couldn't be a poet at all without a landscape filled with bogs and turf. His imagination runs through history, digging its way down into the past to unlock clues to political and historical difficulties, in much the same way the turf-cutters carve their way down-ward through progressively older layers of peat, where they sometimes come upon messages from the past—skeletons of the extinct giant Irish elk, rounds of cheese or butter, Neolithic quern stones, two-thousand-year-old bodies. He makes use of these finds, of course, but he also finds his own truths by digging through the past. If we read Heaney's poetry without understand-ing the geography of his imagination, we risk misun-derstanding what he's all about.

For the last couple of centuries, since Wordsworth and the Romantic poets, the sublime landscape—the dramatic and breathtaking vista—has been idealized, sometimes to the point of cliché. Needless to say, vast and sudden mountains—the geographic features we find most spectacular and dramatic—figure prominently in such views. When, in the middle of the twentieth century, W H. Auden writes "In Praise of Limestone" (1951), he is directly attacking poetic assumptions of the sublime. But he's also writing about places we can call home: the flat or gently rolling ground of limestone country, with its fertile fields and abundant groundwater, with its occasional subterranean caves, and most important with its nonsublime but also nonthreatening vistas. We can live there, he says. The Matterhorn and Mont Blanc, those emblems of the Romantic sublime, may not be for human habitation, but limestone country is. In this case, geography becomes not only a way by which the poet expresses his psyche but also a conveyor of theme. Auden argues for a humanity-friendly poetry, challenging certain inhuman ideas that have dominated poetic thinking for a goodly period before he came along.

It doesn't matter which prairie, which bog, which mountain range, which chalk down or limestone field we envision. The poets are being fairly generic in these instances.

Hills and valleys have a logic of their own. Why did Jack and Jill go up the hill? Sure, sure, a pail of water, probably orders from a parent. But wasn't the real reason so Jack could break his crown and Jill come tumbling after? That's what it usually is in literature. Who's up and who's down? Just what do up and down mean?

First, think about what there is down low or up high. Low: swamps, crowds, fog, darkness, fields, heat, unpleasantness, people, life, death. High: snow, ice, purity, thin air, clear views, isolation, life, death. Some of these, you will notice, appear on both lists, and you can make either environment work for you if you're a real writer. Like Hemingway. In "The Snows of Kilimanjaro" (1936), he contrasts the leopard, dead and preserved in the snow on the peak, with the writer dying of gangrene down on the plain. The leopard's death is clean, cold, pure, while the writer's death is ugly, unpleasant, horrible. The final result may be the same, but one is so much less wholesome than the other.

D. H. Lawrence offers the contrasting view in *Women in Love*. The four main characters, tired of the muck and confusion of life in near-sea-level England, opt for a holiday in the Tyrol. At first the alpine environment seems clean and uncluttered, but as time goes on they—and we—begin to realize that it's also inhuman. The two with the most humanity, Birkin and Ursula, decide to head back downhill to more hospitable climes, while Gerald and Gudrun stay. Their mutual hostility grows to the point where Gerald attempts to murder Gudrun and, deciding the act isn't worth the effort, skis off higher and higher until, only yards from the very top of the mountains, he collapses and dies of, for want of a better term, a broken soul.

So, high or low, near or far, north or south, east or west, the places of poems and fiction really matter. It isn't just setting, that hoary old English class topic. It's place and space and shape that bring us to ideas and psychology and history and dynamism. It's enough to make you read a map.

20

. . . So Does Season

Here's my favorite snippet of poetry:

> That time of year thou mayst in me behold
> When yellow leaves, or none, or few, do hang
> Upon those boughs which shake against the cold:
> Bare, ruined choirs, where late the sweet birds sang.

As you know, that's Shakespeare's sonnet 73, your constant bedside reading. I like it for a lot of reasons. First, it just sounds wonderful—say it out loud a couple of times and you'll start to hear how the words play off each other. Then there's the rhythm. I often recite it in class when I'm explaining meter and scansion—how the stressed and unstressed syllables function in lines of poetry. But the thing that really works here, and in the next ten lines, is the meaning: the speaker is seriously feeling his age here and making us feel it, too, with those boughs shaking in the cold winds, those last faded leaves still hanging, if barely, in the canopy, those empty limbs that formerly were so full of life and song. His leaves, his hair, have mostly departed, we can surmise, and his appendages are less resolute than formerly, and of course, he's entered a quieter period than his youth had been. November in the bones; it makes my joints ache just to think about it.

Now to the nuts and bolts: Shakespeare didn't invent this metaphor. This fall/middle-age cliché was pretty creaky in the knees long before he got hold of it. What he does, brilliantly, is to invest it with a specificity and a continuity that force us to really *see* not only the thing he describes—the end of autumn and the coming of winter—but the thing he's really talking about, namely the speaker's standing on the edge of old age. And of course he, being himself, pulls this off time and again in his poems and plays. "Shall I compare thee to a summer's day?" he asks. "Thou art more lovely and more temperate." What beloved could turn her back on that one? When King Lear is raging in his old man's madness, he's doing it in a winter storm. When the young lovers escape to the enchanted woods to sort out their romantic difficulties and thereby take their proper places in the adult world, it is a midsummer night.

Nor is the issue always age. Happiness and dissatisfaction have their seasons. A thoroughly unpleasant king, Richard III, rails against his situation by saying, his voice dripping with sarcasm, "Now is the winter of our discontent, / Made glorious summer by this son of York." Even if we don't know what he means by that, we know from his tone what he feels and we're pretty sure it doesn't say anything good about this son (with its play on "sun") of York's future. Elsewhere he speaks of seasons as having each their appropriate emotions, as in the song from *Cymbeline,* with its "Fear no more the heat o' th' sun, / Nor the furious winter's rages." Summer is passion and love; winter, anger and hatred. The Book of Ecclesiastes tells us that to everything there is a season. *Henry VI, Part II* gives us the Shakespearean formula for the same thing, although a bit more mixed, "Sometimes hath the brightest day a cloud, / And after summer evermore succeeds / Barren winter, with his wrathful nipping cold; / So cares and joys abound, as seasons fleet." Even his titles tell us seasons matter with him: *A Winter's Tale, Twelfth Night* (that is, the last of the twelve days of Christmas), *A Midsummer Night's Dream.*

Of course, seasons aren't the private playground of our greatest writer. We sometimes treat old Will as if he's the beginning, middle, and end of literature, but he's not. He began some things, continued others, and ended a few, but that's not the same at all. A few other writers have also had something to say about the seasons in connection with the human experience.

Take Henry James, for instance. He wants to write a story in which the youth, enthusiasm, and lack of decorum that mark the still comparatively new American republic come into contact with the stuffy and emotionless and rule-bound world that is Europe. He must overcome an initial problem: nobody wants to read about geopolitical entities in conflict. So he needs people, and he comes up with a pair of real beauties. One is a girl, American, young, fresh, direct, open, naive, flirtatious, maybe a little too much of each; the other is a man, also American but long resident in Europe, slightly older, jaded, worldly, emotionally closed, indirect, even surreptitious, totally dependent on the good opinion of others. She's all spring and sunshine; he's all frosty stiffness. Names, you ask? *Daisy* Miller and Frederic *Winter*bourne. Really, it's just too perfect. And obvious. You wonder why we don't feel our intelligence has been insulted. Well, for one thing, he sort of slips the names in, and then the emphasis is really on her surname, which is beyond ordinary, and her hometown, which is Schenectady, for crying out loud. We get so involved with those aspects that the first name seems to us merely a quaint holdover from the old days, which weren't old to James. In any case, once you pay attention to the name game, you pretty much know things will end badly, since daisies can't flourish in winter, and things do. On one level, everything we need to know is there in those two names, and the rest of the novella pretty much acts as a gloss on these two telling names.

Nor are the seasons the exclusive property of high culture. The Mamas & the Papas, expressing dissatisfaction with winter, gray skies, and brown leaves, do some "California dreamin' " as they wish their way back to the land of perpetual summer. Simon & Garfunkel cover much the same unhappy ground in "A Hazy Shade of Winter." The Beach Boys made a very lucrative career out of happy-summer-land with all those surfing and cruising songs. Head for the beach with your surfboard and your Chevy convertible in a Michigan January and see what that gets you. Bob Seger, who is from Michigan, goes nostalgic for that first summer of freedom and sexual initiation in "Night Moves." All the great poets know how to use the seasons.

For about as long as anyone's been writing anything, the seasons have stood for the same set of meanings. Maybe it's hard-wired into us that spring has to do with childhood and youth, summer with adulthood and romance and fulfillment and passion, autumn with decline and middle age and tiredness but also harvest, winter with old age and resentment and death. This pattern is so deeply ingrained in our cultural experience that we don't even have to stop and think about it. Think about it we should, though, since once we know the pattern is in play, we can start looking at variation and nuance.

W. H. Auden, in his great elegy "In Memory of W. B. Yeats" (1940), emphasizes the coldness of the day Yeats died. Auden had the great good fortune that it happened to be true; Yeats died on January 28, 1939. In the poem rivers are frozen, snow falls, the mercury settles to the bottom of thermometers and won't budge—everything unpleasant winter has to offer, Auden finds it for his poem. Now, the traditional elegy, the *pastoral* elegy, has historically been written for a young man, a friend of the poet, often a poet himself, who died much too young. Typically the elegy turns him into a shepherd taken from his pasture (hence the pastoral part) at the height of spring or summer, and all nature, which should be rejoicing in its fullness, instead is sent into mourning for this beloved youth. Auden, an accomplished ironist and realist, turns this pattern around in memorializing not a youngster but a man, born at the end of the American Civil War and dead on the eve of World War II, whose life and career were very long, who had made it to his own winter and who died in the heart of meteorological winter. That mood in the poem is made colder and more desolate by Yeats's death, but also by our expectations of what we might call "the season of the elegy." Such a tactic requires a very great, very skilled poet; fortunately, Auden was one.

Sometimes the season isn't mentioned specifically or immediately, and this can make the matter a bit trickier. Robert Frost doesn't come right out and say, in "After Apple Picking," that it's now October twenty-ninth or November umpteenth, but the fact that he's finished his apple picking informs us we're in autumn. After all, winesaps and pippins don't ripen in March. Our first response may not be, "Oh, here's another poem about fall," although, in fact, this may be the most autumnal poem in the world. Frost expands on the seasonal implications with time of day (late evening), mood (very tired), tone (almost elegiac), and point of view (backward-looking). He speaks of the overwhelming sense of both tiredness and completion, of bringing in a huge harvest that surpassed even his hopes, of being on a ladder so long that the sense of its swaying will stay with him even after he falls into bed the way a fishing bobber, watched all day, will imprint itself on the visual sense of eyes closed for sleep.

So harvest, and not only of apples, is one element of autumn. When our writers speak of harvests, we know it can refer not only to agricultural but also to personal harvests, the results of our endeavors, whether over the course of a growing season or a life. St. Paul tells us that we will reap whatever it is that we sow. The notion is so logical, and has been with us so long, that it has become a largely unstated assumption: we reap the rewards and punishments of our conduct. Frost's crop is abundant, suggesting he has done something right, but the effort has worn him out. This, too, is part of autumn. As we gather in our harvest, we find we have used up a certain measure of our energies, that in truth we're not as young as we used to be.

Not only has something come before, in other words, but something else is coming. Frost speaks in the poem not only of the coming night and his well-earned sleep but of the longer night that is winter and the longer sleep of the woodchuck. Now this reference to hibernation certainly fits with the seasonal nature of the discussion, but that longer sleep also suggests a longer sleep, the *big sleep*, as Raymond Chandler called it. The ancient Romans named the first month of our calendar after Janus, the god of two faces, the month of January looking back into the year gone by and forward into the one to come. For Frost, though, such a dual gaze applies equally well to the autumn and the harvest season.

Every writer can make these modifications in his or her use of the seasons, and the variation produced keeps seasonal symbolism fresh and interesting. Will she play it straight or use spring ironically? Will summer be warm and rich and liberating or hot and dusty and stifling? Will autumn find us toting up our accomplishments or winding down, arriving at wisdom and peace or being shaken by those November winds? The seasons are always the same in literature and yet always different. What we learn, finally, as readers is that we don't look for a shorthand in seasonal use— summer means *x*, winter *y minus x*—but a set of patterns that can be employed in a host of ways, some of them straightforward, others ironic or subversive. We know those patterns because they have been with us for so long.

How long?

Very long. I mentioned before that Shakespeare didn't invent this fall/middle age connection. It predates him by a bit. Say, a few thousand years. Nearly every early mythology, at least those originating in temperate zones where seasons change, had a story to explain that seasonal change. My guess is that the first thing they had to account for was the fact that when the sun disappeared over the hill or into the sea at night, the disappearance was only temporary; Apollo would drive his sun chariot across the sky again the next morning. About the time the community had a handle on this cosmic mystery, though, the next item on the agenda, or next but one, was probably the matter of spring following winter, the days growing shorter but then growing longer again. This, too, required explanation, and pretty soon the story had priests to carry it on. If they were Greek, they would come up with something like this:

Once upon, etc., there's a beautiful young girl, so stunningly attractive that her beauty is a byword not only on earth but in the land of the dead, where the ruler, Hades, learns of her. And Hades decides he has to have this young beauty, whose name is Persephone, so he comes up to earth just long enough to kidnap her and spirit her away to the underworld, which confusingly enough is also called Hades.

Ordinarily the theft of even a beautiful young girl by a god would go unchecked, but this particular girl is the daughter of Demeter, the goddess of agriculture and fertility (a happy combination), who goes instantly and permanently into mourning, leaving the earth in perpetual winter. Hades doesn't care, because like most gods he's very selfish, and he has what he wants. And Demeter doesn't care, because in her selfishness she can't see beyond her own grief. Fortunately, the other gods do notice that animals and people are dying for lack of food, so they ask Demeter for help. She travels down to Hades (the place) and deals with Hades (the god), and there's a mysterious transaction involving a pomegranate and twelve seeds, of which only six get eaten, in most versions by Persephone although sometimes by Hades, who then discovers he's been tricked. Those six uneaten seeds mean she gets to return to earth for six months of every year, during which time her mother, Demeter, is so happy that she lets the world grow and be fertile, only plunging it back into winter when her daughter has to return to the underworld. Hades, of course, spends six months of every twelve sulking, but he realizes that even a god can't beat pomegranate seeds, so he goes along with the plan. Thus spring always *follows winter, and we humans aren't buried in perpetual winter (no, not even in Duluth), and the olives ripen every year.*

Now, if the tellers of the tale were Celts or Picts or Mongols or Cheyenne, they'd be telling a different version, but the basic impulse—we need a story to explain this phenomenon to ourselves—would remain constant.

Death and rebirth, growth and harvest and death, year after year. The Greeks held their dramatic festivals, which featured almost entirely tragedy, at the beginning of spring. The idea was to purge all the built-up bad feeling of winter from the populace (and to instruct it in right conduct toward the gods) so that no negativity would attach to the growing season and thereby endanger the harvest. Comedy was the genre of fall, once the harvest was in and celebrations and laughter were appropriate. Something of the same phenomenon shows itself in more modern religious practice. Part of the immense satisfaction of the Christian story is that the two great celebrations, Christmas and Easter, coincide with dates of great seasonal anxiety. The story of the birth of Jesus, and of hope, is placed almost on the shortest, and therefore most dismal (pre-electric) day of the year. All saturnalia celebrate the same thing: well, at least this is as far as the sun will run away from us, and now the days will start getting longer and, eventually, warmer. The Crucifixion and Resurrection come very near the spring equinox, the death of winter and beginning of renewed life. There is evidence in the Bible that the Crucifixion did in fact take place at that point in the calendar, although not that the birth took place anywhere near December 25. But that may be beside the point, because from an emotional standpoint, and quite apart from the religious significance of the events for Christians, both holidays derive much of their power from their proximity in the calendar year to moments on which we humans place great emphasis.

So it is with books and poems. We read the seasons in them almost without being conscious of the many associations we bring to that reading. When Shakespeare compares his beloved to a summer's day, we know instinctively, even before he catalogs her advantages, that this is way more flattering than being compared to, say, January eleventh. When Dylan Thomas recalls his enchanted childhood summers in "Fern Hill" (1946), we know something more is afoot than simply school being out. In fact, our responses are so deeply ingrained that seasonal associations are among the easiest for the writer to upend and use ironically. T. S. Eliot knows what we generally think of spring, so when he makes April "the cruellest month" and says we were happier buried under winter snows than we are having the earth warm up and start nature's (and our) juices flowing again, he knows that line of thought will bring us up short. And he's right.

Seasons can work magic on us, and writers can work magic with seasons. When Rod Stewart wants to say, in "Maggie May," that he's hanging around too long and wasting his youth on this older woman, he makes it late September. When Anita Brookner, in her finest novel, *Hotel du Lac* (1984), sends her heroine off to a resort to recover from a romantic indiscretion and to meditate on the way youth and life have passed her by, what point in the calendar does she choose?

Late September?

Excellent. So Shakespeare and Ecclesiastes and Rod Stewart and Anita Brookner. You know, I think we might be onto something here.

Interlude
One Story

We've spent quite a while thinking about specific tasks involved in the activity of reading, such as considering how this means x, that signifies y, and so on. Now of course I believe "this" and "that" and x and y matter, and on some level so do you, else we would not be at this point in our discussion. But there's a greater truth, at least as I see it, behind all these specific interpretive activities, a truth that informs and drives the creation of novels and plays and stories and poems and essays and memoirs even when (as is usually the case) writers aren't aware of it. I've mentioned it before and have employed it throughout, so it's no very great secret. Moreover, it's not my personal invention or discovery, so I'm not looking for credit here, but it needs saying again, so here it is: **there's only one story.**

One story. Everywhere. Always. Wherever anyone puts pen to paper or hands to keyboard or fingers to lute string or quill to papyrus. They all take from and in return give to the same story, ever since Snorgg got back to the cave and told Ongk about the mastodon that got away. Norse sagas, Samoan creation stories, *Gravity's Rainbow*, *The Tale of Genji*, *Hamlet*, last year's graduation speech, last week's Dave Barry column, *On the Road* and *The Road to Rio* and "The Road Not Taken." One story.

What's it about?

That's probably the best question you'll ever ask, and I apologize for responding with a really lame answer: I don't know. It's not about anything. It's about everything. It's not about something the way an elegy is *about* the death of a young friend, for instance, or the way *The Maltese Falcon* is about solving the mystery of the fat man and the black bird. It's about everything that anyone wants to write about. I suppose what the one story, the ur-story, is about is ourselves, about what it means to be human. I mean, what else is there? When Stephen Hawking writes *A Brief History of Time*, what is he doing except telling us what home is like, describing the place where we live? You see, being human takes in just about everything, since we want to know about space and time and this world and the

next, questions I'm pretty sure none of my English set-
ters have ever really pondered. Mostly, though, we're
interested in ourselves in space or time, in the world.
So what our poets and storytellers do for us—drag a
rock up to the fire, have a seat, listen to this one—is
explain us-and-the-world, or us-in-the-world.

Do writers know this? Do they think about it?

a. *Good heavens, no.*

b. *Absolutely, yes.*

c. *Let me try again.*

On one level, everyone who writes anything knows
that pure originality is impossible. Everywhere you
look, the ground is already camped on. So you sigh and
pitch your tent where you can, knowing someone else
has been there before. Think of it this way: can you
use a word no one else has ever used? Only if you're
Shakespeare or Joyce and coin words, but even they
mostly use the same ones as the rest of us. Can you
put together a combination of words that is absolutely
unique? Maybe, occasionally, but you can't be sure.
So too with stories. John Barth discusses an Egyptian
papyrus complaining that all the stories have been told
and that therefore nothing remains for the contempo-
rary writer but to retell them. That papyrus describing

the postmodern condition is forty-five hundred years old. This is not a terrible thing, though. Writers notice all the time that their characters resemble somebody— Persephone, Pip, Long John Silver, La Belle Dame sans Merci—and they go with it. What happens, if the writer is good, is usually not that the work seems derivative or trivial but just the opposite: the work actually acquires depth and resonance from the echoes and chimes it sets up with prior texts, weight from the accumulated use of certain basic patterns and tendencies. Moreover, works are actually more comforting because we recognize elements in them from our prior reading. I suspect that a wholly original work, one that owed nothing to previous writing, would so lack familiarity as to be quite unnerving to readers. So that's one answer.

But here's another. Writers also have to practice a kind of amnesia when they sit down or (like Thomas Wolfe, who was very tall and wrote on top of the refrigerator—really) stand up to write. The downside of the weight of millennia of accumulated practice of any activity is that it's very . . . heavy. I once psyched out a teammate in an over-thirty men's basketball league quite by accident. We were practicing free throws before a game when something occurred to me, and like an idiot I couldn't keep it to myself. "Lee, have you ever considered," I asked, "how many things can go wrong when you shoot a free throw?" He literally stopped in mid-shot to offer his view. "Damn you," he said. "Now I won't make one all night." He was right. Had I known I could have that kind of effect, I'd have warmed up with the other team. Now consider Lee's problem if he had to consider not merely all the biomechanics of shooting a basketball but the whole history of free-throw shooting. You know, not too much like Lenny Wilkins, a bit of Dave Bing, some of Rick Barry before he switched to the two-handed underhand shot, plenty of Larry Bird (but don't plagiarize him outright), none at all of Wilt Chamberlain. What are the chances any of us would ever make a free throw? And basketball only dates back about one century. Now consider trying to write a lyric poem, with everyone from Sappho to Tennyson to Frost to Plath to Verlaine to Li Po looking over your shoulder. That's a lot of hot breath on the back of your neck. So, amnesia. When the writer gets to work, she has to shut out the voices and write what she writes, say what she has to say. What the unremembering trick does is clear out this history from the front of her mind so her own poem can come in. While she may never, or very rarely, think at all about these matters consciously, she's been reading poetry since she was six, when Aunt Tillie gave her Robert Louis Stevenson's *A Child's Garden of Verses,* burns through a couple of volumes of poetry a week, has read most of Wallace Stevens six or seven times. In other words, the history of poetry never leaves her. It's always present, a gigantic subconscious database of poetry (and fiction, since she's read that, too).

You know by now I like to keep things fairly simple. I'm no fan of the latest French theory or of jargon of any stripe, but sometimes we really can't do without it. What I'm talking about here involves a couple of concepts we need to consider. The first, as I mentioned a few chapters back, is *intertextuality.* This highly ungainly word denoting a most useful notion comes to us from the great Russian formalist critic Mikhail Bakhtin, who limits it pretty much to fiction, but I think I'll follow the example of T. S. Eliot, who, being a poet, saw that it operates throughout the realms of literature. The basic premise of intertextuality is really pretty simple: everything's connected. In other words, anything you write is connected to other written things. Sometimes writers are more up front about that than others, openly showing, as John Fowles does in *The French Lieutenant's Woman,* that he's drawing on the tradition of the Victorian novel, and on the works of Thomas Hardy and Henry James in particular. At one point Fowles writes an especially Jamesian sentence, full of embedded clauses, false starts, delayed effects, until, having thoroughly and delightfully aped the master, he declares, "But I must not ape the master." We get the joke, and the punch line makes the parody better than if he'd pretended he was up to nothing very special, since it says with a wink that we're in on the whole thing, that we knew all along.

Other writers pretend their work is completely their own, untutored, immediate, unaffected. Mark Twain claimed never to have read a book, yet his personal library ran to something over three thousand volumes. You can't write *A Connecticut Yankee in King Arthur's Court* (1889) without being familiar with Arthurian romances. Jack Kerouac presents himself as a free spirit performing automatic writing, but there's plenty of evidence that this Ivy Leaguer (Columbia) did a lot of revising and polishing—and reading of quest tales—before his manuscript of *On the Road* (1957) got typed on one long roll of paper. In each case, their work interacts with other works. And those works with others. The result is a sort of World Wide Web of writing. Your novel may contain echoes or refutations of novels or poems you've never read.

Think of intertextuality in terms of movie westerns. You're writing your first western; good for you. What's it about? A big showdown? *High Noon.* A gunslinger who retires? *Shane.* A lonely outpost during an uprising? *Fort Apache, She Wore a Yellow Ribbon*—the woods are full of 'em. Cattle drive? *Red River.* Does it involve, by any chance, a stagecoach?

No, wait, I wasn't thinking about any of them.

Doesn't matter. Your movie will. Here's the thing: you can't avoid them, since even avoidance is a form of interaction. It's simply impossible to write or direct in a vacuum. The movies you have seen were created by men and women who had seen others, and so on, until every movie connects with every other movie ever made. If you've seen Indiana Jones being dragged behind a truck by his whip, then you've been touched by *The Cisco Kid* (1931), even though there's a strong chance you've never seen *The Cisco Kid* itself. Every western has a little bit of other westerns in it, whether it knows it or not. Let's take the most basic element, the hero. Will your hero talk a lot or not? If not, then he's in the tradition of Gary Cooper and John Wayne and (later) Clint Eastwood. If he does speak, just talks his fool head right off, then he's like James Garner and those revisionist films of the sixties and seventies. Or maybe you have two, one talker and one silent type— *Butch Cassidy and the Sundance Kid* (1969). Your guy is going to have a certain amount of dialogue, and whatever type you decide on, audiences are going to hear echoes of some prior film, whether you think those echoes are there or not. And that, dear friends, is intertextuality.

The second concept for our consideration is *archetype*. The late great Canadian critic Northrop Frye took the notion of archetypes from C. G. Jung's psychoanalytical writings and showed that whatever Jung can tell us about our heads, he can tell us a great deal more about our books. "Archetype" is a five-dollar word for "pattern," or for the mythic original on which a pattern is based. It's like this: somewhere back in myth, something—a story component, let's call it—comes into being. It works so well, for one reason or another, that it catches on, hangs around, and keeps popping up in subsequent stories. That component could be anything: a quest, a form of sacrifice, flight, a plunge into water, whatever resonates and catches our imaginations, setting off vibrations deep in our collective consciousness, calling to us, alarming us, inspiring us to dream or nightmare, making us want to hear it again. And again and again and again. You'd think that these components, these archetypes, would wear out with use the way cliché wears out, but they actually work the other way: they take on power with repetition, finding strength in numbers. Here is the *aha!*

factor again. When we hear or see or read one of these instances of archetype, we feel a little frisson of recognition and utter a little satisfied "aha!" And we get that chance with fair frequency, because writers keep employing them.

Don't bother looking for the originals, though. You can't find the archetype, just as you can't find the pure myths. What we have, even in our earliest recorded literature, are variants, embellishments, versions, what Frye called "displacement" of the myth. We can never get all the way to the level of pure myth, even when a work like *The Lord of the Rings* or *The Odyssey* or *The Old Man and the Sea* feels "mythic," since even those works are displacements of myth. Perhaps it's impossible; perhaps there never has been a single, definite version of the myth. Frye thought the archetypes came from the Bible, or so he said at times, but such a notion won't account for the myths and archetypes that lie behind and inform the works of Homer, say, or those of any storyteller or poet who lacked access to the Judeo-Christian tradition. So let's say that somewhere back there in the mists of time when storytelling was completely oral (or pictorial, if you count the cave walls), a body of myth began establishing itself. The unanswerable question, it seems to me, is whether there was ever freestanding myth informing our stories or whether the mythic level grows out of the stories that we tell to explain ourselves and our world. In other words, was there some original master story for any particular myth from which all subsequent stories—pallid imitations—are "displacements," or does the myth take shape by slow accretion as variant story versions are told and retold over time? I incline toward the latter, but I don't know. In fact, I doubt anyone can know. I also doubt whether it matters. What does matter is that there is this mythic level, the level on which archetype operates and from which we borrow the figure of, for instance, the dying-and-reviving man (or god) or the young boy who must undertake a long journey.

Those stories—myth, archetype, religious narrative, the great body of literature—are always with us. Always in us. We can draw upon them, tap into them, add to them whenever we want. One of our great storytellers, country singer Willie Nelson, was sitting around one day just noodling on the guitar, improvising melodies he'd never written down, never heard in quite those forms. His companion, a nonmusician whose name I forget, asked him how he could come up with all those tunes. "They're all around us," old Willie said. "You just reach up and pick them out of the air." Stories are like that, too. That one story that has been going on forever is all around us. We—as readers or writers, tellers or listeners—understand each other, we share knowledge of the structures of our myths, we comprehend the logic of symbols, largely because we have access to the same swirl of story. We have only to reach out into the air and pluck a piece of it.

21

Marked for Greatness

Quasimodo is a hunchback. So is Richard III (Shakespeare's, not history's). Mary Shelley's better-known creation, not Victor Frankenstein, but his monster, is a man of parts. Oedipus has damaged feet. And Grendel—well, he is another monster. All characters who are as famous for their shape as for their behavior. Their shapes tell us something, and probably very different somethings, about them or other people in the story.

First, the obvious but nonetheless necessary observation: in real life, when people have any physical mark or imperfection, it means nothing thematically, metaphorically, or spiritually. Well, a scar on your cheek might tell us something if you got it as a member of a dueling fraternity at Heidelberg, and certain self-inflicted marks—Grateful Dead tattoos for instance—might say something about your musical tastes. But by and large a short leg is just a short leg, and scoliosis is just scoliosis.

But put that scoliosis on Richard III and, voilà, you have something else entirely. Richard, as morally and spiritually twisted as his back, is one of the most completely repugnant figures in all of literature. And while it might strike us as cruel and unjust to equate physical deformity with character or moral deformity, it seemed not only acceptable to the Elizabethans but almost inevitable. Shakespeare is very much a product of his time in suggesting that one's proximity to or distance from God is manifested in external signs. The Puritans, only a few years after him, saw failure in business—ruined crops, bankruptcy, financial mismanagement, even disease in one's herd—as clear evidence of God's displeasure and therefore of moral shortcomings. Evidently the story of Job didn't play in Plymouth.

Right. The Elizabethans and Jacobeans weren't politically correct. So now what? you ask. Meaning, what about four centuries later?

Things have changed pretty dramatically in terms of equating scars or deformities with moral shortcomings or divine displeasure, but in literature we continue to understand physical imperfection in symbolic terms.

It has to do with being different, really. Sameness doesn't present us with metaphorical possibilities, whereas difference—from the average, the typical, the expected—is always rich with possibility.

Vladimir Propp, in his landmark study of folktales back in the 1920s, *Morphology of the Folktale,* separates the story of the folk quester into thirty or so separate steps. One of the initial steps is that the hero is marked in some way. He may be scarred or lamed or wounded or painted or born with a short leg, but he bears some mark that sets him apart. The tales Propp looks at go back hundreds of years and have scores of variants, and while they happen to be Slavic in origin, structurally they resemble the Germanic, Celtic, French, and Italian folktales better known in the West. Many of those tales continue to inform our understanding of how stories are told.

You doubt? How many stories do you know in which the hero is different from everyone else in some way, and how many times is that difference physically visible? Why does Harry Potter have a scar, where is it, how did he get it, and what does it resemble?

Consider the ways Toni Morrison marks her characters. One quester, our old friend Milkman Dead from *Song of Solomon,* bears an initial marking, one leg being shorter than the other. He spends much of his youth adopting ways of walking that will hide his deficiency, as he perceives it. Later he will be scarred twice, once on his cheek by a beer bottle in a fight in Shalimar, Virginia, and once on his hands when his former pal Guitar tries to garotte him and Milkman gets his hands up just in time. In *Beloved*, Sethe has been whipped so severely in her past that she wears elaborate scars resembling a tree on her back. Her mother-in-law and mentor, Baby Suggs, has a bad hip. Beloved herself is perfect, except for three scratches on her forehead; on the other hand, Beloved is something else again, not merely human. These character markings stand as indicators of the damage life inflicts. In the case of Sethe and Beloved, that life involves slavery, so the violence that marks them is of a very specific sort. But even the others bear signs illustrating the way life marks all who pass through it.

Beyond that, though, is another element: character differentiation. At the end of Sophocles' *Oedipus Rex*, the king blinds himself, which is very definitely a kind of marking—of atonement, guilt, and contrition—and one that he will wear throughout the subsequent play, *Oedipus at Colonus*. But he was marked much, much earlier. In fact, being good Greeks, we knew this before we arrived at the theater, just from the meaning of the name, Oedipus—"Wounded Foot." If we were headed to the theater to watch a play called *Wounded Foot the King* (which is what that title means), we'd already know something was up. The oddity of the name, the way it calls attention to a physical problem, suggests that this aspect of his identity will come into play. Indeed, Oedipus's feet are damaged from the thong that was put through his Achilles tendons when, as an infant, he was sent away to die in the wilderness. His parents, fearing the terrible prophecy that he would kill his father and marry his mother, have him taken out to the country to be killed. Knowing how hard it will be for their servant to be the agent of death, they intend for the infant to be left on a mountain where he will perish of exposure. Just to be safe, they cause his feet to be lashed together so he doesn't get up and crawl away. Later his feet will become a piece of evidence proving that he is in fact the doomed infant. You might think that his mother, Jocasta, would be well advised either (a) never to remarry, or (b) to avoid marrying anyone with damaged ankles, but she chooses option (c) instead, thereby providing us with a plot. Quite lucky for Sophocles, if catastrophic for poor Oedipus. His scars speak of his personal history, which of course is hidden from him until it is revealed during the course of the play. Moreover, they address the personality of his parents, especially Jocasta, who tried to elude the curse, and of

Oedipus himself, who seems never to have inquired as to how he came to have these scars. This lack of inquisitiveness is diagnostic, since the basis of his downfall is his inability to know himself.

Something more modern? Sure. Ernest Hemingway. *The Sun Also Rises.* Modern enough? The novel, which deals with the generation that was damaged in so many ways by World War I, is an ironic reworking of the wasteland motif. Like T. S. Eliot's poetic masterpiece *The Waste Land,* it presents a society that has been rendered barren—spiritually, morally, intellectually, and sexually—by the war. Such a treatment is not at all surprising, given the death and destruction of millions of young, virile males. Traditionally, the wasteland myth concerns the struggle, the quest, to restore fertility. This quest is undertaken by or on behalf of the Fisher King, a character who exhibits physical damage in many versions. That's the original. Hemingway's Fisher King? Jake Barnes, newspaper correspondent and wounded war veteran. How do we know he's the Fisher King? He goes fishing. Actually, his fishing trip is quite extensive and, in its own way, restorative. It is also highly symbolic. And what, you ask, is the wound that makes him right for the role? This is tricky, since Jake, who narrates, never says. There's only one thing, though, that can make a grown man, looking at himself naked in the mirror, weep. In real life, Hemingway's own wound was in the upper thigh; in the novel, he moved it just north. Poor Jake, all the sexual desire and none of the ability to act upon it.

So what's going on here? Character differentiation, certainly. The missing member sets Jake apart from everyone else in the novel, or any other novel I know of, for that matter. It also sets up parallels to the operative wasteland myth. Perhaps a touch of Isis and Osiris thrown in; Osiris was torn apart, and the goddess Isis succeeded in reassembling him except for the part that makes Jake Barnes resemble him (the Osiris myth is an Egyptian fertility story). Priestesses of Isis took human lovers as symbolical stand-ins for the damaged Osiris, not unlike the way Lady Brett Ashley in the novel takes other lovers because she and Jake cannot consummate their passion. But chiefly, the injury is symbolic of the destruction of possibilities, spiritual as well as procreative, accomplished by the war. When millions of young men die in war, they take with them not merely reproductive possibilities but also tremendous intellectual, creative, and artistic resources. The war was, in short, the death of culture, or at least of a very great chunk of it. Moreover, those who survived, like Hemingway and his characters, were badly damaged from the experience. The Great War generation probably suffered more devastating psychic damage and spiritual displacement than any other in history. Hemingway captures that damage three times over: once in the Nick Adams stories culminating in "Big Two-Hearted River" (1925), where Nick goes off alone to Michigan's then remote Upper Peninsula on a fishing trip to repair his broken psyche after the horrors of his war experience; a second in Jake Barnes's war wound and the fractured festivities in Pamplona; and a third in Lieutenant Frederic Henry's separate peace, broken by his lover's death in childbirth in *A Farewell to Arms*. All three cover the same ground of mental damage, spiritual despair, the death of hope. Jake's wounding, then, is personal, historical, cultural, mythic. That's a lot of impact for one little piece of shrapnel.

In his *Alexandria Quartet*, Lawrence Durrell introduces numerous characters with disabilities and deformities of various sorts—two with eye patches (although one is faking it) and one with a glass eye, one with a harelip, one who contracts smallpox and is badly scarred, one whose hand, impaled by an accidental speargun shot, must be amputated to save her life, one who is deaf, and several with limbs missing. On one level, being Durrell characters, they are simply versions of the exotic. Yet collectively they come to represent something else: everyone, Durrell seems to be saying, is damaged in some way or other, and no matter how careful or fortunate we might seem to be, we don't get through life without being marked by the experience. Interestingly enough, his damaged characters are not particularly incommoded by their deficiencies. The harelipped Nahfouz becomes a celebrated mystic and preacher, while Clea, the painter, reports late in the final novel that her prosthetic hand can paint. The gift lies not in her hand, in other words, but in her heart, her mind, her soul.

What's Mary Shelley up to then? Her monster doesn't carry the specific historical baggage of a Jake Barnes, so what does his deformity represent? Let's look at where he comes from. Victor Frankenstein builds his spare-parts masterpiece not only out of a graveyard but also out of a specific historical situation. The industrial revolution was just starting up, and this new world would threaten everything people had known during the Enlightenment; at the same time, the new science and the new faith in science—including anatomical research, of course—imperiled many religious and philosophical tenets of English society in the first decades of the nineteenth century. Thanks to Hollywood, the monster looks like Boris Karloff or Lon Chaney and intimidates us by its sheer physical menace. But in the novel it's the *idea* of the monster that is frightening, or perhaps it's really the idea of the man, the scientist-sorcerer, forging an unholy alliance with dark knowledge that scares us. The monster represents, among other things, forbidden insights, a modern pact with the devil, the result of science without ethics. You don't need me to tell you this, naturally. Every time there's an advance in the state of knowledge, a movement into a *brave new world* (another literary reference, of course), some commentator or other informs us that we're closer to meeting a Frankenstein (meaning, of course, the monster).

The monster has several other possible frames of reference. The most obvious literary angle is the Faustian pact with the devil. We keep getting versions of Faust, from Christopher Marlowe's *Dr. Faustus* to Goethe's *Faust* to Stephen Vincent Benét's *The Devil and Daniel Webster* to *Damned Yankees* to movie versions of *Bedazzled* (and, of course, Darth Vader's turn to the Dark Side) to bluesman Robert Johnson's stories of how he acquired his musical skill in a meeting with a mysterious stranger at a crossroads. The enduring appeal of this cautionary tale suggests how deeply embedded it is in our collective consciousness. Unlike other versions, however, *Frankenstein* involves no demonic personage offering the damning bargain, so the cautionary being is the product (the monster) rather than the source (the devil) of the unholy act. In his deformity he projects the perils of man seeking to play God, perils that, as in other (noncomic) versions, consume the power seeker.

Beyond these cautionary elements, though, the real monster is Victor, the monster's maker. Or at least a portion of him. Romanticism gave us the notion, rampant throughout the nineteenth century and still with us in the twenty-first, of the dual nature of humanity, that in each of us, no matter how well made or socially groomed, a monstrous Other exists. The concept explains the fondness for doubles and self-contained Others in Victorian fiction: *The Prince and the Pauper* (1882), *The Master of Ballantrae*, *The Picture of Dorian Gray* (1891), and *Dr. Jekyll and Mr. Hyde.* Significantly, these last two also involve hideous Others, the portrait of Dorian that reveals his corruption and decay while he himself remains beautiful, and the monstrous Mr. Hyde, into whom the good doctor turns when he drinks the fateful elixir. What they share with Shelley's monster is the implication that within each of us, no matter how civilized, lurk elements that we'd really prefer not to acknowledge—the exact opposite of *The Hunchback of Notre Dame* or "Beauty and the Beast," where a hideous outer form hides the beauty of the inner person.

Are deformities and scars therefore always significant? Perhaps not. Perhaps sometimes a scar is simply a scar, a short leg or a hunchback merely that. But more often than not physical markings by their very nature call attention to themselves and signify some psychological or thematic point the writer wants to make. After all, it's easier to introduce characters without imperfections. You give a guy a limp in Chapter 2, he can't go sprinting after the train in Chapter 24. So if a writer brings up a physical problem or handicap or deficiency, he probably means something by it.

Now, go figure out Harry Potter's scar.

22

He's Blind for a Reason, You Know

Here's the setup: You have a man, a largely admirable man—capable, intelligent, strong, if slightly quick to anger—with a problem. Unbeknownst to him, he has committed the two most hideous crimes in the human catalog of evil. So unaware is he of his sins that he agrees to hunt down the criminal, promising all kinds of punishment. An information specialist, someone who can shed light on the search he has undertaken, who can show our hero the truth, is summoned. When the specialist arrives, he's blind. Can't see a thing in the world. As it turns out, though, he is able to see things in the spirit and divine world, can see the truth of what's actually happened, truth to which our hero is utterly oblivious. The blind specialist gets into a heated argument with the protagonist, who accuses the specialist of fraud, and is accused in turn of being the worst sort of malefactor, one who by the way is blind to what really matters.

What did this fellow do?

Nothing much. Just murder his father and marry his mother.

Two and a half millennia ago Sophocles wrote a little play called *Oedipus Rex*. Tiresias, the blind seer, does indeed know the whole truth about King Oedipus, sees everything, although that knowledge is so painful that he tries to hold it back, and when he does blurt it out, it is in a moment of such anger that no one believes him. Oedipus, meanwhile, who until the very end remains in the dark, makes constant reference to sight. He will "bring the matter to light," will "look into things," will "show everyone the truth." Every time he says one of these things, the audience gasps and squirms in its seats, because we see what's going on long before he does. When he finally sees the horror that is his life—children who are also siblings, a wife-mother driven to suicide, a curse like no other on him and his family—he exacts a terrible punishment indeed.

He blinds himself.

There are a lot of things that have to happen when a writer introduces a blind character into a story, and

even more in a play. Every move, every statement by
or about that character has to accommodate the lack
of sight; every other character has to notice, to behave
differently, if only in subtle ways. In other words, the
author has created a minor constellation of difficul-
ties for himself by introducing a blind character into
the work, so something important must be at stake
when blindness pops up in a story. Clearly the author
wants to emphasize other levels of sight and blindness
beyond the physical. Moreover, such references are
usually quite pervasive in a work where insight and
blindness are at issue.

For example, first-time readers or viewers will
observe that Tiresias is blind but sees the real story,
and Oedipus is blind to the truth and eventually blinds
himself. What they may miss, though, is the much
more elaborate pattern running through the fabric of
the play. Every scene, it seems, every ode by the chorus,
contains references to seeing—who saw what, who
failed to see, who is really blind—and images of light
and darkness, which have everything to do with seeing
or not seeing. More than any other work, *Oedipus Rex*
taught me how to read literary blindness, taught me
that as soon as we notice blindness and sight as thematic
components of a work, more and more related images
and phrases emerge in the text. The challenging thing

about literature is finding answers, but equally important is recognizing what questions need to be asked, and if we pay attention, the text usually tells us.

I didn't always know to look for the right questions—I grew into asking. Coming back to "blindness," I distinctly remember the first time I read James Joyce's little story "Araby." The first line tells us that the street the young narrator lives on is "blind." Hmm, I thought, that's an odd expression. I promptly got hung up on what it meant in the literal sense (a blind alley in British/Irish English is a dead-end street, which has another set of connotations, some related and some not), and missed entirely what it "really" meant. I got most of the story, the boy watching the girl at every opportunity, even when the light is poor or he has the "blinds" (I'm not making this up) pulled almost all the way down; the boy blinded by love, then by vanity; the boy envisioning himself as a hero out of a romance; the boy going to the supposedly exotic bazaar, Araby, arriving late to find much of it already in darkness, registering it as the tawdry and antiromantic place that it is; and finally the boy, nearly blinded by his own angry tears, seeing himself for the ridiculous creature he is. I think I had to read the story two more times before I got hooked into North Richmond Street being "blind." The significance of that adjective isn't immediately evident or relevant in itself. What it does, though, is set up a pattern of reference and suggestion as the young boy watches, hides, peeks, and gazes his way through a story that is alternately bathed in light and lost in shadow. Once we ask the right question— something like, "What does Joyce intend by calling the street blind?"—answers begin presenting themselves with considerable regularity. A truly great story or play, as "Araby" and *Oedipus Rex* are, makes demands on us as readers; in a sense it teaches us how to read it. We feel that there's something more going on in the story—a richness, a resonance, a depth—than we picked up at first, so we return to it to find those elements that account for that sensation.

Periodically throughout this book, I have felt obliged to issue disclaimers. This is one of those times. What we have discussed is absolutely true: when literal blindness, sight, darkness, and light are introduced into a story, it is nearly always the case that figurative seeing and blindness are at work. Here's the caveat: seeing and blindness are generally at issue in many works, even where there is no hint of blindness on the part of windows, alleys, horses, speculations, or persons.

If it's there all the time, what's the point of introducing it specifically into some stories?

Good question. I think it's a matter of shading and subtlety—and their opposite. It's a little like music, I suppose. Do you get all those musical jokes in Mozart and Haydn? Well, neither do I. The closest I came to classical music in my youth was Procol Harum ripping off a Bach cantata for "A Whiter Shade of Pale." Eventually I learned a little, including the difference between Beethoven and "Roll Over Beethoven," even if I prefer the latter, and between Miles Davis and John Coltrane at their peak, but I remain a musical numskull. Those subtle jokes for the musical initiates are lost on an ignoramus such as myself. So if you want me to get the point musically, you'd better be fairly obvious. I get Keith Emerson better than I get Bach. Any Bach. And some of the Bachs aren't that subtle.

Same with literature. If writers want us—all of us—to notice something, they'd better put it out there where we'll find it. Please observe that in most works where blindness is manifest, the writer brings it up pretty early. I call this "the Indiana Jones principle": **if you want your audience to know something important about your character (or the work at large), introduce it early, before you need it.** Say we're two-thirds of the way through *Raiders of the Lost Ark* and suddenly Indy, who has heretofore been afraid of absolutely nothing, is terrified of snakes. Do we buy that? Of course not. That's why Steven Spielberg, the director, and Lawrence Kasdan, the writer, installed that snake in the airplane right in the first sequence, before the credits, so that when we get to the seven thousand snakes, we'll know just how badly they frighten our hero.

The principle doesn't always work, of course. In his absurdist dramatic masterpiece *Waiting for Godot* (1954) (about which, more later), Samuel Beckett waits until the second act to introduce a blind character. The first time Lucky and Pozzo show up to relieve the boredom of Didi and Gogo, the main characters, Pozzo is a cruel master who keeps Lucky on a leash. The second time, he's blind and needs Lucky to escort him around, although he's no less cruel for all that. Of course, what this means is up for grabs, since Beckett is employing irony, and not very subtly. More commonly, though, the blind character will show up early. In Henry Green's first novel, *Blindness* (1926), his schoolboy protagonist is blinded by a freak accident when a small boy throws a rock through a railway carriage window. John, the schoolboy, has just become aware of, has just begun to see, life's possibilities, and at that moment in his life a rock and a thousand shards of glass come sailing in to rob him of that vision.

Back to Oedipus. Don't feel too bad. When we meet him again, in *Oedipus at Colonus*, it's many years later, and of course he's suffered greatly, but that suffering has redeemed him in the eyes of the gods, and rather than being a blight on the human landscape, he becomes a favorite of the gods, who welcome him into the next world with a miraculous death. He has acquired a level of vision he never had when he was sighted. Blind as he is, he walks toward that death without assistance, as if guided by an unseen power.

23

It's Never Just Heart Disease . . . And Rarely Just Illness

One of my very favorite novels is a gem of narrative misdirection by Ford Madox Ford called *The Good Soldier* (1915). Its narrator is more fallible, more consistently clueless, than any narrator you're ever likely to meet in all of fiction; at the same time he's completely believable and therefore pathetic. He is part of a pair of couples who meet every year at a European spa. During all these years, and quite unbeknownst to him, his wife, Florence, and the husband of the other couple, Edward Ashburnham, carry on a passionate affair. It gets better: Edward's wife, Leonora, knows all about it, and in fact may have stage-managed its beginning to keep the chronically straying Edward out of a more disastrous relationship. The success of this strategy must be questioned, since the relationship eventually manages to destroy, by my count, six lives. Only poor cuckolded old John Dowell remains ignorant. Consider the possibilities for irony. For an English professor, and for any avid reader, having a blithely ignorant (and only recently clued-in) husband narrate the saga of his wife's longtime infidelity is about as good as it gets.

But I digress. Why, you ask, are they habitués of the spa? Florence and Edward are ill, of course.

Heart trouble. What else?

In literature there is no better, no more lyrical, no more perfectly metaphorical illness than heart disease. In real life, heart disease is none of the above; it's frightening, sudden, shattering, exhausting, but not lyrical or metaphorical. When the novelist or playwright employs it, however, we don't complain that he's being unrealistic or insensitive.

Why? It's fairly straightforward.

Aside from being the pump that keeps us alive, the heart is also, and has been since ancient times, the symbolic repository of emotion. In both *The Iliad* and *The Odyssey* Homer has characters say of other characters that they have "a heart of iron," iron being the newest and hardest metal known to men of the late Bronze Age. The meaning, if we allow for some slight variations of context, is tough-minded, resolute even to the point of hard-heartedness—in other words, just what we might mean by the same statements today. Sophocles uses the heart to mean the center of emotion within the body, as do Dante, Shakespeare, Donne, Marvell, Hallmark . . . all the great writers. Despite this nearly constant use over at least twenty-eight hundred years, the figure of the heart never overstays its welcome, because it always is welcome. Writers use it because we feel it. What shapes were your Valentine's cards in when you were a kid? Or last year, for that matter? When we fall in love, we feel it in our hearts. When we lose a love, we feel heartbroken. When overwhelmed by strong emotion, we feel our hearts are full to bursting.

Everybody knows this, everybody intuitively senses this. What, then, can the writer do with this knowledge? The writer can use heart ailments as a kind of shorthand for the character, which is probably what happens most often, or he can use it as a social metaphor. The afflicted character can have any number of problems for which heart disease provides a suitable emblem: bad love, loneliness, cruelty, pederasty, disloyalty, cowardice, lack of determination. Socially, it may stand for these matters on a larger scale, or for something seriously amiss at the heart of things.

We're not just talking classic literature here. When Colin Dexter decides to kill off his recurrent detective Morse in *The Remorseful Day* (1999), he has a number of options. The chief inspector is a genius at solving crimes and crossword puzzles, but like all geniuses, he has flaws. Specifically, he drinks too much and remains a complete stranger to physical fitness, so much so that in novel after novel his Thames Valley Police superiors mention his excessive fondness for "the beer." His liver and digestive system are seriously compromised, to the point where he is hospitalized for these problems in a previous Morse novel. In fact, he solves a century-old murder from his hospital bed in *The Wench Is Dead* (1989). His major problem, though, is loneliness. Morse has spectacularly bad luck with his women; several wind up as either corpses or culprits in his various adventures, while others just don't work out. Sometimes he's too needy, other times too unbending, but time after time he loses out. So when the time comes for him to collapse amid the spires of his beloved Oxford University, Dexter gives him a heart attack.

Why?

We're into the realm of speculation here, but this is how it strikes me. To have Morse succumb to cirrhosis of the liver turns the whole thing into a straightforward piece of moralizing: see, we told you drinking too much is bad for you. Morse's drinking would go from being a quaint idiosyncrasy to something from one of those old school-guidance films, and that is not what Dexter wants. Of course excessive drinking is bad for you—excessive anything, including irony, is bad for you—but that's not the point. But with a heart attack, the connection to an overfondness for drink is still there if that's what some readers want to see, but now the ailment points not toward his behavior but toward the pain and suffering, the loneliness and regret, of his sad-sack love life, that may well be causing the behavior. The emphasis is on his humanity, not his misdeeds. And authors, as a rule, are chiefly interested in their characters' humanity.

Even when the humanity isn't very humane, or the heart ailment a disease. Nathaniel Hawthorne has a great short story called "The Man of Adamant" (1837). As with a number of his characters, the man of the title is a committed misanthrope, absolutely convinced that everyone else is a sinner. So he moves into a cave to avoid all human contact. Does it sound like a "heart" problem to you? Of course it does. Now the limestone cave he chooses has water, a little drip of water, that's just stiff with calcium. And moment by moment, year by year, the water in that cave seeps its way into his body, so that at the end of the story he turns to stone, or not him entirely, just his heart. The man whose heart was figurative stone at the outset has his heart turn to literal stone at the end. It's perfect.

Or take the case of Joseph Conrad's *Lord Jim*. Early in the novel, Jim's courage has failed him at a crucial moment. His strength of heart, both in terms of bravery and of forming serious attachments, is in question throughout the narrative, at least in his own mind, and at the end he misjudges an enemy and his miscalculation causes the death of his best friend, who happens to be the son of the local chieftain. Jim has promised this leader, Doramin, that if his plan results in the death of any of his people, Jim will forfeit his own life. When it does, he walks with great calm to Doramin, who shoots him through the chest; Jim glances proudly at the assembled crowd—See, I am both brave and true to my word—and falls dead. Conrad doesn't perform a postmortem, but there is one and only one place in the chest where a shot results in instantaneous death, and we know where that place is. The very next comment by Marlow, the narrator, is that Jim was "inscrutable at heart." The novel's all about heart, really, heart in all its senses. Jim's end, then, like the Adamantine Man's, is perfectly apt. A man who in life has put so much stock in "heart"—in loyalty and trust, in courage and fidelity, in having a true heart—can only die by a blow to the heart. Unlike Hawthorne's character's demise, though, Jim's is also heartbreaking—to the woman who is his de facto wife, to old Stein, the trader who sent him in-country, and to readers, who come to hope for something heroic and uplifting, something suitably romantic, for the incorrigibly romantic Jim. Conrad knows better, though: it's tragedy, not epic, as he proves by that shot in the heart.

More commonly, though, heart trouble takes the form of heart disease. Vladimir Nabokov created one of the nastiest villains in modern literature in Lolita's Humbert Humbert. His self-absorption and obsession lead him to cruelty, statutory rape, murder, and the destruction of several lives. His darling Dolores, the Lolita of the title, can never lead a psychologically or spiritually whole adult life. Of her two seducers, Clare Quilty is dead and Humbert is in jail, where he dies, somewhat unexpectedly, of heart failure. Throughout the whole novel he's had a defective heart in the figurative sense, so how else could he die? He may or may not need to die, but if he does buy the farm, there's only one death symbolically appropriate to his situation. Nobody had to tell that to Nabokov.

As a practical matter, then, we readers can play this two ways. If heart trouble shows up in a novel or play, we start looking for its signification, and we usually don't have to hunt too hard. The other way around: if we see that characters have difficulties of the heart, we won't be too surprised when emotional trouble becomes the physical ailment and the cardiac episode appears.

Now, about that irony. Remember Florence and Edward, the wayward spouses with heart trouble? Just what, you ask, is wrong with their hearts? Not a thing in the world. Physically, that is. Faithlessness, selfishness, cruelty—those things are wrong, and ultimately those things kill them. But physically, their hearts are completely sound. So why did I say earlier they suffer from heart disease? Haven't I just violated the principle of this chapter? Not really. Their *choice* of illness is quite telling: each of them elects to employ a fragile heart as a device to deceive the respective spouse, to be able to construct an elaborate personal fiction based on heart disease, to announce to the world that he or she suffers from a "bad heart." And in each case the lie is, on another level, absolutely true. As I said earlier, it doesn't get better than that.

At the beginning of James Joyce's wonderful story "The Sisters" (1914), the unnamed young narrator mentions that his old friend and mentor, a priest, is dying. There is "no hope" for him this time, we're told. Already your reader's radar should be on full alert. A priest with no hope? Not hard to recognize in such a statement a host of possibilities for interpretive play, and indeed those possibilities are realized throughout the story. What's of immediate interest here, though, is how the priest got that way. He's had a stroke, not his first, and it has left him paralyzed. "Paralysis" is a word that fascinates the young boy, quite apart from its meaning; he yokes it with "simony" and "gnomon" in a triad of words to obsess over. For us, however, it's the notion of paralysis—and stroke—that intrigues.

Anyone who has ever had to watch a loved one deteriorate after a massive stroke will no doubt look askance at the very idea of such frustration and misery being in some way intriguing, fascinating, or picturesque, and quite rightly. But as we've seen time and again, what we feel in real life and what we feel in our reading lives can be quite different.

From this little story the condition of paralysis grows into one of Joyce's great themes: Dublin is a city in which the inhabitants are paralyzed by the strictures laid upon them by church, state, and convention. We see it throughout *Dubliners*—a girl who cannot let go of the railing to board a ship with her lover; men who know the right thing to do but fail because their bad habits limit their ability to act in their own best interest; a man confined to bed after a drunken fall in a public-house rest room; political activists who fail to act after the death of their great leader, Charles Stewart Parnell, some ten years earlier. It shows up again and again in *A Portrait of the Artist as a Young Man* and *Ulysses* and even in *Finnegans Wake* (1939). Of course, most maladies in most short stories, or even novels, are not quite so productive of meaning. For Joyce, however, paralysis—physical, moral, social, spiritual, intellectual, political—informs his whole career.

Until the twentieth century, disease was mysterious. Folks began to comprehend the germ theory of disease in the nineteenth century, of course, after Louis Pasteur, but until they could do something about it, until the age of inoculation, illness remained frightening and mysterious. People sickened and died, often with no discernible preamble. You went out in the rain, three days later you had pneumonia; ergo, rain and chills cause pneumonia. That still occurs, of course. If you're like me, you were told over and over again as a child to button your coat or put on a hat lest you catch your death of cold. We've never really accepted microbes into our lives. Even knowing how disease is transmitted, we remain largely superstitious. And since illness is so much a part of life, so too is it a part of literature.

There are certain principles governing the use of
disease in works of literature:

1) *Not all diseases are created equal.* Prior to
   modern sanitation and enclosed water systems in
   the twentieth century, cholera was nearly as
   common as, much more aggressive than, and
   more devastating than tuberculosis (which was
   generally called consumption). Yet cholera
   doesn't come close to TB in its frequency of lit-
   erary occurrence. Why? Image mostly. Cholera
   has a bad reputation, and there's almost nothing
   the best public relations firm in the world could
   do to improve it. It's ugly, horrible. Death by
   cholera is unsightly, painful, smelly, and violent.
   In that same period of the late nineteenth cen-
   tury, syphilis and gonorrhea reached near-
   epidemic proportions, yet except for Henrik
   Ibsen and some of the later naturalists, venereal
   diseases were hardly on the literary map. Syphi-
   lis, of course, was prima facie evidence of sex
   beyond the bounds of marriage, of moral cor-
   ruption (you could only get it, supposedly, by
   visiting prostitutes), and therefore taboo. In its
   tertiary stages, of course, it also produced
   unpleasant results, including loss of control of

one's limbs (the sudden, spastic motions Kurt Vonnegut writes of in his 1973 *Breakfast of Champions*) and madness. The only treatment known to the Victorians employed mercury, which turned the gums and saliva black and carried its own hazards. So these two, despite their widespread occurrence, were never A-list diseases.

Well, then, what makes a prime literary disease?

2) *It should be picturesque.* What, you don't think illness is picturesque? Consider consumption. Of course it's awful when a person has a coughing fit that sounds like he's trying to bring up a whole lung, but the sufferer of tuberculosis often acquires a sort of bizarre beauty. The skin becomes almost translucent, the eye sockets dark, so that the sufferer takes on the appearance of a martyr in medieval paintings.

3) *It should be mysterious in origin.* Again, consumption was a clear winner, at least with the Victorians. The awful disease sometimes swept through whole families, as it would when one member nursed a dying parent or sibling or child, coming into daily contact with contaminated

droplets, phlegm, blood for an extended period. The mode of transmission, however, remained murky for most people in that century. Certainly John Keats had no idea that caring for his brother Tom was sealing his own doom, any more than the Brontës knew what hit them. That love and tenderness should be rewarded with a lengthy, fatal illness was beyond ironic. By the middle of the nineteenth century, science discovered that cholera and bad water went together, so it had no mystery points. As for syphilis, well, its origins were entirely too clear.

4) *It should have strong symbolic or metaphorical possibilities.* If there's a metaphor connected with smallpox, I don't want to know about it. Smallpox was hideous in both the way it presented and the disfigurement it left without really offering any constructive symbolic possibilities. Tuberculosis, on the other hand, was a *wasting disease*, both in terms of the individual wasting away, growing thinner and thinner, and in terms of the waste of lives that were often barely under way.

Throughout the nineteenth and early twentieth centuries, TB joined cancer in dominating the literary imagination regarding illness. Here's a partial list: Ralph Touchett in Henry James's novel *The Portrait of a Lady* (1881) and Milly Theale in his later *The Wings of the Dove* (1902), Little Eva in Harriet Beecher Stowe's *Uncle Tom's Cabin* (1852), Paul Dombey in Charles Dickens's *Dombey and Son* (1848), Mimi in Puccini's opera *La Bohème* (1896), Hans Castorp and his fellow patients at the sanatorium in Thomas Mann's *Magic Mountain* (1924), Michael Furey in Joyce's "The Dead," Eugene Gant's father in Thomas Wolfe's *Of Time and the River* (1935), and Rupert Birkin in Lawrence's *Women in Love*. In fact, Lawrence encodes his illness into the physiognomy, personality, and general health of his various alter egos. Not every one of these was labeled "tubercular." Some were "delicate," "fragile," "sensitive," "wasting away"; others were said to "have a lung" or "suffer from lung disease" or were merely identified as having a persistent cough or periods of low energy. A mere symptom or two would suffice for the contemporary audience, to whom the symptoms were all too familiar. So many characters contracted tuberculosis in part because so many writers either suffered from it themselves or watched friends, colleagues, and loved ones deteriorate in its grasp. In addition to Keats and the Brontës, Robert Louis Stevenson, Katherine Mansfield, Lawrence, Frédéric Chopin,

Ralph Waldo Emerson, Henry David Thoreau, Franz Kafka, and Percy Bysshe Shelley form a fair beginning toward a Who's Who of artistic consumptives. In her study *Illness as Metaphor* (1977), Susan Sontag brilliantly discusses the reasons for the disease's popularity as a subject and the metaphorical uses to which it was put. For now, we're less interested in all the implications she identifies, and more interested in recognizing that when a writer employs TB directly or indirectly, he's making a statement about the victim of the disease. His choice, while no doubt carrying a strong element of verisimilitude, also very likely houses symbolic or metaphorical intentions.

This fourth consideration—the metaphorical possibilities a disease offers—generally overrides all others: a sufficiently compelling metaphor can induce an author to bring an otherwise objectionable illness into a work. A good example would be plague. As an instance of individual suffering, bubonic plague is no bonus, but in terms of widespread, societal devastation, it's a champion. In two works written a mere twenty-five hundred years apart, plague successfully takes center stage. In *Oedipus Rex* Sophocles has Thebes hit by various plagues—withered crops, stillborn children, the works—but here as in general use, plague carries with it the implication of bubonic. It comes to mean what we think of as plague, in fact, because it can lay waste to whole cities in short order, because it sweeps through populations as a visitation of divine wrath. And of course divine wrath is the order of the day at the beginning of Sophocles' play. Two and a half millennia later, Albert Camus not only uses the malady, he calls his novel *The Plague* (1947). Again, he is not interested so much in the individual sufferer as he is in the communal aspect and the philosophical possibilities. In examining how a person confronts the wholesale devastation wrought by disease, Camus can set his existentialist philosophy into motion in a fictional setting: the isolation and uncertainty caused by the disease, the absurdly random nature of infection, the despair felt by a doctor in the face of an unstoppable epidemic, the desire to act even while recognizing the pointlessness of action. Now neither Camus's nor Sophocles' use is particularly subtle or hard to get, but in their overt way they teach us how other writers may use illness when it is less central.

When Henry James has had enough of Daisy Miller and decides to kill her off, he gives her *Roman fever* or what we would now call *malaria*. If you read that beautiful little novella and neither of these names suggests anything to you, you really need to pay more attention. Malaria works great, metaphorically: it translates as "bad air." Daisy has suffered from figurative bad air—malicious gossip and hostile public opinion—throughout her stay in Rome. As the name implies, it was formerly thought that the illness was contracted from harmful vapors in hot, moist night air; no one suspected that the problem might lie with those darned mosquitoes that were biting them on those hot, moist nights. So the notion of poisonous vapors would work nicely. Still, the older name used by James, Roman fever, is even better. Daisy does indeed suffer from Roman fever, from the overheated state that makes her frantic to join the elite ("We're dying to be exclusive," she says early on) while at the same time causing the disapproval of the Europeanized Americans who reside permanently in Rome at every turn. When she makes her fatal midnight trip to the Colosseum and she sees the object of, if not her affections, then at least her interests, Winterbourne, he ignores her, prompting her to say, "He cuts me dead." And the next thing we know, she is dead. Does the manner of her death matter? Of course. Roman fever perfectly captures what happens to Daisy, this fresh young thing from the wilds of Schenectady who is destroyed by the clash between her own vitality and the rotten atmosphere of this oldest of Old World cities. James is a literary realist, hardly the most flamboyantly symbolic of writers, but when he can kill off a character in a highly lifelike way while employing an apt metaphor for her demise, he doesn't hesitate.

Another great nineteenth-century realist who sees the figurative value of illness is Henrik Ibsen. In his breakthrough play *A Doll's House* (1879), he includes a neighbor to the Helmer family, Dr. Rank, who is dying of tuberculosis of the spine. Dr. Rank's illness is uncommon only in terms of its location; tuberculosis can settle in any part of the body, although the respiratory system is the one we always think of. Here's the interesting part: Rank says he inherited the disease from his father's dissolute living. Aha! Now instead of being a mere ailment, his condition becomes an indictment of parental misdeeds (a strong thematic statement in its own right) and, as we latter-day cynics can recognize, a coded reference to an entirely different pair of letters. Not TB, but VD. As I suggested earlier, syphilis and its various brethren were off-limits for most of the nineteenth century, so any references needed to be in code, as here. How many people suffer from consumption because their parents led immoral lives? Some, certainly, but inherited syphilis is much more likely. In fact, emboldened by his experiment here, Ibsen returned to the notion several years later in *Ghosts* (1881), in which he has a young man losing his mind as the result of inherited tertiary syphilis. Intergenerational tensions, responsibilities, and misdeeds are some of Ibsen's abiding themes, so it's not surprising that such an ailment would resonate with him.

Naturally, what gets encoded in a literary disease is largely up to the writer and the reader. When, in the course of *Justine*, the first novel of Lawrence Durrell's *Alexandria Quartet*, the narrator's lover, Melissa, succumbs to tuberculosis, he means something very different from what Ibsen means. Melissa, the dancer/escort/prostitute is a victim of life. Poverty, neglect, abuse, exploitation have all combined to grind her down, and the grinding nature of her illness—and of Darley's (the narrator's) inability to save her or even to recognize his responsibilities to her—stands as the physical expression of the way life and men have quite literally used her up. Moreover, her own acceptance of the disease, of the inevitability of her mortality and suffering, mirrors her self-sacrificing nature: perhaps it is best for everyone else, Darley especially, if she dies. What's best for her never seems to enter her mind. In the third novel of the series, *Mountolive*, Leila Hosnani contracts smallpox, which she takes as a sign of divine judgment against her vanity and her marital lapse. Durrell, however, sees it otherwise, as symptomatic of the ravages that time and living take on us all. In each case, of course, we're free to draw our own conclusions.

What about AIDS?

Every age has its special disease. The Romantics and Victorians had consumption; we have AIDS. For a while in the middle of the twentieth century, it looked like polio would be the disease of the century. Everyone knew people who died, or wound up on crutches, or lived in iron lungs because of that terrible, and terrifying, disease. Although I was born the year Dr. Jonas Salk made his blessed discovery of a vaccine, I can remember parents during my youth who still wouldn't let their children go into a public swimming pool. Even when conquered, polio had a powerful grip on the imaginations of my parents' generation. For some reason, though, that imagination did not become literary; polio rarely shows up in novels of the period.

Now AIDS, on the other hand, has been an epidemic that does occupy the writers of its time. Why? Let's run the list. *Picturesque?* Certainly not, but it shares that terrible, dramatic wasting quality of consumption. *Mysterious?* It was when it showed up, and even now this virus that can mutate in infinite ways to thwart nearly any treatment eludes our efforts to corral it. *Symbolic?* Most definitely. AIDS is the mother lode of symbol and metaphor. Its tendency to lie dormant for so long, then make an appearance, its ability because of that dormant period to turn every victim into an unknowing carrier, its virtual one hundred percent mortality rates over the first decade or so of its history, all these things offer strong symbolic possibilities. The way it has visited itself disproportionately on young people, hit the gay community so hard, devastated so many people in the developing world, been a scourge in artistic circles—the tragedy and despair, but also the courage and resilience and compassion (or their lack) have provided metaphor, theme, and symbol as well as plot and situation for our writers. Because of the demographic distribution of its infection history, AIDS adds another property to its literary usage: *the political angle.* Nearly everybody who wants to can find something in HIV/AIDS that somehow works into their political view. Social and religious conservatives almost immediately saw the element of divine retribution, while AIDS activists saw the slow response of government as evidence of official hostility to ethnic and sexual constituencies hardest hit by the disease. That's a lot of freight for a disease which is really just about transmission, incubation, and duration—which is what all diseases have always been about.

Given the highly charged nature of the public experience, we would expect to see AIDS show up in places occupied by other ailments in earlier times. Michael Cunningham's novel *The Hours* (1998) is a reworking of Virginia Woolf's modern classic, *Mrs. Dalloway*, in which a shell-shocked veteran of the Great War disintegrates and commits suicide. In the aftermath of that terrible war, shell shock was a hot-button medical item. Did it exist, were these men simply malingerers, were they predisposed to psychological unfitness, could they be cured, what had they seen that caused them but not others to succumb? Cunningham clearly can't use shell shock and is even too far out of the Vietnam era for PTSD to have much resonance. Besides, he's writing about the contemporary urban experience, as Woolf was doing earlier in the century, and part of that experience for him is the gay and lesbian community and part of *that* experience is HIV/AIDS. His suicide, therefore, is a patient with very advanced AIDS. Other than the illness that occasions them, the two deaths resemble each other greatly. We recognize in them a personal calamity that is particular to its time but that has the universality of great suffering and despair and courage, of a "victim" seeking to wrest control over his own life away from the condition that has controlled him. It's a situation, Cunningham reminds us, that differs from age to age only in the specific details, not in the humanity those details reveal. That's what happens when works get reenvisioned: we learn something about the age that produced the original as well as about our own.

Often, though, the most effective illness is the one the writer makes up. Fever—the non-Roman sort—worked like a charm in times past. The character merely contracted fever, took to her bed, and died in short or long order as the plot demanded, and there you were. The fever could represent the randomness of fate, the harshness of life, the unknowability of the mind of God, the playwright's lack of imagination, any of a wide array of possibilities. Dickens kills off all sorts of characters with fevers that don't get identified; of course, he had so many characters that he needed to dispatch some of them periodically just for housekeeping purposes. Poor little Paul Dombey succumbs with the sole purpose of breaking his father's heart. Little Nell hovers between life and death for an unbearable real-time month as readers of the original serialized version waited for the next installment to be issued and reveal her fate. Edgar Allan Poe, who in real life saw plenty of tuberculosis, gives us a mystery disease in "The Masque of the Red Death." It may be an encoding of TB or of some other malady, but chiefly it is what no real disease can ever be: exactly what the author wants it to be. Real illnesses come with baggage, which can be useful or at least overcome in a novel. A made-up illness, though, can say whatever its maker wants it to say.

It's too bad modern writers lost the generic "fever" and the mystery malady when modern medicine got so it could identify virtually any microbe and thereby diagnose virtually any disease. This strikes me as a case where the cure is definitely worse than the disease, at least for literature.

24

Don't Read with Your Eyes

Remember the Twelfth Night party in Joyce's story "The Dead" that we looked at earlier? To a child of late-twentieth-century America (or early-twenty-first, for that matter), the meal is no big deal. Except for the goose. Not that many households in this country roast a goose for the holiday, or any holiday. But the rest looks pretty ordinary to us. A vase with stalks of celery, American apples and oranges on the sideboard, floury potatoes. Nothing very remarkable. Unless you live, as do the old ladies who provide the meal, in pre-electrification Dublin, where it happens to be the sixth of January. So if you're going to understand the ladies, and the meal, and the story, you have to read through eyes that are not your own, eyes that, while not those of Aunts Kate and Julia, can take in the meaning of the meal they have provided. And those eyes did not grow up watching *Animaniacs*. The aunts have provided a meal beyond their limited means, in which they feed exotic and expensive produce to a substantial number of guests. Celery does not grow in Ireland in January, and the fruit is from *America* and therefore quite expensive. They have gone to considerable expense on Epiphany, the second most important day of the Christmas season, the day the Christ child was revealed to the wise men. In addition to its religious significance, the evening is also the old ladies' one big extravagance of the year, the party by which they cling to a fading gentility and memories of greater comfort as members of the middle class. We cannot understand their anxiety over the success of this gathering unless we see how important it is in their lives.

Or take this situation. James Baldwin's wonderful short story "Sonny's Blues" deals with a rather uptight math teacher in Harlem in the 1950s whose brother serves time in prison for heroin possession. At the end of the story there's a scene we looked at in an earlier chapter, where the brother, Sonny, has returned to playing in a club and the math teacher, our narrator, goes to hear him for the first time ever. There's been a lot of tension throughout the story since the two don't comprehend each other and the math teacher really can't fathom the troubles that drive Sonny and his music and his drug problem. Nor does he understand jazz; the only jazz name he can come up with is Louis Armstrong, proving to Sonny that he's hopelessly square. As the brother sits listening to Sonny with the jazz combo, however, he begins to hear in this beautiful, troubled music the depths of feeling and suffering and joy that lie behind it. So he sends an offering, a scotch and milk, that indicates understanding and brotherhood; Sonny sips, sets the drink back on the piano, and acknowledges the gift, which shimmers like "the very cup of trembling," in the closing words of the story. It's deep and emotional and biblical, with a resonance that very few stories ever achieve—about as close to perfection as we're likely to encounter. Now here's where the business of interpretation gets interesting. At my school, there are sociology/social work classes on substance abuse. And two or three times I've had a recent student in said substance abuse classes show up at discussions of "Sonny's Blues," very earnestly saying something like, "You should never give alcohol to a recovering addict." Perfectly true, I'm sure. In this context, though, not helpful. This story was published in 1957, using the best information Baldwin had at that time, and it is meant as a study of relations between brothers, not as a treatise on addiction. It's about redemption, not recovery. If you read it as the latter, that is, if you don't adjust your eyes and mind to transport you from contemporary reality to Baldwin's 1957, whatever the ending has to offer will be pretty well lost on you.

We all have our own blind spots, and that's normal. We expect a certain amount of verisimilitude, of faithfulness to the world we know, in what we watch and what we read. On the other hand, a too rigid insistence on the fictive world corresponding on all points to the world we know can be terribly limiting not only to our enjoyment but to our understanding of literary works. So how much is too much? What can we reasonably demand of our reading?

That's up to you. But I'll tell you what I think, and what I try to do. It seems to me that if we want to get the most out of our reading, as far as is reasonable, we have to try to take the works as they were intended to be taken. The formula I generally offer is this: **don't read with *your* eyes**. What I really mean is, don't read only from your own fixed position in the Year of Our Lord two thousand and some. Instead try to find a reading perspective that allows for sympathy with the historical moment of the story, that understands the text as having been written against its own social, historical, cultural, and personal background. There are dangers in this, and I'll return to them. I also need to acknowledge here that there is a different model of professional reading, *deconstruction*, that pushes skepticism and doubt to its extreme, questioning nearly everything in the story or poem at hand, to deconstruct the work and show how the author is not really in charge of his materials. The goal of these deconstructive readings is to demonstrate how the work is controlled and reduced by the values and prejudices of its own time. As you will have discerned, this is an approach with which I have limited sympathy. At the end of the day, I prefer to like the works I analyze. But that's another story.

Let's return for a moment to Baldwin's math teacher and Sonny's addiction. The comment about giving alcohol to an addict betrays a certain mind-set about social problems as well as a unique history of artistic and popular culture experiences on the part of the reader that are at odds with the story's own goals. "Sonny's Blues" is about redemption, but not the one students have been conditioned to expect. So much of our popular culture—daytime talk shows, made-for-television movies, magazine articles—leads us to think in terms of identifying a problem, such as addiction, and seeking a simple, direct solution. In its place, such thinking makes perfect sense. On the other hand, Baldwin is only slightly interested in Sonny's addiction in and of itself;

what he really cares about is the brother's emotional turmoil. Everything in the story points to this interest. The point of view (the brother's), the depth of detail about the brother's life relative to Sonny's, the direct access to the brother's thoughts, all remind us this is about the narrator and not the jazzman. Most tellingly, it is the brother who is removed from his world, taken out of his comfort zone, when he follows Sonny to meet with other musicians and then to hear Sonny play. If you want to put pressure on a character to cause him to change or crumble, take him away from home, make him inhabit an alien world. For the middle-class math teacher, the world of jazz might as well be Neptune.

Here's why this business of the reader's perspective matters. This story falls into that very large category that I call "last-chance-for-change" stories. Not a terribly scientific name, I'll grant, but that's what they are. Here's how they work: the character—sufficiently old to have experienced a number of opportunities to grow, to reform, to get it right, but of course he never has—is presented with one more chance, one last opportunity to educate himself in this most important area (and it varies with the story) where up to now he has remained stunted. The reason he's older is just the opposite of why the quester is typically younger: his possibilities for growth are limited and time is running

out. In other words, there is a time imperative, a sort
of urgency as the sands run out. And then the situation
in which he finds himself needs to be compelling. Our
guy? He's never understood or sympathized with his
brother, even to the point of not visiting him in prison.
When the narrator's daughter dies and Sonny writes a
caring letter of sympathy, he makes the narrator (I'm
sorry he doesn't have a name) feel even greater guilt.
Now that Sonny is out of prison and not using heroin,
the narrator has a chance to get to know his younger,
troubled brother as he never has before. If he can't
do that this time, he never will. And this leads us to
the point of the last-chance-for-change story, which is
always the same: **can this person be saved?** This is
the question Baldwin is asking in the story, but he's not
asking it about Sonny. In fact (such is the heartlessness
of authors), for the question to really matter to us in
terms of the narrator, Sonny's own future must be very
cloudy. Whether he can do the one thing in the world
he's good at and not be drawn back into the addic-
tion that is rife within the jazz community, we cannot
know. Our doubts on his behalf add to the urgency of
the narrator's growth; anyone can love and understand
a reformed junkie, but one who may not be reformed,
who admits the perils are still there for him, offers real
difficulties. Now if we read the story through the filter

of daytime talk shows and social work classes, we not only miss the focus of the story, we misunderstand it at its most basic level. Sonny's trouble is interesting, of course, but it's merely the hook to draw us in; the real issues the story raises all concern the narrator/brother. If we see it as Sonny's story, the resolution will be profoundly dissatisfying. If we understand it as the brother's, it works beautifully.

And this is a fairly recent story. How much harder to understand the mind-set behind, say, *Moby-Dick. The Last of the Mohicans. The Iliad.* All that violence. A diet that is almost purely carnivorous. Blood sacrifices. Looting. Multiple gods. Concubines. Those readers who have been raised in a monotheistic culture (which is all of us, whatever our religious persuasion or lack thereof, who live within the Western tradition) might have a little trouble with the piety of the Greeks, whose chief implement of religious practice is the carving knife. Indeed, the very setup of the epic, in which Achilles throws a fit and withdraws from the war because his sex slave has been taken from him, does not engage our sympathies as it would have those of the ancient Greek audience. For that matter, his "redemption," in which he proves he's back on track by slaughtering every Trojan in sight, strikes us as distinctly barbaric. So what can this "great work" and its spirituality, sexual politics, code of machismo, and overwrought violence teach us? Plenty, if we're willing to read with the eyes of a Greek. A really, really old Greek. Achilles destroys the thing he holds most dear, his lifelong friend Patroclus, and dooms himself to an early death by allowing excessive pride to overrule his judgment. Even great men must learn to bend. Anger is unbecoming. One day our destiny will come for us, and even the gods can't stop it. There are lots of useful lessons in *The Iliad*, but while it may at times read like an episode of *The Jerry Springer Show*, we'll miss most of them if we read it through the lens of our own popular culture.

Now, about that danger I mentioned earlier. Too much acceptance of the author's viewpoint can lead to difficulties. Do we have to accept the values of a three-thousand-year-old blood culture as depicted in the Homeric epics? Absolutely not. I think we should frown on the wanton destruction of societies, on the enslavement of conquered peoples, on keeping concubines, on wholesale slaughter. At the same time, though, we need to understand that the Mycenaean Greeks did not. So if we would understand *The Iliad* (and it is worth understanding), we have to accept those values for those characters. Must we accept the novel that is full of racial hatred, that vilifies persons of African or Asian or Jewish ancestry? Of course not. Is *The Merchant of Venice* anti-Semitic? Probably. More or less so than its historical moment? Much less, I should think. Shylock, while hardly a glowing picture of the Jew, is at least given reasons for being as he is, is invested with a kind of humanity that many nonfiction tracts of the Elizabethan period do not credit Jews with having. Shakespeare does not blame him for the Crucifixion, nor does he recommend burning Jews at the stake (as was happening in the century of the play's composition in other parts of Europe). So accept the play or reject it? Do as you see fit. What I would suggest is that we see Shylock's villainy in the context of the difficult and complex situation Shakespeare creates for him, see if he makes sense as an individual and not merely as a type or representative of a hated group, see if the play works independently of whatever bigotry might lie behind it or if it requires that bigotry to function as art. For me, if it must rely on hatred in order to function, it has to go. I don't see *Merchant* working only or even primarily as a product of bigotry, and I will go on reading it, although there are many works by Shakespeare that I like better and return to more regularly. Each reader or viewer must decide this one for himself. The one thing I find unacceptable is to reject it, or any work, sight unseen.

Let's take, briefly, a more recent and more troubling example. The *Cantos* of Ezra Pound have some marvelous passages, but they also contain some very ugly views of Jewish culture and Jewish people. More to the point, they are the product of a man who was capable of being much more anti-Semitic than he is in the poems, as he proved in his wartime broadcasts on Italian radio. I sort of weaseled my way around the issue with Shakespeare, claiming that he was somewhat less bigoted than his time; I can make no such claim for Pound. Moreover, that he made such statements at precisely the time that millions of Jews were being put to death by the Nazis only compounds our sense of outrage toward him. Nor can we write it off as insanity, which is what the defense counsel did at his trial for treason (he was charged with broadcasting for the enemy). So what about the poetry? Well, you decide. I know Jewish readers who still read Pound and claim to gain something from the experience, others who refuse to have anything to do with him, and still others who read him but rant against him all the while. Nor does one have to be Jewish. I do still read Pound, some. I find much that is astonishing, beautiful, haunting, powerful. Very much worthwhile. I also find, with some regularity, myself asking, How could someone so talented be so blind, so arrogant, so bigoted? The answer is, I don't know. The more time I spend with him, the more I'm astonished by his capacity for folly. It's unfortunate that genius was harnessed to someone who may not have worn it well. I find the *Cantos*, for all its brilliance, a very flawed masterpiece; flawed for reasons other than the anti-Semitism, but certainly more flawed because of it. It remains one of the half dozen or so most important works in my field of specialization, however, so I can't turn my back on it even if I want to. I've been telling you earlier in this chapter that you generally want to adopt the worldview the work requests of its audience. Sometimes, though, as in the case of Pound and his *Cantos*, the work asks too much.

Now here is where I envy you. If you are a professor, you have to deal with some pretty unsavory characters and some questionable works. If you only want to read like one, you can walk away whenever you want to.

25

It's My Symbol and
I'll Cry If I Want To

So far we've been talking about figures that are fairly common and well-known. A lot of things in the world have more or less ready-made associations—or associations so long in use that they seem ready-made to us latecomers. Rivers? Change, flow, flood, or drought. Rocks? Stasis, resistance to change, permanence. When Yeats puts an imagined stone in his hypothetical river in "Easter 1916," he contrasts the flux of the river with the unyielding stone, and we all get it without having to think very deeply. So far, so good.

Now, what if it's not something seen around the house of literature every day? What if it's, oh, I don't know, a cow? Or a goat? Lots of sheep in pastoral poems, not so many goats. Let's go off the deep end here; how about a flea? You think I'm kidding, right?

John Donne went there long ago, getting a lot of mileage out of the tiny pest. I mentioned earlier that Donne was a lawyer and clergyman by trade—he was dean of St. Paul's Cathedral in London for the last decade of his life—but earlier he was a rake as well as a writer fond of sexy metaphors. It was the task of every literary rake to talk his romantic targets into giving him what he wanted in the cleverest fashion possible. Here's one of Donne's efforts:

> Mark but this flea, and mark in this,
> How little that which thou deniest me is;
> It suck'd me first, and now sucks thee,
> And in this flea our two bloods mingled be.
> Thou know'st that this cannot be said
> A sin, nor shame, nor loss of maidenhead;
> Yet this enjoys before it woo,
> And pamper'd swells with one blood made of two;
> And this, alas! is more than we would do.

This is just the first stanza of "The Flea," but, allowing for a thee and thou, we can make sense of it. The male speaker is asking his reluctant lover to consider that the flea has done what she won't let him do: it has mingled their two beings, in this case by taking blood from each of them. See, he says, our blood is already joined, so what's the big deal about having a roll in the hay? There's no shame in the flea, or in our having been bitten by it; why should there be shame in our having sex?

He goes on in this vein in the next two stanzas, first asking her not to kill the flea, since that would amount to killing, in a funny bit of illogic, all three of them, and speaking of the insect as "our marriage bed." We understand throughout that he is not entirely sincere, that the flea is an occasion for comic posing as well as sexual begging. In stanza three, she does kill the flea—not a happy sign for the imploring lover—and he suggests that there will be no more dishonor in her consenting to sex than there is in her having killed the flea. This kind of extended metaphor running through the poem as an organizing device is called a *conceit*, something at which Donne and his so-called metaphysical poet colleagues excelled. Often, as here, the device seems more important than the subject, the latter seeming to have been dreamt up in order to employ the former. The occasion, a lover's urgent request, may be amusing, but not nearly so much as using an annoying flea as the basis for such an argument.

So here's the payoff: how many times have you seen a strategy like this? Not the sexual request, the use of a flea (or, alternatively, a mosquito, tick, horsefly, or any other biting insect). Pretty much never, right? One of the things we've been talking about in this book is how we can build a sort of literary database of imagery and its uses: rain, check; shared meals, check; quests, check; and so on. What that database relies upon, naturally, is repetition. If enough writers use a given object or situation in enough works, we start to recognize and understand the range of possible meanings. They don't have to say, "Hey, pay attention! It's raining!" They can simply make it rain and we'll do the rest. The writers don't even have to think about it; it can rain because that's what the plot demands. We can figure things out from there.

The point is, we have, as writers, artists, and readers, a common pool of figurative data built up over centuries of use in a host of situations and for a multiplicity of purposes—a store of images, symbols, similes, and metaphors that we not only can access but do, almost automatically. We may not think our way through the implications of a flood in a movie, but we can feel its impact—apart from the surface fact of things getting washed away—at a level before conscious thought. This warehouse of implications, as it were, permits texts to mean more than one thing simultaneously.

Let's be clear, just so no one runs off the rails: these implications are invariably *secondary*. The *primary* meaning of the text is the story it is telling, the surface discussion (landscape description, action, argument, and so on). There comes a point in our literary development when we nearly all lose sight of that fact. If you want to trip up an advanced English class, ask them, "What's this story about?" They fall all over themselves coming up with "hidden" meanings, many of which may actually be correct. They just forget to say that it's about a bigot whose wife invites a blind man to dinner. Any fourth grader can do it, but eventually we lose the skill as we pursue what lies beneath, so it's worth exercising that muscle every so often. Think of it this way: if the novel is a complete disaster as a piece of storytelling, it can't be saved by all the symbols in the world. No, I did not just condemn *Moby-Dick*; it succeeds by rules of narrative that not many people can grasp (especially at seventeen or twenty, when most of us get fouled in its lines).

None of this diminishes the importance of those secondary meanings; they still matter. They are what provide texture and depth to a work; without them, the literary world would be a little flat. They instill resonance as we recognize something in a new work that we might have seen elsewhere or that deepens the meaning of the surface story. It's one thing, say, for a young woman to feel passionately toward her rescuer, quite another if the rescue was from drowning (as opposed to from a runaway carriage or a pack of wolves), since in almost drowning she has experienced something quite close to death. She has been, in a sense, reborn. That shared storehouse of *figuration*—that is, types of figurative representation such as symbols, metaphors, allegory, imagery—allows us, even encourages us, to discover possibilities in a text beyond the literal. We have spent a great deal of time discussing various items stored in that vault, from gardens to baptisms to journeys to weather and seasons to food to illness, but its contents are vastly greater than any book can possibly cover. Happily, once you understand the principle, you can uncover and grapple with individual instances as you go. After all, you've been doing it all your life without knowing, so the only difference is that you're moving ahead thoughtfully.

On the other hand, what about those figurative elements that are not part of the common share? I suggested that Donne's tiny bloodsucker was a private symbol. Here's another one from the same guy. In "A Valediction: Forbidding Mourning," he is bidding farewell to his beloved. In attempting to soften the blow he says, in effect, "Just think of it like this: you are the foot of a compass [think geometry, not geography], while I am the pencil point. No matter how far I must range out, we are always connected, so I cannot break free of you. You are the center of my existence even when we are far apart." Actually, he provides twin compasses, with each of the lovers being the center of the other's existence. I'm not sure that allows for a lot of movement, but we'll pass on that for now; after all, it's a great image. It's a lot of fun to debate in class whether he is sincere or just using a line to make a quick morning-after getaway (evidence in the poem runs in both directions), but for right now, that's beside the point. For our purposes, there's a problem: no map exists for this new territory. There just aren't a lot of poems that make use of mathematical devices. Oh, three hundred or so years later Louis MacNeice will refer to "slide snide rules" in his "Variation on Heraclitus," leaving the hapless instructor to explain to mystified students that in the old days (i.e., before calculators) the slide rule was something we used for math and physics calculations. There may also be a poem or two out there somewhere that allude to the abacus, although I've not seen them. But you just won't find a lot of references to protractors and compasses. So what to do with such a reference?

Figure it out.

I know, I know. That sounds really lame, but sometimes the truth does hobble. In a situation where we encounter purely private symbols, there are some things we can fall back on. Most important, there's context. Where in the poem does the image reside? (In this case, the final three stanzas, after he has discussed disappearances of a more permanent sort.) How does he use the image? What does he seem to mean by it? In other words, what are the words, read carefully, telling us? We also have another set of tools available: our own good sense and reading savvy. As we become expert readers through practice, we gain the ability to transfer knowledge from one area to another. True, before this poem we have no practice with compass imagery, but we do have experience with figures of distance and connectedness. We know how other forms of staying in touch work, from letters to telephone calls to messages by courier (although those often go badly). We understand lovers' oaths and all that goes with them. What we learn pretty quickly is that this is not the hardest image we'll ever have to deal with. We can do this.

Of course, some writers make it hard. I mentioned Yeats and a fairly public symbol earlier, but he is notorious for his capacity to employ very private images and symbols. One of his favorites involves a tower. And not just any tower, not the ivory tower of popular cliché, but a very specific example. His tower. Around

1915 or 1916 he bought a fifteenth- or sixteenth-century (dates on these matters are a little fuzzy) Anglo-Norman tower, a sort of bastion-minus-its-castle, although it was called Ballylee Castle. Using the Gaelic word for tower, he rechristened it Thoor Ballylee, a curious affectation given the poet's signature inability to master the old language. But then, Yeats was a funny guy. Once he acquires the tower from his great friend Lady Gregory, it quickly dominates his poetry. Sometimes it merely stands for being rooted in the soil of Co. Galway, which was a great desire of his. At others, it can be an emblem of imperfect art, as when he goes up to the roof and leans on a broken stone crenel. Frequently, it is most significantly itself, the place from which he can, in relative safety, watch the competing military forces move up and down the road during the Irish Civil War ("Meditations in Time of Civil War"). Or it is the building on which he intends to have a dedicatory poem inscribed ("To Be Carved on a Stone at Thoor Ballylee"). It is a retreat from the modern world, a refuge, a connection to an aristocratic past, an object of great solidity. It becomes the title of successive books, such as *The Tower* (1928) and *The Winding Stair* (1933), after its most notable interior feature. And then there are the gyres.

What do you mean—what are gyres?

Okay, so here's where private systems of symbols really kick in. Yeats has an entire visionary system that he articulates in *A Vision* (1925). This system has lots of moving parts, but key among them are the gyres—which he always pronounced with a hard *g*. His gyres are spinning conical things with the point of one resting (if spinning things rest) in the base of the other. Clear as mud, right? Imagine an hourglass. Now, split it at the narrowest point. If you can somehow cause those two halves to intersect with each other (easier with nonsolid objects) and cause them to spin in opposite directions, you've got it. The gyres embody opposing historical or philosophical or spiritual forces, so they're a little like Hegel's or Marx's dialectic, in which opposing forces clash together to create a new reality. Except that dialectics don't spin or whirl.

There is no end to the fun Yeats has with gyres, and once they pop up in his thinking—shortly after his marriage in 1917—they are everywhere, from the wheeling flights of birds taking off from water to whirlwinds to anything vaguely circular. But one of his favorites involves that winding stair inside a tower, something at once exotic and homey that he would have encountered every day in his summer residence. Like gyres, the tower and spiral stairway are inseparable; one is not much use without the other. One of the great beauties—and challenges—of reading Yeats is that you find symbols and metaphors that you will find nowhere else in all of literature. His system of figuration is private, idiosyncratic, even, as some claim, hermetic, sealed off, airless. You'll never get some parts of him on a first reading; it may require special information (I have studied *A Vision*, but that's a lot to ask of civilians). So it takes some work to get everything you want from some of his poetry.

And here's the thing: there's no road map. You can work with stock symbolism till the cows are back in the barn, and it won't help. These symbols are private. That doesn't mean no visitors allowed. I don't claim to offer a comprehensive examination of figuration in literature, but even if I did manage such a thing, in this instance you would still be on your own. If, instead of twenty-some chapters, this book had a hundred twenty-some, or two hundred twenty-some, it still wouldn't have a chapter on gyres. In order to warrant such a chapter, we would need at least two poets dealing in them. To date, there is only one. I suspect that statement will always be true. Singular systems don't get general discussions.

That, however, doesn't mean we can't decode his writing. We may not get it all, but we can do a good bit. When Yeats, for instance, in "The Wild Swans at

Coole" has his swans go wheeling up in "great broken rings," we have no trouble with the image itself, that of a great flock of huge, white birds rising in loose circles into the air. Does it matter if readers don't get the larger symbolic implications? Not really. There are layers and layers of possible meanings here, and we take what we can find, what we are prepared to deal with at the moment of our reading. Besides, in this case, the contrast between the aging, earthbound speaker and the always young, airborne birds is worth all the gyres that ever were. Or weren't.

So here's a strategy: **use what you know**. I have spent many years teaching twentieth-century writing— Joyce, Faulkner, Woolf, Eliot, Pound, Fowles, O'Brien (several of those), all the heavy hitters of innovative writing. You know, the scary ones. And without exception, those writers produce books that we must learn to read as we go. *Ulysses* isn't like, well, anything. It isn't *Dubliners* or *A Portrait of the Artist as a Young Man*, Joyce's two earlier works, nor is it much like works by other so-called stream-of-consciousness writers, whatever affinities it may have with them. The only thing that can really prepare you to read *Ulysses* is reading *Ulysses*. As you can tell, I'm a lot of help in class. Still, it's true; there are some narrative strategies in the novel that readers will never have seen before and, likely, will never see again. Oh, by the way, what you learn there will also not really prepare you for *Finnegans Wake*. That novelty is part of the excitement as well as the challenge of the book. There's so much that's just plain new. I don't know how you can't love that, although students routinely remind me that it's possible. The same can be said for *Mrs. Dalloway* or *The Waste Land* or *As I Lay Dying* or *The French Lieutenant's Woman* or even *The Great Gatsby*, if in slightly less gaudy ways. What I've learned from all these modern and postmodern works has led me to conclude that it is true of others as well: **every work teaches us how to read it as we go along**. The big lessons, for best results, occur early on. Context helps a lot in reading new or unfamiliar forms of literature. Page three helps with page four, which helps with pages eight and fifteen, and so on. Not every book presents the same level of challenge; the lessons in Dickens are somewhat more modest than those in Joyce (and have mainly to do with endurance). Even so, every page of a literary work is part of an education in reading.

The other thing, aside from immediate context, that helps us with the occasional rough patch is everything else we have read. And by "reading" here, I am taking a liberal view. You read novels and poems, of course. But you also "read" a play even if you see it in its proper setting, a theater, and not between the covers of a book. Well, then, do you also "read" a movie? I believe so, although some films may reward reading more than others. Hollywood has always produced a certain number of films that do not repay the application of brainwaves—think gross-out comedies; titles whose last name is a number, as in *Rambo 17½*; and some adaptations of comic books. But since I have invoked comic books, yes, you read those as well. And in reading all those forms of narrative and presentation, you prepare yourself for new works. In the present instance, in analyzing the more familiar and shared examples of symbolic representation, we gain practice in understanding figuration. From there, we can move forward to encounter new and stranger examples. Most of the time, we do this without thinking about it, but thinking about it might be useful. When I suggest to students that they use their past reading experiences, their response is on the order of, "We don't have any." Which, as we have just seen, is untrue. And here's what I say in reply: **You know more than you think you do**. No, you have not read everything. But you have probably read enough—enough novels, memoirs, poems, news stories, movies, television shows, plays, songs, enough everything when it's all added up. The real problem is that "inexperienced" readers tend to deny themselves credit for the experience they do have. Get over it! Focus on all that you do know, not all that you don't. And use it.

Not every private symbol is entirely idiosyncratic. Sometimes an image or scene is merely turned to innovative uses. Usually, if someone introduces a tight-rope or high wire into a work, our attention is turned entirely to matters of balance, to the void beneath the wire. Such a pattern is perfectly logical; the thrill and fascination of the performance lies not merely in the difficulty but also in the possibility of calamity. For persons of a certain age (mine, for instance), the most notable example would be Leon Russell's song "Tight Rope" (1972), in which the twin perils, the chasms on either side, are described variously as ice and fire, hate and hope, and life and death. But there's another way of viewing the wire. Especially the highest wire act ever performed. On a bright August morning in 1974, the French aerialist Philippe Petit walked a wire between the then-still-new twin towers of the World Trade Center. This was, of course, twenty-seven years before two jetliners commandeered by terrorists reduced the buildings to rubble, with terrible loss of life. Eight years after that atrocity, Colum McCann published his novel *Let the Great World Spin* (2009), in

which Petit's feat acts as the framing device that con-
nects stories of diverse New Yorkers on that summer's
day. A few of them have witnessed the walk, while
most have only heard about it second- or thirdhand,
as indeed most residents of the city would have. But
here's the thing: McCann does not use the wire as a
metaphor for hazard and disaster, although that pos-
sibility is always present both in Petit's performance
and in the lives—and deaths—of the characters in
the framed narrative. Rather, McCann points out the
other dimension of a tightrope, not its narrowness
but its length. To accomplish his stunt, Petit connects
the two towers by means of his cable. The novel fol-
lows this metaphor throughout, showing how lives are
joined together by the most unlikely and seemingly
flimsy of filaments. The brilliance of the novel grows
out of its insistence that the real star is not the walker
but the wire; everyone, including the narrator, gives
full due to the "crazy man," as most see him, walk-
ing between the buildings, but it is the braided cable
supporting him that constitutes the real magic. The
novel has been described as "kaleidoscopic" and "daz-
zling," and properly so. If those adjectives are apt, and
I believe they are, the dazzling part is McCann's find-
ing a conceit, a controlling metaphor, that enables him
to string together disparate lives from Bronx hookers

to a Manhattan district court judge to art poseurs to a ruined Irish monk to the owner of a Park Avenue penthouse—in other words, to portray a city that is itself dazzlingly kaleidoscopic.

The way McCann deploys his dominant figure is uncommon, possibly unique, yet it is by no means difficult to read or comprehend. The reason that this seeming paradox is true is that for the most part humans are very good at entering these "private" realms, at inferring meanings, at judging the implications of texts—in other words, we're good at reading. So when Samuel Beckett sticks characters in ash cans or Edward Albee plants them in a sandbox, or when Eugène Ionesco turns them into rhinoceroses, we may scratch our heads at first, given that we've never seen that situation, but with a little time and imagination, we'll figure it out. Even the weird stuff usually makes sense on some level. Maybe especially the weird stuff.

26

Is He Serious?
And Other Ironies

Now hear this: **irony trumps everything.**

Consider roads. Journey, quest, self-knowledge. But what if the road doesn't lead anywhere, or, rather, if the traveler chooses not to take the road. We know that roads (and oceans and rivers and paths) exist in literature only so that someone can travel. Chaucer says so, as do John Bunyan, Mark Twain, Herman Melville, Robert Frost, Jack Kerouac, Tom Robbins, *Easy Rider, Thelma and Louise.* If you show us a thoroughfare, you better put your hero on it. But then there's Samuel Beckett. Known as the poet of stasis, he puts one of his heroes, literally, in an ash can. The great actress Billie Whitelaw, who was in virtually every Beckett play that called for a woman, said his work repeatedly put her in the hospital, sometimes by demanding too much strenuous activity, but just as often by not letting her move at all. In his masterpiece *Waiting for Godot*, he creates two tramps, Vladimir and Estragon, and plants them beside a road they never take. Each day they return to the same spot, hoping the unseen Godot will show up, but he never does, they never take the road, and the road never brings anything interesting their way. In some places writing something like that will get you a fifteen-yard penalty for improper use of a symbol. Of course, we catch on pretty fast and soon understand that the road exists *for* Didi and Gogo to take, and that their inability to do so indicates a colossal failure to engage life. Without our ingrained expectations about roads, however, none of this works: our hapless duo become nothing more than two guys stranded in desolate country. But they're not merely in desolate country but in desolate country beside an avenue of escape they fail to take. And that makes all the difference.

Irony? Yes, on a variety of levels. First, the entire play exists in what the late literary theorist Northrop Frye calls the "ironic mode." That is, we watch characters who possess a lower degree of autonomy, self-determination, or free will than ourselves. Whereas normally in literary works we watch characters who are our equals or even superiors, in an ironic work we watch characters struggle futilely with forces we might be able to overcome. Second, the specific situation of the road offers another level of irony. Here are two men, Didi and Gogo, who wish to find possibilities for change or improvement, yet they can only understand the road they wait beside passively, in terms of what it brings to them. We in the audience can see the implication that eludes them (this is where our expectations concerning roads enter the equation), so much so that we may want to scream at them to walk up the road to a new life. But of course they never do.

Or take rain. Of course, we already know that it has nearly limitless cultural associations, but even those won't cover the literary possibilities once irony kicks in. If you read a scene in which new life was coming into being, the rain outside would almost inevitably lead you (based on your previous reading) to a process of association in which you thought, or felt (since this really works as much at the visceral as at the intellectual level): rain-life-birth-promise-restoration-fertility-continuity. What, you don't always run that cycle when rain and new life are on the table? If you begin to read like an English professor, you will. But then there's Hemingway. At the end of *A Farewell to Arms* his hero, Frederic Henry, having just experienced the death of his lover, Catherine Barkley, and her baby during childbirth, distraught, walks out into the rain. None of those expectations we just listed are going to prevail; in fact, quite the opposite. It might help to know Hemingway's background in World War I, during which the novel is set, or his earlier life experiences, or his psychology and worldview, or the difficulty of writing this passage (he rewrote the last page twenty-six times, he said) in order to make sense of this scene. Most of all, we need to know that it's ironic. Like most of his generation, Hemingway learned irony early, then met it firsthand in the war as he watched youth meet death on a daily basis. His book is ironic from its first words. Literally. His title is taken from a sixteenth-century poem by George Peele, "A Farewell," about soldiers rallying enthusiastically to the call to war, the first two words of which are "To arms!" By conjoining these two in one seamless phrase, Hemingway makes a title as nearly opposite Peele's rousing meaning as it's possible to get. That ironic stance pervades the novel right up to the end, where mother and child, rather than existing for each other, as experience has taught us to expect, slay each other, the infant strangled by the umbilical cord, the mother dead after a series of hemorrhages. Frederic Henry walks out into rain in a season that is still winter but comes on the heels of a false spring. There's nothing cleansing or rejuvenating about the whole thing. That's irony—take our expectations and upend them, make them work against us.

You can pretty much do this with anything. Spring comes and the wasteland doesn't even notice. Your heroine is murdered at dinner with the villain, during a toast in her honor no less. The Christ figure causes the destruction of others while he survives very nicely. Your character crashes his car into a billboard but is unhurt because his seat belt functions as designed. Then, before he can get it off, the billboard teeters, topples, and crushes him. Its message? Seat belts save lives.

Is the billboard the same as those other instances of irony?

Sure, why not? It's a sign that's used in a way other than the intended one. So are the others. What is a sign? It's something that signifies a message. The thing that's doing the *signifying,* call it the *signifier,* that's stable. The message, on the other hand, the thing being signified (and we'll call that the *signified*), that's up for grabs. The signifier, in other words, while being fairly stable itself, doesn't have to be used in the planned way. Its meaning can be deflected from the expected meaning.

Here's an instance. G. K. Chesterton, a mystery writer and contemporary of Arthur Conan Doyle, has a story, "The Arrow of Heaven" (1926), in which a man is killed by an arrow. Of the cause of death there is never a flicker of doubt. That's too bad, since it sets up an insoluble problem: no one could have shot him but God. The victim is in a high tower with higher windows, so there is no way for a straight shot except from heaven. Father Brown, Chesterton's little hero/detective/priest, studies the matter a while, listening to all the stories, including one intended to misdirect him about how those Indian swamis could throw a knife from an impossible distance and kill a man, so maybe they worked their magic in this case with an arrow. This story immediately reveals the solution: no divine bow, but a murderer in the room with the victim. If a knife, which is intended for close use, can be thrown, then an arrow can be used to stab. Everyone except Father Brown makes the error of assuming that the arrow can only mean one thing. Our expectations about the arrow, like those of the characters in the story, point us in one direction, but Chesterton deflects the meaning away from those expectations. Mysteries, like irony, make great use of deflection. The arrow itself is stable; arrows are arrows. The uses to which arrows can be put and the meanings we attach to them, however, are not so stable.

Well, the seat belt billboard is an arrow. So are the deadly dinner, the failed Christ figure, Hemingway's rain and Beckett's road. In each case, the sign carries with it a customary meaning, but that doesn't guarantee it will deliver that received meaning. The signifier is stable. The rain is neither ironic nor not ironic; it's simply rain. That simple rain, however, is placed in a context where its conventional associations are upended. The signified's meaning stands opposed to what we expect. Since one half of the sign is stable and the other is not, the sign itself becomes unstable. It may mean many things, but what it won't mean is the thing we came in expecting that it would. Still, that expected meaning keeps hanging around, and since we experience this phantom meaning as an echo at the same time as the newly created, dominant meaning, all sorts of reverberations can be set off. It's kind of like the way jazz improvisation works. Jazz musicians don't just launch into random sound; rather, the combo begins by laying out a melody which is the basis for everything that will follow. Then, when the trumpeter or the pianist cuts loose, running through the chorus two, three, fifteen times, each one a little different, we hear each of those improvisations, those changes, against our memory of the original melody. That memory is largely what makes the experience of the solo meaningful: this is where he started and now this is where he's taken us.

What irony chiefly involves, then, is a deflection from expectation. When Oscar Wilde has one character in *The Importance of Being Earnest* (1895) say of another, recently widowed, that "her hair has gone quite gold from grief," the statement works because our expectation is that stress turns people's hair white. Someone becoming blond in widowhood suggests something else entirely, that perhaps her grief has not been so all-consuming as the pronouncement suggests on the surface. Wilde is the master of comic irony in both verbal and dramatic modes, and he succeeds because he pays attention to expectations. Verbal irony forms the basis for what we mean when we say irony. In ancient Greek comedy, there was a character known as the *eiron* who seemed subservient, ignorant, weak, and he played off a pompous, arrogant, clueless figure called the *alazon*. Northrop Frye describes the *alazon* as the character who "doesn't know that he doesn't know," and that's just about perfect. What happens, as you can tell, is that the *eiron* spends most of his time verbally ridiculing, humiliating, undercutting, and generally getting the best of the *alazon*, who doesn't get it. But we do; irony works because the audience understands something that eludes one or more of the characters. By the time we get to Wilde, we can have verbal irony that needs no *alazon* but that uses an assumed innocence as the basis against which it plays.

The irony with which we're dealing in this discussion, though, is chiefly structural and dramatic rather than verbal. We know what *should* happen when we see a journey start, or when the novel cycles through the seasons and ends in spring, or when characters dine together. When what should happen doesn't, then we have Chesterton's arrow.

E. M. Forster only wrote a handful of books early in the twentieth century, but two of them, *A Passage to India* and *Howards End* (1910), are among the truly great novels. The latter deals with the class system and issues of individual worth. One of its important characters is a working-class man, Leonard Bast, who is determined to improve himself. He reads books approved for the purpose, such as John Ruskin on art and culture, he goes to lectures and concerts, always struggling to better himself. His efforts do lead him to meet people of the higher classes, the bourgeois Schlegel sisters and, through them, the aristocratic Wilcox family. We might expect this pattern to hold true and to lead him up and out of his wretched existence; instead he ends up finding greater wretchedness and death where he had hoped for his soul's ascent. Henry Wilcox advises him, through Helen Schlegel, to leave his banking position for a more secure firm, but the advice proves to be completely wrong, as his old bank continues to prosper while his new post is eliminated. Moreover, in his despair he has spent a night with Helen that has left her pregnant, and when Charles Wilcox attempts to exact retribution, Leonard dies of a heart attack. Irony, right? But there's more. We would normally see his love of books as something that is affirming of values, improving, and educational—all of which we know as positive virtues. As Leonard collapses, however, the last thing he sees are the books from the bookcase he has pulled over on himself. We sense the disjunction between what books ought to be and the function assigned to them here by Forster.

It goes on and on. In Virginia Woolf's *Mrs. Dalloway*, her damaged Great War veteran, Septimus Warren Smith, commits suicide because his enemies are coming to get him. His enemies? Two doctors. We customarily associate physicians with healing, but in this novel they are interfering and threatening figures. Characters in Iris Murdoch's *Unicorn* spend a great deal of time trying to identify one of their number as the title creature, which is associated in folk mythology with Christ. Yet their first choice, who also seems to be the princess held captive in the tower, turns out to be selfish, manipulative, and murderous, while the second candidate winds up drowning another character (named Peter, no less). Hardly the image of Christ one would expect in either case. In each of these novels, the dislocation between our expectations and the reality constitutes a dual awareness, a kind of double-hearing that is the hallmark of irony.

That dual awareness can be tricky to achieve at times. I can bring a discussion of *A Clockwork Orange* to silence by suggesting that we consider Alex, its protagonist, as a Christ figure.

Alex? The rapist and murderer Alex?

No doubt Anthony Burgess's protagonist has some high negatives. He is supremely violent, arrogant, elitist, and worst of all unrepentant. Moreover, his message is not one of love and universal brotherhood. If he's a Christ figure at all, it's not in any conventional sense.

But let's consider a few facts. He leads a small band of followers, one of whom betrays him. He is succeeded by a man named Pete (although this fact is troubling, since this Pete, unlike Peter, is also the betrayer). He is offered a bargain by the devil (he relinquishes his soul, in the form of spiritual autonomy, in exchange for the freedom awarded for undergoing aversion therapy). He wanders in the wilderness after his release from prison, then launches himself from a great height (one of the temptations Christ resists). He seems to be dead but then revivifies. Finally the story of his life carries a profound religious message.

None of these attributes looks right. They look instead like parodies of Christ's attributes. Or, rather, none of the attributes but that last one. This is very tricky business. No, Alex is not like Jesus. Nor is Burgess using Alex to denigrate or mock Jesus. It can look that way, however, if we approach the matter from the wrong angle or consider it carelessly.

It's a help, of course, to know that Burgess himself held deep Christian convictions, that issues of goodness and spiritual healing occupy a major place in his thought and work. More important, though, is the item I place at the end of my list, that the purpose of telling Alex's story is to convey a message of religious and spiritual profundity. The book is really Burgess's entry in the very old debate over the problem of evil, namely, why would a benevolent deity permit evil to exist in his creation? His argument runs like this: there is no goodness without free will. Without the ability to freely choose—or reject—the good, an individual possesses no control over his own soul, and without that control, there is no possibility of attaining grace. In the language of Christianity, a believer cannot be saved unless the choice to follow Christ is freely made, unless the option not to follow him genuinely exists. Compelled belief is no belief at all.

The Gospels offer us a positive model for their argument: Jesus is the embodiment of the behaviors Christian believers should embrace as well as the spiritual goal toward which they strive. *A Clockwork Orange*, on the other hand, provides a negative model. In other words, Burgess reminds us that for goodness to mean anything, not only must evil exist, but so must the option of choosing evil. Alex freely, and joyously, chooses evil (although in the final chapter he has begun to outgrow that choice). When his capacity to choose is taken away, evil is replaced not with goodness but with a hollow simulacrum of goodness. Because he still wants to choose evil, he is in no way reformed. In acquiring the desired behavior through the "Ludovico Technique," as the aversion therapy is called in the novel, society has not only failed to correct Alex but has committed a far worse crime against him by taking away his free will, which for Burgess is the hallmark of the human being.

In this regard, and only in this one, is Alex a modern version of Christ. Those other aspects are a bit of ironic window dressing the author embeds in his text as cues for how to understand Alex's story and the message he unwittingly conveys.

Nearly all writers employ irony sometimes, although the frequency of occurrence varies greatly. With some writers, particularly modern and postmodern writers, irony is a full-time business, so that as we read them more and more, we come to expect that they will inevitably thwart conventional expectations. Franz Kafka, Samuel Beckett, James Joyce, Vladimir Nabokov, Angela Carter, and T. Coraghessan Boyle are only a few of those twentieth-century masters of the ironic stance. If we were wise, we would never open a Boyle novel or short story expecting him to do the conventional thing. Some readers find relentless irony difficult to warm to, and some writers find that being ironic carries perils. Salman Rushdie's irony in *The Satanic Verses* did not register with certain Muslim clerics. So there's our second ironic precept: **irony doesn't work for everyone**. Because of the multivocal nature of irony—we hear those multiple voices simultaneously—readers who are inclined toward univocal utterances simply may not register that multiplicity.

For those who do, though, there are great compensations. Irony—sometimes comic, sometimes tragic, sometimes wry or perplexing—provides additional richness to the literary dish. And it certainly keeps us readers on our toes, inviting us, compelling us, to dig through layers of possible meaning and competing signification. We must remember: **irony trumps everything.** In other words, every chapter in this book goes out the window when irony comes in the door.

How do you know if it's irony?

Listen.

27

A Test Case

THE GARDEN PARTY
by Katherine Mansfield

And after all the weather was ideal. They could not have had a more perfect day for a garden-party if they had ordered it. Windless, warm, the sky without a cloud. Only the blue was veiled with a haze of light gold, as it is sometimes in early summer. The gardener had been up since dawn, mowing the lawns and sweeping them, until the grass and the dark flat rosettes where the daisy plants had been seemed to shine. As for the roses, you could not help feeling they understood that roses are the only flowers that impress people at garden-parties; the only flowers that everybody is certain of knowing. Hundreds, yes, literally hundreds, had come out in a single night; the green bushes bowed down as though they had been visited by archangels.

Breakfast was not yet over before the men came to put up the marquee.

"Where do you want the marquee put, mother?"

"My dear child, it's no use asking me. I'm determined to leave everything to you children this year. Forget I am your mother. Treat me as an honoured guest."

But Meg could not possibly go and supervise the men. She had washed her hair before breakfast, and she sat drinking her coffee in a green turban, with a dark wet curl stamped on each cheek. Jose, the butterfly, always came down in a silk petticoat and a kimono jacket.

"You'll have to go, Laura; you're the artistic one."

Away Laura flew, still holding her piece of bread-and-butter. It's so delicious to have an excuse for eating out of doors, and besides, she loved having to arrange things; she always felt she could do it so much better than anybody else.

Four men in their shirt-sleeves stood grouped together on the garden path. They carried staves covered with rolls of canvas, and they had big tool-bags slung on their backs. They looked impressive. Laura wished now that she had not got the bread-and-butter, but there was nowhere to put it, and she couldn't possibly throw it away. She blushed and tried to look severe and even a little bit short-sighted as she came up to them.

"Good morning," she said, copying her mother's voice. But that sounded so fearfully affected that she was ashamed, and stammered like a little girl, "Oh—er—have you come—is it about the marquee?"

"That's right, miss," said the tallest of the men, a lanky, freckled fellow, and he shifted his tool-bag, knocked back his straw hat and smiled down at her. "That's about it."

His smile was so easy, so friendly that Laura recovered. What nice eyes he had, small, but such a dark blue! And now she looked at the others, they were smiling too. "Cheer up, we won't bite," their smile seemed to say. How very nice workmen were! And what a beautiful morning! She mustn't mention the morning; she must be business-like. The marquee.

"Well, what about the lily-lawn? Would that do?"

And she pointed to the lily-lawn with the hand that didn't hold the bread-and-butter. They turned, they stared in the direction. A little fat chap thrust out his under-lip, and the tall fellow frowned.

"I don't fancy it," said he. "Not conspicuous enough. You see, with a thing like a marquee," and he turned to Laura in his easy way, "you want to put it somewhere where it'll give you a bang slap in the eye, if you follow me."

Laura's upbringing made her wonder for a moment whether it was quite respectful of a workman to talk to her of bangs slap in the eye. But she did quite follow him.

"A corner of the tennis-court," she suggested. "But the band's going to be in one corner."

"H'm, going to have a band, are you?" said another of the workmen. He was pale. He had a haggard look as his dark eyes scanned the tennis-court. What was he thinking?

"Only a very small band," said Laura gently. Perhaps he wouldn't mind so much if the band was quite small. But the tall fellow interrupted.

"Look here, miss, that's the place. Against those trees. Over there. That'll do fine."

Against the karakas. Then the karaka-trees would be hidden. And they were so lovely, with their broad, gleaming leaves, and their clusters of yellow fruit. They were like trees you imagined growing on a desert island, proud, solitary, lifting their leaves and fruits to the sun in a kind of silent splendour. Must they be hidden by a marquee?

They must. Already the men had shouldered their staves and were making for the place. Only the tall fellow was left. He bent down, pinched a sprig of lavender, put his thumb and forefinger to his nose and snuffed up the smell. When Laura saw that gesture she forgot all about the karakas in her wonder at him caring for things like that—caring for the smell of lavender. How many men that she knew would have done such a thing? Oh, how extraordinarily nice workmen were, she thought. Why couldn't she have workmen for her friends rather than the silly boys she danced with and who came to Sunday night supper? She would get on much better with men like these.

It's all the fault, she decided, as the tall fellow drew something on the back of an envelope, something that was to be looped up or left to hang, of these absurd class distinctions. Well, for her part, she didn't feel them. Not a bit, not an atom . . . And now there came the chock-chock of wooden hammers. Some one whistled, some one sang out,

"Are you right there, matey?" "Matey!" The friendliness of it, the—the—Just to prove how happy she was, just to show the tall fellow how at home she felt, and how she despised stupid conventions, Laura took a big bite of her bread-and-butter as she stared at the little drawing. She felt just like a work-girl.

"Laura, Laura, where are you? Telephone, Laura!" a voice cried from the house.

"Coming!" Away she skimmed, over the lawn, up the path, up the steps, across the veranda, and into the porch. In the hall her father and Laurie were brushing their hats ready to go to the office.

"I say, Laura," said Laurie very fast, "you might just give a squiz at my coat before this afternoon. See if it wants pressing."

"I will," said she. Suddenly she couldn't stop herself. She ran at Laurie and gave him a small, quick squeeze. "Oh, I do love parties, don't you?" gasped Laura.

"Ra-ther," said Laurie's warm, boyish voice, and he squeezed his sister too, and gave her a gentle push. "Dash off to the telephone, old girl."

The telephone. "Yes, yes; oh yes. Kitty? Good morning, dear. Come to lunch? Do, dear. Delighted of course. It will only be a very scratch meal—just the sandwich crusts and broken meringue-shells and what's left over. Yes, isn't it a perfect morning? Your white? Oh, I certainly should. One moment— hold the line. Mother's calling." And Laura sat back. "What, mother? Can't hear."

Mrs. Sheridan's voice floated down the stairs. "Tell her to wear that sweet hat she had on last Sunday."

"Mother says you're to wear that sweet hat you had on last Sunday. Good. One o'clock. Bye-bye."

Laura put back the receiver, flung her arms over her head, took a deep breath, stretched and let them fall. "Huh," she sighed, and the moment after the sigh she sat up quickly. She was still, listening. All the doors in the house seemed to be open. The house was alive with soft, quick steps and running voices. The green baize door that led to the kitchen regions swung open and shut with a muffled thud. And now there came a long, chuckling absurd sound. It was the heavy piano being moved on its stiff castors. But the air! If you stopped to notice, was the air always like this? Little faint winds were playing chase, in at the tops of the windows, out at the doors. And there were two tiny spots of sun, one on the inkpot, one on a silver photograph frame, playing too. Darling little spots. Especially the one on the inkpot lid. It was quite warm. A warm little silver star. She could have kissed it.

The front door bell pealed, and there sounded the rustle of Sadie's print skirt on the stairs. A man's voice murmured; Sadie answered, careless, "I'm sure I don't know. Wait. I'll ask Mrs. Sheridan."

"What is it, Sadie?" Laura came into the hall.

"It's the florist, Miss Laura."

It was, indeed. There, just inside the door, stood a wide, shallow tray full of pots of pink lilies. No other kind. Nothing but lilies—canna lilies, big pink flowers, wide open, radiant, almost frighteningly alive on bright crimson stems.

"O-oh, Sadie!" said Laura, and the sound was like a little moan. She crouched down as if to warm herself at that blaze of lilies; she felt they were in her fingers, on her lips, growing in her breast.

"It's some mistake," she said faintly. "Nobody ever ordered so many. Sadie, go and find mother."

But at that moment Mrs. Sheridan joined them.

"It's quite right," she said calmly. "Yes, I ordered them. Aren't they lovely?" She pressed Laura's arm. "I was passing the shop yesterday, and I saw them in the window. And I suddenly thought for once in my life I shall have enough canna lilies. The garden-party will be a good excuse."

"But I thought you said you didn't mean to interfere," said Laura. Sadie had gone. The florist's man was still outside at his van. She put her arm round her mother's neck and gently, very gently, she bit her mother's ear.

"My darling child, you wouldn't like a logical mother, would you? Don't do that. Here's the man."

He carried more lilies still, another whole tray.

"Bank them up, just inside the door, on both sides of the porch, please," said Mrs. Sheridan. "Don't you agree, Laura?"

"Oh, I do, mother."

In the drawing-room Meg, Jose and good little Hans had at last succeeded in moving the piano.

"Now, if we put this chesterfield against the wall and move everything out of the room except the chairs, don't you think?"

"Quite."

"Hans, move these tables into the smoking-room, and bring a sweeper to take these marks off the carpet and—one moment, Hans—" Jose loved giving orders to the servants, and they loved obeying her. She always made them feel they were taking part in some drama. "Tell mother and Miss Laura to come here at once."

"Very good, Miss Jose."

She turned to Meg. "I want to hear what the piano sounds like, just in case I'm asked to sing this afternoon. Let's try over 'This Life is Weary.' "

Pom! Ta-ta-ta Tee-ta! The piano burst out so passionately that Jose's face changed. She clasped her hands. She looked mournfully and enigmatically at her mother and Laura as they came in.

"This Life is Wee-ary,
A Tear—a Sigh.
A Love that Chan-ges,
This Life is Wee-ary,
A Tear—a Sigh.
A Love that Chan-ges,
And then . . . Good-bye!"

But at the word "Good-bye," and although the piano sounded more desperate than ever, her face broke into a brilliant, dreadfully unsympathetic smile.

"Aren't I in good voice, mummy?" she beamed.

"This Life is Wee-ary,
Hope comes to Die.
A Dream—a Wa-kening."

But now Sadie interrupted them. "What is it, Sadie?"

"If you please, m'm, cook says have you got the flags for the sandwiches?"

"The flags for the sandwiches, Sadie?" echoed Mrs. Sheridan dreamily. And the children knew by her face that she hadn't got them. "Let me see." And she said to Sadie firmly, "Tell cook I'll let her have them in ten minutes."

Sadie went.

"Now, Laura," said her mother quickly, "come with me into the smoking-room. I've got the names somewhere on the back of an envelope. You'll have to write them out for me. Meg, go upstairs this minute and take that wet thing off your head. Jose, run and finish dressing this instant. Do you hear me, children, or shall I have to tell your father when he comes home tonight? And—and, Jose, pacify cook if you do go into the kitchen, will you? I'm terrified of her this morning."

The envelope was found at last behind the dining-room clock, though how it had got there Mrs. Sheridan could not imagine.

"One of you children must have stolen it out of my bag, because I remember vividly—cream cheese and lemon-curd. Have you done that?"

"Yes."

"Egg and—" Mrs. Sheridan held the envelope away from her. "It looks like mice. It can't be mice, can it?"

"Olive, pet," said Laura, looking over her shoulder.

"Yes, of course, olive. What a horrible combination it sounds. Egg and olive."

They were finished at last, and Laura took them off to the kitchen. She found Jose there pacifying the cook, who did not look at all terrifying.

"I have never seen such exquisite sandwiches," said Jose's rapturous voice.

"How many kinds did you say there were, cook? Fifteen?"

"Fifteen, Miss Jose."

"Well, cook, I congratulate you."

Cook swept up crusts with the long sandwich knife, and smiled broadly.

"Godber's has come," announced Sadie, issuing out of the pantry. She had seen the man pass the window.

That meant the cream puffs had come. Godber's were famous for their cream puffs. Nobody ever thought of making them at home.

"Bring them in and put them on the table, my girl," ordered cook.

Sadie brought them in and went back to the door. Of course Laura and Jose were far too grown-up to really care about such things. All the same, they couldn't help agreeing that the puffs looked very attractive. Very. Cook began arranging them, shaking off the extra icing sugar.

"Don't they carry one back to all one's parties?" said Laura.

"I suppose they do," said practical Jose, who never liked to be carried back. "They look beautifully light and feathery, I must say."

"Have one each, my dears," said cook in her comfortable voice. "Yer ma won't know."

Oh, impossible. Fancy cream puffs so soon after breakfast. The very idea made one shudder. All the same, two minutes later Jose and Laura were licking their fingers with that absorbed inward look that only comes from whipped cream.

"Let's go into the garden, out by the back way," suggested Laura. "I want to see how the men are getting on with the marquee. They're such awfully nice men."

But the back door was blocked by cook, Sadie, Godber's man and Hans.

Something had happened.

"Tuk-tuk-tuk," clucked cook like an agitated hen. Sadie had her hand clapped to her cheek as though she had a toothache. Hans's face was screwed up in the effort to understand. Only Godber's man seemed to be enjoying himself; it was his story.

"What's the matter? What's happened?"

"There's been a horrible accident," said cook. "A man killed."

"A man killed! Where? How? When?"

But Godber's man wasn't going to have his story snatched from under his very nose.

"Know those little cottages just below here, miss?" Know them? Of course, she knew them. "Well, there's a young chap living there, name of Scott, a carter. His horse shied at a traction-engine, corner of Hawke Street this morning, and he was thrown out on the back of his head. Killed."

"Dead!" Laura stared at Godber's man.

"Dead when they picked him up," said Godber's man with relish. "They were taking the body home as I come up here." And he said to the cook, "He's left a wife and five little ones."

"Jose, come here." Laura caught hold of her sister's sleeve and dragged her through the kitchen to the other side of the green baize door. There she paused and leaned against it. "Jose!" she said, horrified, "however are we going to stop everything?"

"Stop everything, Laura!" cried Jose in astonishment. "What do you mean?"

"Stop the garden-party, of course." Why did Jose pretend?

But Jose was still more amazed. "Stop the garden-party? My dear Laura, don't be so absurd. Of course we can't do anything of the kind. Nobody expects us to. Don't be so extravagant."

"But we can't possibly have a garden-party with a man dead just outside the front gate."

That really was extravagant, for the little cottages were in a lane to themselves at the very bottom of a steep rise that led up to the house. A broad road ran between. True, they were far too near. They were the greatest possible eyesore, and they had no right to be in that neighbourhood at all. They were little mean dwellings painted a chocolate brown. In the garden patches there was nothing but cabbage stalks, sick hens and tomato cans. The very smoke coming out of their chimneys was poverty-stricken. Little rags and shreds of smoke, so unlike the great silvery plumes that uncurled from the Sheridans' chimneys. Washerwomen lived in the lane and sweeps and a cobbler, and a man whose house-front was studded all over with minute bird-cages. Children swarmed. When the Sheridans were little they were forbidden to set foot there because of the revolting language and of what they might catch. But since they were grown up, Laura and Laurie on their prowls sometimes walked through. It was disgusting and sordid. They came out with a shudder. But still one must go everywhere; one must see everything. So through they went.

"And just think of what the band would sound like to that poor woman," said Laura.

"Oh, Laura!" Jose began to be seriously annoyed. "If you're going to stop a band playing every time some one has an accident, you'll lead a very strenuous life. I'm every bit as sorry about it as you. I feel just as sympathetic." Her eyes hardened. She looked at her sister just as she used to when they were little and fighting together. "You won't bring a drunken workman back to life by being sentimental," she said softly.

"Drunk! Who said he was drunk?" Laura turned furiously on Jose. She said, just as they had used to say on those occasions, "I'm going straight up to tell mother."

"Do, dear," cooed Jose.

"Mother, can I come into your room?" Laura turned the big glass door-knob.

"Of course, child. Why, what's the matter? What's given you such a colour?" And Mrs. Sheridan turned round from her dressing-table. She was trying on a new hat.

"Mother, a man's been killed," began Laura.

"Not in the garden?" interrupted her mother.

"No, no!"

"Oh, what a fright you gave me!" Mrs. Sheridan sighed with relief, and took off the big hat and held it on her knees.

"But listen, mother," said Laura. Breathless, half-choking, she told the dreadful story. "Of course, we can't have our party, can we?" she pleaded.

"The band and everybody arriving. They'd hear us, mother; they're nearly neighbours!"

To Laura's astonishment her mother behaved just like Jose; it was harder to bear because she seemed amused. She refused to take Laura seriously.

"But, my dear child, use your common sense. It's only by accident we've heard of it. If some one had died there normally—and I can't understand how they keep alive in those poky little holes—we should still be having our party, shouldn't we?"

Laura had to say "yes" to that, but she felt it was all wrong. She sat down on her mother's sofa and pinched the cushion frill.

"Mother, isn't it terribly heartless of us?" she asked.

"Darling!" Mrs. Sheridan got up and came over to her, carrying the hat. Before Laura could stop her she had popped it on. "My child!" said her mother, "the hat is yours. It's made for you. It's much too young for me. I have never seen you look such a picture. Look at yourself!" And she held up her hand-mirror.

"But, mother," Laura began again. She couldn't look at herself; she turned aside.

This time Mrs. Sheridan lost patience just as Jose had done.

"You are being very absurd, Laura," she said coldly. "People like that don't expect sacrifices from us. And it's not very sympathetic to spoil everybody's enjoyment as you're doing now."

"I don't understand," said Laura, and she walked quickly out of the room into her own bed-room. There, quite by chance, the first thing she saw was this charming girl in the mirror, in her black hat trimmed with gold daisies, and a long black velvet ribbon. Never had she imagined she could look like that. Is mother right? she thought. And now she hoped her mother was right. Am I being extravagant? Perhaps it was extravagant. Just for a moment she had another glimpse of that poor woman and those little children, and the body being carried into the house. But it all seemed blurred, unreal, like a picture in the newspaper. I'll remember it again after the party's over, she decided. And somehow that seemed quite the best plan . . .

Lunch was over by half-past one. By half-past two they were all ready for the fray. The green-coated band had arrived and was established in a corner of the tennis-court.

"My dear!" trilled Kitty Maitland, "aren't they too like frogs for words? You ought to have arranged them round the pond with the conductor in the middle on a leaf."

Laurie arrived and hailed them on his way to dress. At the sight of him Laura remembered the accident again. She wanted to tell him. If Laurie agreed with the others, then it was bound to be all right. And she followed him into the hall.

"Laurie!"

"Hallo!" He was half-way upstairs, but when he turned round and saw Laura he suddenly puffed out his cheeks and goggled his eyes at her. "My word, Laura! You do look stunning," said Laurie. "What an absolutely topping hat!"

Laura said faintly "Is it?" and smiled up at Laurie, and didn't tell him after all.

Soon after that people began coming in streams. The band struck up; the hired waiters ran from the house to the marquee. Wherever you looked there were couples strolling, bending to the flowers, greeting, moving on over the lawn. They were like bright birds that had alighted in the Sheridans' garden for this one afternoon, on their way to— where? Ah, what happiness it is to be with people who all are happy, to press hands, press cheeks, smile into eyes.

"Darling Laura, how well you look!"

"What a becoming hat, child!"

"Laura, you look quite Spanish. I've never seen you look so striking."

And Laura, glowing, answered softly, "Have you had tea? Won't you have an ice? The passion-fruit ices really are rather special." She ran to her father and begged him. "Daddy darling, can't the band have something to drink?"

And the perfect afternoon slowly ripened, slowly faded, slowly its petals closed.

"Never a more delightful garden-party . . ." "The greatest success . . ." "Quite the most . . ."

Laura helped her mother with the good-byes. They stood side by side in the porch till it was all over.

"All over, all over, thank heaven," said Mrs. Sheridan. "Round up the others, Laura. Let's go and have some fresh coffee. I'm exhausted. Yes, it's been very successful. But oh, these parties, these parties! Why will you children insist on giving parties!" And they all of them sat down in the deserted marquee.

"Have a sandwich, daddy dear. I wrote the flag."

"Thanks." Mr. Sheridan took a bite and the sandwich was gone. He took another. "I suppose you didn't hear of a beastly accident that happened to-day?" he said.

"My dear," said Mrs. Sheridan, holding up her hand, "we did. It nearly ruined the party. Laura insisted we should put it off."

"Oh, mother!" Laura didn't want to be teased about it.

"It was a horrible affair all the same," said Mr. Sheridan. "The chap was married too. Lived just below in the lane, and leaves a wife and half a dozen kiddies, so they say."

An awkward little silence fell. Mrs. Sheridan fidgeted with her cup. Really, it was very tactless of father . . .

Suddenly she looked up. There on the table were all those sandwiches, cakes, puffs, all uneaten, all going to be wasted. She had one of her brilliant ideas.

"I know," she said. "Let's make up a basket. Let's send that poor creature some of this perfectly good food. At any rate, it will be the greatest treat for the children. Don't you agree? And she's sure to have neighbours calling in and so on. What a point to have it all ready prepared. Laura!" She jumped up. "Get me the big basket out of the stairs cupboard."

"But, mother, do you really think it's a good idea?" said Laura.

Again, how curious, she seemed to be different from them all. To take scraps from their party. Would the poor woman really like that?

"Of course! What's the matter with you to-day? An hour or two ago you were insisting on us being sympathetic, and now—"

Oh well! Laura ran for the basket. It was filled, it was heaped by her mother.

"Take it yourself, darling," said she. "Run down just as you are. No, wait, take the arum lilies too. People of that class are so impressed by arum lilies."

"The stems will ruin her lace frock," said practical Jose.

So they would. Just in time. "Only the basket, then. And, Laura!"—her mother followed her out of the marquee—"don't on any account—"

"What, mother?"

No, better not put such ideas into the child's head! "Nothing! Run along."

It was just growing dusky as Laura shut their garden gates. A big dog ran by like a shadow. The road gleamed white, and down below in the hollow the little cottages were in deep shade. How quiet it seemed after the afternoon. Here she was going down the hill to somewhere where a man lay dead, and she couldn't realize it. Why couldn't she? She stopped a minute. And it seemed to her that kisses, voices, tinkling spoons, laughter, the smell of crushed grass were somehow inside her. She had no room for anything else. How strange! She looked up at the pale sky, and all she thought was, "Yes, it was the most successful party."

Now the broad road was crossed. The lane began, smoky and dark. Women in shawls and men's tweed caps hurried by. Men hung over the palings; the children played in the doorways. A low hum came from the mean little cottages. In some of them there was a flicker of light, and a shadow, crab-like, moved across the window. Laura bent her head and hurried on. She wished now she had put on a coat. How her frock shone! And the big hat with the velvet streamer—if only it was another hat! Were the people looking at her? They must be. It was a mistake to have come; she knew all along it was a mistake. Should she go back even now?

No, too late. This was the house. It must be. A dark knot of people stood outside. Beside the gate an old, old woman with a crutch sat in a chair, watching. She had her feet on a newspaper. The voices stopped as Laura drew near. The group parted. It was as though she was expected, as though they had known she was coming here.

Laura was terribly nervous. Tossing the velvet ribbon over her shoulder, she said to a woman standing by, "Is this Mrs. Scott's house?" and the woman, smiling queerly, said, "It is, my lass."

Oh, to be away from this! She actually said, "Help me, God," as she walked up the tiny path and knocked. To be away from those staring eyes, or to be covered up in anything, one of those women's shawls even. I'll just leave the basket and go, she decided. I shan't even wait for it to be emptied.

Then the door opened. A little woman in black showed in the gloom.

Laura said, "Are you Mrs. Scott?" But to her horror the woman answered, "Walk in please, miss," and she was shut in the passage.

"No," said Laura, "I don't want to come in. I only want to leave this basket. Mother sent—"

The little woman in the gloomy passage seemed not to have heard her. "Step this way, please, miss," she said in an oily voice, and Laura followed her.

She found herself in a wretched little low kitchen, lighted by a smoky lamp. There was a woman sitting before the fire.

"Em," said the little creature who had let her in. "Em! It's a young lady." She turned to Laura. She said meaningly, "I'm 'er sister, miss. You'll excuse 'er, won't you?"

"Oh, but of course!" said Laura. "Please, please don't disturb her. I—I only want to leave—"

But at that moment the woman at the fire turned round. Her face, puffed up, red, with swollen eyes and swollen lips, looked terrible. She seemed as though she couldn't understand why Laura was there. What did it mean? Why was this stranger standing in the kitchen with a basket? What was it all about? And the poor face puckered up again.

"All right, my dear," said the other. "I'll thenk the young lady."

And again she began, "You'll excuse her, miss, I'm sure," and her face, swollen too, tried an oily smile.

Laura only wanted to get out, to get away. She was back in the passage. The door opened. She walked straight through into the bedroom, where the dead man was lying.

"You'd like a look at 'im, wouldn't you?" said Em's sister, and she brushed past Laura over to the bed. "Don't be afraid, my lass,"—and now her voice sounded fond and sly, and fondly she drew down the sheet—" 'e looks a picture. There's nothing to show. Come along, my dear."

Laura came.

There lay a young man, fast asleep—sleeping so soundly, so deeply, that he was far, far away from them both. Oh, so remote, so peaceful. He was dreaming. Never wake him up again. His head was sunk in the pillow, his eyes were closed; they were blind under the closed eyelids. He was given up to his dream. What did garden-parties and baskets and lace frocks matter to him? He was far from all those things. He was wonderful, beautiful. While they were laughing and while the band was play-ing, this marvel had come to the lane. Happy . . . happy . . . All is well, said that sleeping face. This is just as it should be. I am content.

But all the same you had to cry, and she couldn't go out of the room without saying something to him. Laura gave a loud childish sob.

"Forgive my hat," she said.

And this time she didn't wait for Em's sister. She found her way out of the door, down the path, past all those dark people. At the corner of the lane she met Laurie. He stepped out of the shadow. "Is that you, Laura?"

"Yes."

"Mother was getting anxious. Was it all right?"

"Yes, quite. Oh, Laurie!" She took his arm, she pressed up against him.

"I say, you're not crying, are you?" asked her brother.

Laura shook her head. She was.

Laurie put his arm round her shoulder. "Don't cry," he said in his warm, loving voice. "Was it awful?"

"No," sobbed Laura. "It was simply marvellous. But Laurie—" She stopped, she looked at her

brother. "Isn't life," she stammered, "isn't life—"
But what life was she couldn't explain. No matter.
He quite understood.

"Isn't it, darling?" said Laurie.

What a terrific story! If you have any aspirations to fiction writing, the perfection of this story has to inspire awe and envy. Before the questions, a bit of background. Katherine Mansfield was a writer who came from New Zealand, although she spent her adult years in England. She was married to John Middleton Murry, a writer and critic, was friends with D. H. and Frieda Lawrence (in fact, she was the model, at least in part, for Gudrun in his *Women in Love*), produced a sizable handful of very lovely and accomplished stories, and died young of tuberculosis. Despite her slim output, there are those who would rank her as one of the unquestioned masters of the short story form. The story printed here appeared in 1922, the year before she died. It is not autobiographical in any ways that matter for our purposes. So are you ready for those questions?

First question: what does the story signify?

What is Mansfield saying in the story? What do you see it as meaning?

Second question: how does it signify?

> *What elements does Mansfield employ to cause the story to signify whatever it signifies? What elements, in other words, cause it to mean the things you take it to mean?*

Okay, here are the ground rules:

1) Read carefully

2) Use any interpretive strategies you've picked up from this book or elsewhere

3) Employ no outside sources about the story

4) No peeking at the rest of this chapter

5) Write down your results, so there's no fudging. Neatness doesn't count, nor spelling, just observations. Give the story careful thought and record your results, then bring them back here and we'll compare notes.

Take as long as you like.

Oh, you're back. That didn't take too long. Not too arduous, I hope? What I've done in the meantime is hand it out to a few college students of my acquaintance, some of them veterans of my classes, some of them close relatives who owe me a favor. I'll give you three different versions and you can see if they sound familiar. The first, a college freshman, said, "I know that story. We read it junior year. It's the one about a rich family that lives up on a hill and has no clue about the working class that's trapped down in the valley." This is pretty much what all my respondents noticed. So far, so good. The beauty of this story is that everybody gets it. You feel what's important in it, see the tensions of family and class.

The second, a history major who has taken several of my courses, expanded on that initial assessment a bit:

> To have the party or not, that is the question. An element of indifference is the ultimate overtone. These things happen, how could we not celebrate? For our main character, her guilt is heightened by the fact that these mourners live down the hill. It is brought to extremes when at the end of the party it is suggested that in an act of goodwill and charity, those below should be given the leftovers. What does this signify? The indifference of the dominant class of people to the suffering of others. Our main character is somewhere in between, caught between

what is expected of her and how she feels. She faces
it. She takes the food, the waste of the party, to the
widow in mourning, she faces the horrible reality
of humanity. Afterward, she seeks the comfort of
the only person who could possibly understand the
situation, her brother, and finds no answers because
there are no answers, just shared perceptions of
reality.

That's pretty good. A number of themes are beginning to emerge. Both of these first two readings have picked up what is most central to the story, namely the growing awareness of the main character to class differentiation and snobbery. Consider the third response. The writer, Diane, is a recent graduate who took several classes from me in both literature and creative writing. Here's what she said:

What does the story signify?

Mansfield's "The Garden Party" shows the clash
between the social classes. More specifically, it
shows how people insulate themselves from what
lies outside their own narrow view of the world—
how to put up blinders (be they with velvet rib-
bons), if you will.

How does it signify?

Birds and Flight

Mansfield uses the metaphor of birds and flight as a strategy to show how the Sheridans insulate themselves from the lower classes. Jose is a "butterfly." Mrs. Sheridan's voice "floats" and Laura must "skim over the lawn, up the path, up the steps" to reach her. They are all perched high on an aerie up a "steep rise" from the cottages below. But Laura is a fledgling. Her mother steps back and encourages her to flit around in her preparations for the party, but Laura's wings aren't quite experienced enough—she "flung her arms over her head, took a deep breath, stretched and let them fall," then sighed, so that even a workman "smiled down at her." From her vantage on the ground, Laura still has a foot in their lower-class world. They are her "neighbors." She has not yet separated herself from them. Remote sympathy is fine, but intimate empathy directly conflicts with the Sheridans' manner of living. If Laura is to rise to the level of her family and class, then she is going to need instruction.

Like her siblings before her, she learns from her mother. Mrs. Sheridan teaches Laura how to put on a garden party, but more to the point, she teaches the strategy to see the world from a loftier—though somewhat myopic—perspective. Like a mother bird teaching her young to fly, Mrs. Sheridan encourages Laura to go so far on her own until it becomes clear that her inexperience requires intervention. When Laura pleads with her mother to cancel the party because of the carter's death, Mrs. Sheridan diverts her with a gift of a new hat. Though Laura is reluctant to abandon her base instincts, she does manage a compromise: "I'll remember it again after the party's over." She chooses to put a little space between her life on the hill and the outside world.

Laura sees her peers, her fellow partygoers, as "birds that had alighted in the Sheridans' garden for this one afternoon, on their way to—where?" The answer is left vague. There is a danger below at the cottages of the lower-classes; when the Sheridan children were young they "were forbidden to set foot there." A man down there has a "housefront . . . studded all over with minute bird-cages." Those cages represent a threat to the way of life of the high-flying birds of the social elite. As long as they remain aloft, they evade the danger.

But it is now time for Laura to try her wings. Mrs. Sheridan pushes her from the nest. She tells her to go down to the cottages to give the widow a sympathy basket of their leftovers. Laura must confront her conflict between the worldview that nags at her and the more slivered view of her advantaged upbringing. She faces her conscience. She goes down from the safety of her home, crosses the "broad road" to the cottages, and becomes caged in the house of the dead man. She becomes self-conscious of her appearance, shiny and streaming, something apart from the people who live here. She sees herself through the eyes of the young widow and is confused that the woman does not know why Laura has come. She begins to recognize that her world does not belong here, and the realization frightens her. She wants to flee, but she must ultimately view the dead man. It is while looking at him that she chooses to see, instead of the reality of the hardship the man's death leaves to his family, an affirmation of her own lifestyle. She reasons that his death has nothing at all to do with "garden-parties and baskets and lace frocks," and she is thereby lifted from moral obligation. The revelation is "marvelous." If Laura cannot explain what life is to her brother, "Isn't life . . . isn't life—" it is because as Mansfield writes, it is of "no matter." Laura has learned to look at it from a loftier perspective. She needn't pretend to look short-sighted anymore.

Wow. I'd like to say I taught her everything she knows, but that would be a lie. She never got those insights from me. In fact, that's not the primary direction my reading tends, but if it were, I don't believe I could improve upon it. It's neat, carefully observant, fully realized, elegantly expressed, if obviously the product of a much more intense study of the text than I had asked you to undertake. In fact, as a group, the student observations I solicited were on the money. If your response was like any of them, give yourself an A.

If we express the act of reading in scientific or religious terms (since I'm not sure if this will fall into the realm of physics or metaphysics), all these student readings represent, with varying degrees of specificity and depth, almost clinical analysis of the observable *phenomena* of the story. This is as it should be. Readers need to deal with the obvious—and not so obvious—material of the story before going anywhere else. The most disastrous readings are those that are wildly inventive and largely independent of the story's factual content, those that go riffing off on a word out of context or a supposed image that is in truth not at all the image presented in the text. What I want to do, on the other hand, is consider the *noumenal* level of the story, its spiritual or essential level of being. If you don't think such a thing is possible, neither does my spell-checker, but here we go. This is an exercise in feeling my way into the text.

I'll be honest here. I'm about to cheat. I asked you to tell me what the story signifies first, but for my own response, I'm going to hold that for last. It's more dramatic that way.

Way back I mentioned that Joyce's *Ulysses* makes heavy use of Homer's tale of long-suffering Odysseus wending his way home from Troy. You may recall that I also mentioned that, except for the title, there are almost no textual cues to suggest that these Homeric parallels are at work in the novel. That's a pretty big level of signification to hang on one word, even a very prominent one. Well, if you can do that with the title of an immense novel, why not with a little story? "The Garden Party." Now, all the student respondents worked with it, too, chiefly with its last word. Me, I like the middle one. I like looking at gardens and thinking about them. For years I've lived next to one of the great agricultural universities, and its campus is a giant garden filled with a number of spectacular smaller gardens. Every one of those gardens, and every garden that's ever been, is on some level an imperfect copy of another garden, the paradise in which our first parents lived. So when I see a garden in a story or poem, the first thing I do is to see how well it fits that Edenic template, and I must admit that in Mansfield's story, the fit is also imperfect. That's okay, though, because the story from Genesis of Adam and Eve is only one version, and on the level of myth, it has many cousins. For now I think I'll reserve judgment for a little bit about what sort of garden this particular one might turn out to be.

What I notice first in the text is that word "ideal"; how many times have you described *your* weather as ideal? They couldn't have had a more "perfect" day. Those two words may just be hyperbole, but coming in the first two sentences of the story, they feel suggestive. The sky is without a cloud (just so we can't but expect some sort of cloud is coming), and the gardener has been at work since dawn. Later, this perfect afternoon will "ripen" and then "slowly fade," as a fruit or flower would. By then we will have seen that flowers permeate this story, as befits a garden party. Even the places emptied of daisies are "rosettes." And the real roses themselves have bloomed "in the hundreds" overnight, as if by magic or, since Mansfield mentions a visitation by archangels, by divinity. This first paragraph is

bracketed by the ideal and archangels—not a particu-
larly human environment, is it?

When I see an unreal, idealized setting such as this,
I generally want to know who's in charge. No mystery
here: everyone defers to Mrs. Sheridan. Whose garden
is it? Not the gardener's; he's just a servant doing the
bidding of the mistress. And what a garden, with its
hundreds of roses, lily lawn, karaka trees with broad
leaves and bunches of yellow fruit, lavender, plus
trays and trays and trays of canna lilies, of which,
Mrs. Sheridan believes, one cannot have too many.
This excess of canna lilies she describes as "enough"
for once in her life. Even the guests become part of
her garden realm, seeming to be "bright birds" as
they stroll the lawn and stoop to admire the flow-
ers, while her hat, which she passes on to Laura, has
"gold daisies." Clearly she is the queen or goddess of
this garden world. Food is the other major element of
her realm. She is responsible for food for the party,
sandwiches (fifteen different kinds including cream-
cheese-and-lemon-curd and egg-and-olive) and cream
puffs and passion fruit ices (so we know it is New
Zealand and not Newcastle). The final component is
children, of which she has four. So a queen oversee-
ing her realm of living plants, food, and progeny. Mrs.
Sheridan begins to sound suspiciously like a fertility

goddess. Since, however, there are lots of kinds of fertility goddesses, we need more information.

I'm not done with that hat. It's a black hat with black velvet ribbon and gold daisies, equally incongruous at the party and at the later visitation, although I'm less impressed by what it is than by whose it is. Mrs. Sheridan has purchased it, but she insists that Laura take it, declaring it "much too young" for herself. Although Laura resists, she does accept the hat and is later captivated by her own "charming" image in the mirror. No doubt she does look charming, but part of that is transferral. When a younger character takes on an older character's talisman, she also assumes some of the elder's power. This is true whether it's a father's coat, a mentor's sword, a teacher's pen, or a mother's hat. Because the hat has come from Mrs. Sheridan, Laura instantly becomes more closely associated than any of her siblings with her mother. This identification is furthered first by Laura's standing beside her mother to help with the good-byes and then by the contents of her charity basket: leftover food from the party and, but for the destruction they would have wrought on her lace frock, arum lilies. This growing identification between Mrs. Sheridan and Laura is significant on a couple of levels, and we'll return to that presently.

First, though, let's look at Laura's trip. The perfect afternoon on the high promontory is ending and "growing dusky as Laura shut[s] their garden gates." From here on her trip grows progressively darker. The cottages down in the hollow are in "deep shade," the lane "smoky and dark." Some of the cottages show a flicker of light, just enough to project shadows on the windows. She wishes she had put on a coat, since her bright frock shines amid the dismal surroundings. Inside the dead man's house itself, she goes down a "gloomy passage" to a kitchen "lighted by a smoky lamp." When her visit ends, she makes her way past "all those dark people" to a spot where her brother, Laurie, "steps out of the shadow."

There are a couple of other odd features here. For one thing, on her way to the lane, Laura is gratuitously accosted by a large dog "running by like a shadow." Upon getting to the bottom, she crosses the "broad road" to go into the dismal lane. Once in the lane, there's an old, old woman with a crutch sitting with her feet on newspaper. On her way in and out Laura passes individuals and small knots of shadowy figures, but they don't speak to her, and the one by the old woman (she alone speaks) parts to make way for her. When the old woman says the house is indeed that of the dead man, she "smiles queerly." Although Laura hasn't wanted to see the dead man, when the sheets are folded back, she finds him "wonderful, beautiful," echoing her admiration in the morning for the workman who stoops to pick and smell the lavender. Laurie, it turns out, has come to wait at the end of the lane—almost as if he can't enter—because "Mother was getting quite anxious."

What just happened here?

For one thing, as my student respondents note, Laura has seen how the other half lives—and dies. One major point of the story is unquestionably the confrontation she has with the lower class and the challenge that meeting throws at her easy class assumptions and prejudices. And then there is the story of a young girl growing up, part of which involves seeing her first dead man. But I think something else is going on here.

I think Laura has just gone to hell. Hades, actually, the classical underworld, the realm of the dead. Not only that, she hasn't gone as Laura Sheridan, but as Persephone. I know what you're thinking: *now he's lost his mind.* It wouldn't be the first time and probably not the last.

Persephone's mother is Demeter, the goddess of agriculture, fertility, and marriage. Agriculture, fertility, marriage. Food, flowers, children. Does that sound like anyone we know? Remember: the guests admiring the flowers at Mrs. Sheridan's garden party go about in couples, as if she has in some way been responsible for their pairing off, so marriage is in there. Okay, the long version is in Chapter 19, but here's the lightning-round version: fertility-goddess mother, beautiful daughter, kidnap and seduction by god of underworld, permanent winter, pomegranate-seed monkey business, six-month growing season, happy parties all round. What we get here, of course, is the myth explaining the seasons and agricultural fertility, and what sort of culture would it be that didn't have a myth to cover that? Highly remiss, in my book.

But that's not the only thing this myth covers. There's the business of the young woman arriving at adulthood, and this constitutes a huge step, since it involves facing and comprehending death. The myth involves the tasting of the fruit, as with Eve, and the stories share the initiation into adult knowledge. With Eve, too, the knowledge gained is of our mortality, and while that's not quite the point of the Persephone story, it's sort of unavoidable when she marries the CEO of the land of the dead.

So how does that make Laura into Persephone, you ask? First, there's her mother as Demeter. That one is, as I suggested, pretty obvious, once the flowers and food and children and couples are considered.

Moreover, we should recall that they live on this Olympian height, towering geographically and in class terms over the ordinary mortals in the hollow below. In this divine world the summer's day is perfect, ideal, as the world was before the loss of her daughter plunged Demeter into mourning and outrage. Then there is the trip down the hill and into a self-contained world full of shadows and smoke and darkness. She crosses the broad road as if it were the River Styx, which one has to cross to enter Hades. No entry is possible without two things: one must pass by Cerberus, the three-headed dog who stands guard, and one must have the admission ticket (Aeneas's Golden Bough). Oh, and a guide wouldn't hurt. Laura has her confrontation with the dog just outside her garden gate, and her Golden Bough turns out to be the gold daisies on her hat. As for guides (and no traveler to the underworld should be without one), Dante in the *Divine Comedy* (1321 A.D.) has the Roman poet Virgil; in Virgil's epic, *The Aeneid* (19 B.C.), Aeneas has the Cumaean Sibyl as his guide. Laura's Sibyl is that very old woman with the queer smile: her manner is no stranger than that of the Cumaean version, and the newspaper under her feet suggests the oracles written on leaves in the Sibyl's cave, where, when the visitor entered, winds whipped the leaves around, scrambling the messages. Aeneas is told to only accept the message from her own lips. As for the knot of unspeaking people who make way for Laura, every visitor to the lower world finds that the shadows pay him or her very little mind, the living having nothing to offer those whose living is done. Admittedly, these elements of the trip to Hades are not native to the Persephone myth, but they have become part and parcel of our understanding of such a trip. Her admiration for the deceased man's form, her identification with the grieving wife, and her audible sob all suggest a symbolic marriage. That world is dangerous, though; her mother has started to warn her before she sets out, as Demeter warns her daughter against eating anything in some versions of the original. Moreover, Mrs. Sheridan sends Laurie, a latter-day Hermes, to escort Laura back from this world of the dead.

Okay, so *why* all this business from three or four thousand years ago? That's what you're wondering, right? There are a couple of reasons, it seems to me, or perhaps a couple of major ones out of many possibilities. Remember, as many commentators have said about the Persephone myth, it encompasses the youthful female experience, the archetypal acquisition of knowledge of sexuality and of death. Our entry into adulthood, the myth suggests, depends on our understanding of our sexual natures and of our mortality.

These modes of knowledge are part of Laura's day in the story. She admires the workmen, comparing them favorably to the young men who come to Sunday supper, presumably as prospective beaux for one or another of the sisters, and later she finds the dead man beautiful—a response encompassing both sex and death. Her inability at the very end of the story to articulate what life is—as caught in the repeated fragment of speech, "Isn't life"—suggests an involvement with death so strong that she cannot at this moment formulate any statement about life. This pattern of entry into adult life, Mansfield intimates, has been a recognizable part of our culture for thousands of years; of course it has always been there, but the myth embodying the archetype has continued unbroken through Western culture since the very early Greeks. In tapping into this ancient tale of initiation, she invests the story of Laura's initiation with the accumulated power of the prevailing myth. The second reason is perhaps less exalted. When Persephone returns from the underworld, she has in a sense become her mother; in fact, some Greek rituals did not distinguish between mother and daughter. That may be a good thing if your mother is really Demeter, less so if she is Mrs. Sheridan. In wearing her mother's hat and carrying her basket, she also takes on her mother's views. Although

Laura struggles against the unconscious arrogance of her family throughout the story, she cannot finally break away from their Olympian attitudes toward the merely mortal who reside below the hill. That she is relieved to be rescued by Laurie, even though she has found the experience "marvelous," suggests that her efforts to become her own person have been only partially successful. We must surely recognize our own incomplete autonomy in hers, for how many of us can deny that there is a great deal of our parents, for good or ill, in us?

What if you don't see all this going on in the story, if you read it simply as a narrative of a young woman making an ill-advised trip on which she learns something about her world, if you don't see Persephone or Eve or any other mythic figures in the imagery? The modernist poet Ezra Pound said that a poem has to work first of all on the level of the reader for whom "a hawk is simply a hawk." The same goes for stories. An understanding of the story in terms of what literally happens, if the story is as good as this one, is a great starting point. From there, if you consider the pattern of images and allusions, you'll begin to see more going on. Your conclusions may not resemble mine or Diane's, but if you're observing carefully and meditating on the possibilities, you'll reach valid conclusions of

your own that will enrich and deepen your experien
of the story.

So what does the story signify, then? Many things.
It offers a critique of the class system, a story of ini-
tiation into the adult world of sex and death, an amus-
ing examination of family dynamics, and a touching
portrait of a child struggling to establish herself as an
independent entity in the face of nearly overwhelming
parental influence.

What else could we ask of a simple little story?

Postlude
Who's in Charge Here?

T he inquiry came in innocently, as the troubling
ones often do. A student. A question. A swirl of
issues demanding to be untangled: "Dear Professor
Foster, what about . . ."

As it happens, this is one I've been wrestling with my
whole life. Someone I'll call Steven sent me an e-mail
with a question many others have asked, directly or
indirectly. The short version is this: "How do I know
I'm right?" The full version is more vexing. I'll give
you a sort of composite between "Steven's" question
and those I've received before:

> I do have one question. Say I see something in the
> story that I think is a symbol (e.g. a blind man),
> and I share my thought with my friends and they

think the same. But in fact the writer created the character of the blind man simply because he happened to see a blind man walking down the street while he was writing.

My question is, should we really give so much credit to writers by interpreting their works in such a special and meaningful way, especially when he/she hasn't been proven to be a good writer yet?

This, of course, is the great and troubling question of literary analysis: how do we ever know that we're right, that we're accurate, that we're justified? Actually, there are several questions here, so let's deal with the main two first: can we ever be certain that our reading is correct, and if so, how?

In answer to that one, I would say that if you are reading carefully—not skipping pieces or inserting words that aren't really there—and you see something, you can assume it's really present. Take your example of the blind man. Does his presence, taken with other elements of the story, suggest something about seeing or the failure to see? Is someone failing to understand a truth right in front of him? Seeing that connection is not always easy or quick, and sometimes it doesn't exist. In that case, the blindness may not mean much at all. But consider this: introducing a blind character into the narrative commands the reader's attention, and the logistics of moving him around, if he is significant, are so difficult that you need a pretty good reason for deploying him. So assume that he means something until you can prove otherwise.

The second part of the inquiry is more intriguing: how can we be sure that we're doing what the author wants us to do? The wise guy in me wants to say, we can't, so get over it. If I could wave a wand and get rid of everyone's sense of obligation to the writer, I would do it in a heartbeat. A reader's only obligation, it seems to me, is to the text. We can't interrogate the writer as to intentions, so the only basis of authority must reside in the text itself. Trust the words and the words only. You can never find the motivation behind them. Even if the writer told you his intent, as a group they're notorious liars and not to be trusted. Plus, writers do things sometimes because they "just feel right"; that is, not every choice is made consciously, although that doesn't mean there's no reason behind it.

The real issue, though, is the one I framed in the title of this piece: who's in charge here? First a bit of context. In 1967, a little-known (in America, anyway) French thinker on matters literary and cultural named

Roland Barthes published a short essay in the equally little-known *Aspen* magazine called "The Death of the Author." The fallout from that bit of whimsy has been the opposite of little known. On one level, it became a cornerstone of the poststructuralist theoretical program; on another, it became a symbol of everything Anglo-Americans hate about continental, and especially Gallic, thought. In other words, it had something for everyone. I have taught this essay a number of times, always with the same results, and those are illustrative of our problems with Barthes and his ilk: "Oh, my gosh, he's saying that writers don't even matter. That can't be right! Writers have to be important. Otherwise, how can what we do as English majors, as English graduate students, matter?" And so on.

What first-time readers of the essay often miss, aside from the playfulness and archness of the piece, is that "author" does not equal "writer" perfectly. Yes, we generally use them interchangeably. Yes, that works just fine most of the time. Barthes, however, carefully avoids the French word for "writer," *écrivain*, sticking with *auteur*. This is, in fact, his point: the writer, he or she who writes, is just fine; the problem comes in with the author, the ultimate *authority* on the text. That personage, the Author (and he consistently capitalizes it so we don't miss the point) as Divine Creator, is dead.

Look at it another way. Most writers whose work you have read are dead. The others will be. At some point, all writers are beyond our reach. I'm not being morbid here, although I'm fully capable of it, but for once I merely state facts. All writers eventually reach the big Remainder Table in the sky. Simply part of the human condition. By definition, then, they reach a point where we cannot appeal to them for clues to meaning. Unlike their physical being, their written work survives, and it is that on which we must base our conclusions.

On that same topic, here's a question: when is a writer dead? Easy, you say? A mere medical question? I think not. Granted, the writer as biological organism can be said to have died on the date on his or her death certificate. But think about it from another angle: what about the writer as creator of her work? Is there any difference, really, between the day after publication of her novel and a hundred years hence? Have the words changed? Does her ability to control our response to the work change in that century? I think not.

Oh, he could be like Henry James and bring out his "New York Edition" of his work years later, possibly even introducing numerous changes and revisions to the party. In our (well, my) time, Louise Erdrich and John Fowles brought out revised versions of *Love Medicine* and *The Magus*, respectively, so it does happen. Some poets, and William Butler Yeats springs to mind, tinker mightily with poems from the journal to the book stage of development, and sometimes from the initial collection to the *Collected Poems*. But most writers write their work once and, for better or worse, leave it at that. Mostly better. Do it right the first time and be done with it. Said the guy writing a revised version of his book.

This argument also gets around Steven's other concern, about the "unproven" author. If we judge the text, the age or experience of the author does not matter. An example? Sure, why not? Maybe even two. In 1983, no one had heard of Louise Erdrich, including me, although she was only two years behind me at a college that isn't all that large. That's fair; she hadn't produced any novels yet. But then she did, and what a novel. *Love Medicine* won the 1984 National Book Critics Circle award for fiction. First novels are rarely best or even near-best novels (Hemingway and Harper Lee provide two of the few exceptions), but this one ranks right up there. Now, we can argue that because chapters had been appearing as stand-alone stories in literary journals and national magazines for four or five years prior to publication, Erdrich was not completely unknown or unread, but the point stands that this was a first novel. If we accept the premise that significance is only valid once a track record has been established, then we will miss a wonderful novel—until, at least, the writer "grows up" in terms of reputation. For my part, I would prefer to read the novel rather than the reputation.

Or try this. In the week I was writing this postlude in the summer of 2013, an interesting publishing revelation occurred. In April, a debut mystery novel was published in Britain to good reviews and near-zero sales. In mid-July, at approximately the moment when remaining copies were being rounded up for a bath in the acid vats, the *Sunday Times* newspaper outed the real writer, a first-timer in adult mysteries sure enough, but also maybe the most famous novelist in the world (although Stephen King might argue that one). Robert Galbraith, it turns out, was J. K. Rowling, who wanted to publish *The Cuckoo's Calling* anonymously just to see how it fared with critics when it wasn't under her name. Her previous novel, *The Casual Vacancy*, sold more than a million copies but had not been treated kindly by critics, so she had some motivation. In the weeks following the revelation of her authorship, the new novel shot to number one on Amazon's bestseller list, chiefly on the basis of e-book sales, all physical copies having been swept up instantly, while the publisher, Little, Brown, ordered hundreds of thousands of new copies to be printed. So here's my question: what's the fuss? From a marketing standpoint, I completely understand, but looked at as an aesthetic proposition, does it really matter? Is the book any better or worse as the work of Ms. Rowling than it was as the product of her retired military-intelligence alter ego? Ultimately, the book must stand or fall on the merits of the text, not the strength of the authorial brand. And to establish those merits, we need to read the book. We all find, all the time, that critics don't speak for us. Often, sales don't speak for us. Some of my worst reading experiences have involved books that "everyone" was reading and praising. Time and again, experience has shown that while I might be "just anyone," I'm definitely not "everyone." What I like, what I admire, what I dismiss, I can only find out by reading for myself.

The same is true of analysis or interpretation or whatever you want to call what we've been up to for the last few hundred pages. I can usually make a persuasive case for my reading of a novel or poem, but I can't make it your reading. Yes, I do know a good deal about literature and how to have fun with it, but I'm not you and you are not me. For that, you should be profoundly grateful. No one in the world can read *Life of Pi* or *Wuthering Heights* or *The Hunger Games* exactly the way you will—except you. Often, too often, I find students apologizing for the way they see a work: "It's only my opinion, but" or "I'm probably wrong, but" or some other iteration of this lame act of contrition. Stop apologizing! It doesn't help, and it sells the speaker short. Be intelligent, be bold, be assertive, be self-confident in your reading. It *is* your opinion (but not "just") and you might be wrong, although that's less likely than most students think. So here's my final piece of advice: **Own the books you read**. Also poems, stories, flash fiction, plays, memoirs, movies, creative nonfiction, and all the rest. I don't mean this literally, although as a person who makes a living through books, I'm not against the idea. What I really mean is that you need to take ownership of your reading. It's yours. It's special. It is exactly like nobody else's in the whole world. As much a part of you as your nose or your thumb. We all learn from each other when we read and discuss literature, and our readings change based on those discussions. I know mine do, in all sorts of ways. But that doesn't mean I abandon my own viewpoint, and neither should you.

Don't cede control of your opinions to critics, teach-
ers, famous writers, or know-it-all professors. Listen
to them, but read confidently and assertively, and don't
be ashamed or apologetic about your reading. You and
I both know you're capable and intelligent, so don't let
anyone tell you otherwise. Trust the text and trust your
instincts. You'll rarely go far wrong.

Envoi

There's a very old tradition in poetry of adding a little stanza, shorter than the rest, at the end of a long narrative poem or sometimes a book of poems. The function differed from poem to poem. Sometimes it was a very brief summation or conclusion. My favorite was the apology to the poem itself: "Well, little book, you're not that much but you're the best I could make you. Now you'll just have to make your way in the world as best you can. Fare thee well." This ritual sending-off was called the *envoi* (I told you that all the best terms are French—and the worst), meaning, more or less, to send off on a mission.

If I told you that I didn't owe my book an apology, we'd both know it was untrue, and every author wraps up a manuscript with some trepidation as to its future welfare. That trepidation, however, becomes pointless once the manuscript becomes a book, as the old writers understood, which is why they told the poor book that it was now an orphan, that whatever parental protections the writer could offer had ended. On the other hand, I figure my little enterprise can get along without me pretty well, so I'll spare it the send-off.

Instead I would address my *envoi* to the reader. You've really been very good about all this, very sporting. You've borne my guff and my wisecracks and my annoying mannerisms much better than I have any right to expect. A first-class audience, really. Now that it's time for us to part, I have a few thoughts with which to send you on your way.

First, a confession and a warning. If I have given the impression somehow—by reaching an end point, for instance—that I have exhausted the codes by which literature is written and understood, I must apologize. It simply isn't true. In fact, we've only scratched the surface here. It now strikes me as highly peculiar, for instance, that I could have brought you this far with no mention of fire. It's one of the original four elements, along with water, earth, and air, yet somehow it didn't come up in our discussion. There are dozens of other topics we could have addressed as easily and as profitably as the ones we did. In fact, my original conception was for somewhat fewer chapters, and a slightly different lineup. The chapters that wound up getting included reflect the noisiness and persistence of their topics: some ideas refused to be denied, crowding their way in and sometimes crowding out those that were less ill-mannered. Looking back over the text, it strikes me as highly idiosyncratic. To the extent that my colleagues would agree that this mode of reading is at least a strong part of what we do, they would no doubt squawk over my categories. Quite right, too. Every professor will have a unique set of emphases. I gather my thoughts into groupings that seem inevitable, but different groupings or formulations may seem inevitable to someone else.

What this book represents is not a database of all the cultural codes by which writers create and readers understand the products of that creation, but a template, a pattern, a grammar of sorts from which you can learn to look for those codes on your own. No one could include them all, and no reader would want to plow through the resulting encyclopedia. I'm pretty sure I could have made this book, with not too much effort, twice as long. I'm also pretty sure neither of us wants that.

Second, a felicitation. All those other codes? You don't need them. At least you don't need them all

spelled out. There comes a point in anyone's read-
ing where watching for pattern and symbol becomes
almost second nature, where words and images start
calling out for attention. Consider the way Diane
picked up on the birds in "The Garden Party." No one
taught her to go looking for birds per se in her read-
ing; rather, what happens is that, based on other read-
ing experiences in a variety of courses and contexts,
she learned to watch for distinctive features of a text,
for repetitions of a certain kind of object or activ-
ity for resonances. One mention of birds or flight is
an occurrence, two may be a coincidence, but three
constitutes a definite trend. And trends, as we know,
cry out for examination. You can figure out fire. Or
horses. Characters in stories have ridden horses—and
sometimes bemoaned their absence—for thousands of
years. What does it mean to be mounted on a steed,
as opposed to being on foot? Consider some examples:
Diomedes and Odysseus stealing the Thracian horses
in *The Iliad*, the Lone Ranger waving from astride
the rearing Silver, Richard III crying out for a horse,
Dennis Hopper and Peter Fonda roaring down the
road on their choppers in *Easy Rider*. Any three or
four examples will do. What do we understand about
horses and riding them or driving them—or not? See?
You can do it just fine.

Third, some suggestions. In the Appendix, I offer some ideas for further reading. There's nothing systematic or even particularly orderly about the suggestions. I'm certainly not weighing in on the culture wars, offering a prescribed reading list to make you . . . whatever. Mostly, these are works I've mentioned along the way, works I like and admire for a variety of reasons, works I think you might like as well. I hope you'll find them even better now than you would have a number of pages ago. My main suggestion, though, is to read things you like. You're not stuck with my list. Go to your bookstore or library and find novels, poems, plays, stories that engage your imagination and your intelligence. Read "Great Literature," by all means, but read good writing. Much of what I like best in my reading I've found by accident as I poked around bookshelves. And don't wait for writers to be dead to be read; the living ones can use the money. Your reading should be fun. We only call them literary *works*. Really, though, it's all a form of play. So play, Dear Reader, play.

And fare thee well.

Appendix
Reading List

I've tossed book and poem titles at you, sometimes at a dizzying pace. I remember that sense of disorientation from my very early undergraduate days (it took me years to figure out "Alain Robbe-Grillet" from the passing references one of my first professors was wont to make). The result can be intoxicating, in which case you go on to study more literature, or infuriating, in which case you blame the authors and works you never heard of for making you feel dumb. Never feel dumb. Not knowing who or what is ignorance, which is no sin; ignorance is simply the measure of what you haven't got to yet. I find more works and writers every day that I haven't got to, haven't even heard of.

What I offer here is a list of items mentioned throughout the book, plus some others I probably should have mentioned, or would have if I had more essays to write. In any event, what all these works have in common is that a reader can learn a lot from them. I have learned a lot from them. As with the rest of this book, there is very little order or method to them. You won't, if you read these, magically acquire *culture* or *education* or any of those scary abstractions; nor do I claim for them (in general) that they are better than works I have not chosen, that *The Iliad* is better than *Metamorphoses* or that Charles Dickens is better than George Eliot. In fact, I have strong opinions about literary merit, but that's not what we're about here. All I would claim for these works is that if you read them, you will become more learned. That's the deal. We're in the learning business. I am, and if you've read this far, so are you. Education is mostly about institutions and getting tickets stamped; learning is what we do for ourselves. When we're lucky, they go together. If I had to choose, I'd take learning.

Oh, there's another thing that will happen if you read the works on this list: you will have a good time, mostly. I promise. Hey, I can't guarantee that everyone will like everything or that my taste is your taste. What I can guarantee is that these works are entertaining. Classics aren't classic because they're old, they're classic because they're great stories or great poems, because they're beautiful or entertaining or exciting or funny or all of the above. And the newer works, the ones that aren't classics? They may grow to that status or they may not. But for now they're engaging, thought-provoking, maddening, fun. We speak, as I've said before, of literary *works*, but in fact literature is chiefly play. If you read novels and plays and stories and poems and you're not having fun, somebody is doing something wrong. If a novel seems like an ordeal, quit; you're not getting paid to read it, are you? And you surely won't get fired if you don't read it. So enjoy.

Primary Works

Julia Alvarez, *How the Garcia Girls Lost Their Accents* (1991), *In the Time of the Butterflies* (1994), *Yo* (1997). Lyrical, riveting stories of violence under the brutal Dominican dictatorship, loss, dislocation, and the experience of new immigrants in the United States. Alvarez writes with a combination of power and beauty; good work if you can get it.

W. H. Auden, "Musée des Beaux Arts" (1940), "In Praise of Limestone" (1951). The first is a meditation on human suffering, based on a Pieter Brueghel painting. The second is a great poem extolling the virtues of gentle landscapes and those of us who live there. There's a lot more great Auden where those came from.

James Baldwin, "Sonny's Blues" (1957). Heroin and jazz and sibling rivalry and promises to dead parents and grief and guilt and redemption. All in twenty pages.

Samuel Beckett, *Waiting for Godot* (1954). What if there's a road but characters don't travel it? Would that mean something?

Beowulf (eighth century A.D.). I happen to like Seamus Heaney's translation, which was published in 2000, but any translation will give you the thrill of this heroic epic.

T. Coraghessan Boyle, *Water Music* (1981), "The Overcoat II" (1985), *World's End* (1987). Savage comedy, scorching satire, astonishing narrative riffs.

Anita Brookner, *Hotel du Lac* (1984). Don't let the French title fool you; it's really in English, a lovely little novel about growing older and heartbreak and painfully bought wisdom.

Lewis Carroll, *Alice in Wonderland* (1865), *Through the Looking-Glass* (1871). Carroll may have been a mathematician in real life, but he understood the imagination and the illogic of dreams as well as any writer we've ever had. Brilliant, loopy fun.

Angela Carter, *The Bloody Chamber* (1979), *Nights at the Circus* (1984), *Wise Children* (1992). Subversiveness in narrative can be a good thing. Carter upends the expectations of patriarchal society.

Raymond Carver, "Cathedral" (1981). One of the most perfectly realized short stories ever, this is the tale of a guy who doesn't get it but learns to. This one has several of our favorite elements: blindness, communion, physical contact. Carver pretty much perfected the minimalist/realist short story, and most of his are worth a look.

Geoffrey Chaucer, *The Canterbury Tales* (1384). You'll have to read this one in a modern translation unless you've had training in Middle English, but it's wonderful in any language. Funny, heartbreaking, warm, ironic, everything a diverse group of people traveling together and telling stories are likely to be.

Joseph Conrad, *Heart of Darkness* (1899), *Lord Jim* (1900). No one looked longer or harder into the human soul than Conrad, who found truth in extreme situations and alien landscapes.

Robert Coover, "The Gingerbread House" (1969). A short, ingenious reworking of "Hansel and Gretel."

Hart Crane, *The Bridge* (1930). A great American poem sequence, centered around the Brooklyn Bridge and the great national rivers.

Colin Dexter, *The Remorseful Day* (1999). Really, any of the Morse mysteries is a good choice. Dexter is great at representing loneliness and longing in his detective, and it culminates, naturally, in heart trouble.

Charles Dickens, *The Old Curiosity Shop* (1841), *A Christmas Carol* (1843), *David Copperfield* (1850), *Bleak House* (1853), *Great Expectations* (1861). Dickens is the most humane writer you'll ever read. He believes in people, even with all their faults, and he slings a great story, with the most memorable characters you'll meet anywhere.

E. L. Doctorow, *Ragtime* (1975). Race relations and the clash of historical forces, all in a deceptively simple, almost cartoonish narrative.

Emma Donoghue, *Room* (2010). A captivity narrative told by the product of that kidnapping. Five-year-old Jack frequently doesn't understand the things he tells us about; most important, he doesn't understand that living locked inside a tiny, soundproofed room is not the norm. He also doesn't have mastery of the definite article, so the room is Room; the bed, Bed— because they are the only ones, to his knowledge, that exist. A tour de force of the use of point of view.

Lawrence Durrell, *The Alexandria Quartet* (*Justine, Balthazar, Mountolive, Clea*) (1957–60). A brilliant realization of passion, intrigue, friendship, espionage, comedy, and pathos, in some of the most seductive prose in modern fiction. What happens when Europeans go to Egypt.

T. S. Eliot, "The Love Song of J. Alfred Prufrock" (1917), *The Waste Land* (1922). Eliot more than any other person changed the face of modern poetry. Formal experimentation, spiritual searching, social commentary.

Louise Erdrich, *Love Medicine* (1986). The first of a number of novels set on a North Dakota Chippewa reservation, told as a series of linked short stories. Passion, pain, despair, hope, and courage run through all her books.

William Faulkner, *The Sound and The Fury* (1929), *As I Lay Dying* (1930), *Absalom, Absalom!* (1936). Difficult but rewarding books that mix social history, modern psychology, and classical myths in narrative styles that can come from no one else.

Helen Fielding, *Bridget Jones's Diary* (1999). A comic tale of modern womanhood, replete with dieting, dating, angst, and self-help—and an intertextual companion to Jane Austen's *Pride and Prejudice* (1813).

Henry Fielding, *Tom Jones* (1741). The original Fielding/Jones comic novel. Any book about growing up that can still be funny after more than 250 years is doing something right.

F. Scott Fitzgerald, *The Great Gatsby* (1925), "Babylon Revisited" (1931). If modern American literature consisted of only one novel, and if that novel were *Gatsby*, it might be enough. What does the green light mean? What does Gatsby's dream represent? And what about the ash heaps and the eyes on the billboard?

Ford Madox Ford, *The Good Soldier* (1915). The greatest novel about heart trouble ever written.

E. M. Forster, *A Room with a View* (1908), *Howards End* (1910), *A Passage to India* (1924). Questions of geography, north and south, west and east, the caves of consciousness.

John Fowles, *The Magus* (1966), *The French Lieutenant's Woman* (1969). Literature can be play, a game, and in Fowles it often is. In the first of these, a young egoist seems to be the audience for a series of private performances aimed at improving him. In the second, a man must choose between two women, but really between two ways of living his life. That's Fowles: always multiple levels going on. He also writes the most wonderful, evocative, seductive prose anywhere.

Robert Frost, "After Apple Picking," "The Woodpile," "Out, Out—" "Mowing" (1913–16). Read all of him. I can't imagine poetry without him.

William H. Gass, "The Pedersen Kid," "In the Heart of the Heart of the Country" (both 1968). These stories make clever use of landscape and weather and are wildly inventive—have you ever thought of high school basketball as a religious experience?

Henry Green, *Blindness* (1926), *Living* (1929), *Party Going* (1939), *Loving* (1945). The first of these really does deal with blindness in its metaphorical as well as literal meanings, and *Party Going* has travelers stranded in fog, so that's kind of like blindness. *Loving* is a kind of reworked fairy tale, beginning with "Once upon" and ending with "ever after"; who could resist. *Living,* aside from being a fabulous novel about all the classes involved with a British factory, is the only book I know in which "a," "an," and "the" hardly ever appear. It's a bizarre and wonderful stylistic experiment. Almost no one has read or even heard of Green, and that's too bad.

Dashiell Hammett, *The Maltese Falcon* (1929). The first truly mythic American detective novel. And don't miss the film version.

Thomas Hardy, "The Three Strangers" (1883), *The Mayor of Casterbridge* (1886), *Tess of the D'Urbervilles* (1891). You'll believe landscape and weather are characters after reading Hardy. You'll certainly believe that the universe is not indifferent to our suffering but takes an active hand in it.

Nathaniel Hawthorne, "Young Goodman Brown" (1835), "The Man of Adamant" (1837), *The Scarlet Letter* (1850), *The House of the Seven Gables* (1851). Hawthorne is perhaps the best American writer at exploring our symbolic consciousness, at finding the ways we displace suspicion and loneliness and envy. He just happens to use the Puritans to do it, but it's never really about Puritans.

Seamus Heaney, "Bogland" (1969), "Clearances" (1986), *North* (1975). One of our truly great poets, powerful on history and politics.

Ernest Hemingway, the stories from *In Our Time* (1925), especially "Big Two-Hearted River," "Indian Camp," and "The Battler," *The Sun Also Rises* (1926), "Hills Like White Elephants" (1927), *A Farewell to Arms* (1929), "The Snows of Kilimanjaro" (1936), *The Old Man and the Sea* (1952).

Homer, *The Iliad*, *The Odyssey* (ca. eighth century B.C.). The second of these is probably more accessible to modern readers, but they're both great. Every time I teach *The Iliad* I have students say, I had no idea this was such a great story.

Henry James, *The Turn of the Screw* (1898). Scary, scary. Is it demonic possession or madness, and if the latter, on whose part? In any case, it's about the way humans consume each other, as is, in a very different way, his "Daisy Miller" (1878).

James Joyce, *Dubliners* (1914), *Portrait of the Artist as a Young Man* (1916). First, the stories in *Dubliners*, of which I've made liberal use of two. "Araby" has so much going on in it in just a few pages: initiation, experience of the Fall, sight and blindness imagery, quest, sexual desire, generational hostility. "The Dead" is just about the most complete experience it's possible to have with a short story. Small wonder Joyce left stories behind after he wrote it: what could he do after that? As for *Portrait*, it's a great story of growth and development. Plus it has a child take a dunk in a cesspool (a "square ditch" in the parlance of the novel) and one of the most harrowing sermons ever committed to paper. Falls, rises, salvation and damnation, Oedipal conflicts, the search for self, all the things that make novels of childhood and adolescence so rewarding.

Franz Kafka, "The Metamorphosis" (1915), "A Hunger Artist" (1924), *The Trial* (1925). In the strange world of Kafka, characters are subjected to unreal occurrences that come to define and ultimately destroy them. It's much funnier than that sounds, though.

Barbara Kingsolver, *The Bean Trees* (1988), *Pigs in Heaven* (1993), *The Poisonwood Bible* (1998). Her novels resonate with the strength of primal patterns. Taylor Greer takes one of the great road trips into a new life in the first of these novels.

D. H. Lawrence, *Sons and Lovers* (1913), *Women in Love* (1920), "The Horse Dealer's Daughter" (1922), "The Fox" (1923), *Lady Chatterley's Lover* (1928), *The Virgin and the Gypsy* (1930), "The Rocking-Horse Winner" (1932). The king of symbolic thinking.

Sir Thomas Malory, *Le Morte Darthur* (late fifteenth century). Very old language, but writers and filmmakers continue to borrow from him. A great story.

Yann Martel, *Life of Pi* (2001). A boy, a tiger, a lifeboat—what more do you need? One of the more unusual versions of the hero's journey, compellingly told.

Colum McCann, *This Side of Brightness* (1998), *Let the Great World Spin* (2009). One low (the men who dug the subway tunnels under New York), one high (a disparate group of New Yorkers on the day Philippe Petit walked a high wire between the twin towers), two brilliant examples of storytelling by a master of English prose.

Iris Murdoch, *A Severed Head* (1961), *The Unicorn* (1963), *The Sea, the Sea* (1978), *The Green Knight* (1992). Murdoch's novels follow familiar literary patterns, as the title of *The Green Knight* would suggest. Her imagination is symbolic, her logic ruthlessly rational (she was a trained philosopher, after all).

Sena Jeter Naslund, *Ahab's Wife* (1999). Ever wonder what happens to those left behind by "great men"? We can debate how terrific Ahab is in *Moby-Dick*, but in one of the major feminist reenvisionings of literary works and figures, Naslund looks into the experience of the woman the crazed captain—and his creator—doesn't even grace with a name.

Vladimir Nabokov, *Lolita* (1958). Yes, that one. No, it isn't a porn novel. But it is about things we might wish didn't exist, and it does have one of literature's creepier main characters. Who thinks he's normal.

Tim O'Brien, *Going After Cacciato* (1978), *The Things They Carried* (1990). Besides being perhaps the two finest novels to come out of the Vietnam War, O'Brien's books give us lots of fodder for thought. A road trip of some eight thousand statute miles, to Paris no less, site of the peace talks. A beautiful native guide leading our white hero west. *Alice in Wonderland* parallels. Hemingway parallels. Symbolic implications enough to keep you busy for a month at your in-laws'.

Edgar Allan Poe, "The Fall of the House of Usher" (1839), "The Mystery of the Rue Morgue" (1841), "The Pit and the Pendulum" (1842), "The Tell-Tale Heart" (1843), "The Raven" (1845), "The Cask of Amontillado" (1846). Poe gives us one of the first really free plays of the subconscious in fiction. His stories (and poems, for that matter) have the logic of our nightmares, the terror of thoughts we can't suppress or control, half a century and more before Sigmund Freud. He also gives us the first real detective story ("Rue Morgue"), becoming the model for Sir Arthur Conan Doyle, Agatha Christie, Dorothy Sayers, and all who came after.

Thomas Pynchon, *The Crying of Lot 49* (1965). My students sometimes struggle with this short novel, but they're usually too serious. If you go into it knowing it's cartoonish and very much from the sixties, you'll have a great time.

Theodore Roethke, "In Praise of Prairie" (1941), *The Far Field* (1964). A great poet from—and of—the American heartland.

William Shakespeare (1564–1616). Take your pick. Here's mine: *Hamlet, Romeo and Juliet, Julius Caesar, Macbeth, King Lear, Henry V, A Midsummer Night's Dream, Much Ado About Nothing, The Tempest, A Winter's Tale, As You Like It, Twelfth Night*. And then there are the sonnets. Read all of them you can. Hey, they're only fourteen lines long. I particularly like sonnet 73, but there are lots of wonderful sonnets in there.

Mary Shelley, *Frankenstein* (1818). The monster isn't simply monstrous. He says something about his creator and about the society in which Victor Frankenstein lives.

Sir Gawain and the Green Knight (late fourteenth century). Not for beginners, I think. At least it wasn't for me when I was a beginner. Still, I learned to really enjoy young Gawain and his adventure. You might, too.

Sophocles, *Oedipus Rex, Oedipus at Colonus, Antigone* (fifth century B.C.). These plays constitute a trilogy dealing with a doomed family. The first (which is the first really great detective story in Western literature) is about blindness and vision, the second about traveling on the road and the place where all roads end, and the third a meditation on power, loyalty to the state, and personal morality. These plays, now over twenty-four hundred years old, never go out of style.

Sir Edmund Spenser, *The Faerie Queen* (1596). Spenser may take some work and a fair bit of patience. But you'll come to love the Redcrosse Knight.

Robert Louis Stevenson, *Treasure Island* (1883), *The Strange Case of Dr. Jekyll and Mr. Hyde* (1886), *The Master of Ballantrae* (1889). Stevenson does fascinating things with the possibilities of the divided self (the one with a good and an evil side), which was a subject of fascination in the nineteenth century.

Bram Stoker, *Dracula* (1897). What, you need a reason?

Dylan Thomas, "Fern Hill" (1946). A beautiful evocation of childhood/summer/life and everything that lives and dies.

Mark Twain, *The Adventures of Huckleberry Finn* (1885). Poor Huck has come under attack in recent decades, and yes, it does have that racist word in it (not surprising in a work depicting a racist society), but *Huck Finn* also has more sheer humanity than any three books I can think of. And it's one of the great road/buddy stories of all time, even if the road is soggy.

Anne Tyler, *Dinner at the Homesick Restaurant* (1982). Tyler has a number of wonderful novels, including *The Accidental Tourist* (1985), but this one really works for my money.

John Updike, "A&P" (1962). I don't really use his story when I create my quest to the grocery, but his is a great little story.

Derek Walcott, *Omeros* (1990). The exploits of a Caribbean fishing community, paralleling events from Homer's two great epics. Fascinating stuff.

Fay Weldon, *The Hearts and Lives of Men* (1988). A delightful novel, comic and sad and magical, with just the right lightness of touch.

Virginia Woolf, *Mrs. Dalloway* (1925), *To the Lighthouse* (1927). Explorations of consciousness, family dynamics, and modern life in luminous, subtle prose.

William Butler Yeats, "The Lake Isle of Innisfree" (1892), "Easter 1916" (1916), "The Wild Swans at Coole" (1917). Or any of a hundred others. A medievalist professor of mine once said that he believed Yeats was the greatest poet in the English language. If we could only have one, he'd be my choice.

Fairy Tales We Can't Live Without

"Sleeping Beauty," "Snow White," "Hansel and Gretel," "Rapunzel," "Rumpelstiltskin." See also later uses of these tales in Angela Carter and Robert Coover.

Movies to Read

Annie Hall (1977), *Manhattan* (1979), *Hannah and Her Sisters* (1986). Woody Allen has directed a film almost every year for nearly fifty years. Are they all perfect? No way. Is the body of work terrific? Absolutely. He's witty, neurotic, inventive, and always very human. See them all if you can, from the silliness of *Take the Money and Run* (1969) and *Bananas* (1971) through the late magic of *Midnight in Paris* (2011) and *To Rome with Love* (2012). If you must choose, however, see his so-called New York Trilogy, listed above, with its great portraits of women.

The Artist (2011). A black-and-white silent film with subtitles and French stars in the twenty-first century? You betcha. It doesn't hurt that the secondary stars—John Goodman, James Cromwell, Penelope Ann Miller—are American or that the real star is Uggie the Jack Russell terrier. Or that the story and acting are terrific. Director Michel Hazanavicius proves for a new generation that pure cinema can get by without dialogue, color, 3-D, or any other newfangled innovations. And we also discover that the stars' names, Jean Dujardin and Bérénice Bejo, are really fun to say.

Avatar (2009). James Cameron, the man who gave us *Titanic*, takes us to the land of the ten-foot-tall blue Na'vi in this sci-fi action fable of imperialism and environmental defilement. Its historical significance may rest on its being one of the first films to rely so comprehensively on computer-generated imagery, or CGI, although it is also a great tale of the hero's journey.

Citizen Kane (1941). I'm not sure this is a film to watch, but you sure can read it.

The Gold Rush (1925), *Modern Times* (1936). Charlie Chaplin is the greatest film comedian ever. Accept no substitutes. His little tramp is a great invention.

Notorious (1946), *North by Northwest* (1959), *Psycho* (1960). Somebody's always copying Hitchcock. Meet the original.

O Brother, Where Art Thou? (2000) Not only a reworking of *The Odyssey* but an excellent road/buddy film with a great American sound track.

Pale Rider (1985). Clint Eastwood's fullest treatment of his mythic avenging-angel hero.

Raiders of the Lost Ark (1981), *Indiana Jones and the Temple of Doom* (1984), *Indiana Jones and the Last Crusade* (1989). Great quest stories. You know when you're searching for the Lost Ark of the Covenant or the Holy Grail that you're dealing with quests. Take away Indy's leather jacket, fedora, and whip and give him chain mail, helmet, and lance and see if he doesn't look considerably like Sir Gawain.

Shane (1953). Without which, no *Pale Rider.*

Stagecoach (1939). Its handling of Native Americans doesn't wear well, but this is a great story of sin and redemption and second chances. And chase scenes.

Star Wars (1977), *The Empire Strikes Back* (1981), *Return of the Jedi* (1983). George Lucas is a great student of Joseph Campbell's theories of the hero (in, among other works, *The Hero with a Thousand Faces*), and the trilogy does a great job of showing us types of heroes and villains. If you know the Arthurian legends, so much the better. Personally I don't care if you learn anything about all that from the films or not; they're so much fun you deserve to see them. Repeatedly.

Tom Jones (1963). The Tony Richardson film starring Albert Finney—accept no substitutes. This has the one and only eating scene I've ever seen that can make me blush. The film, and Henry Fielding's eighteenth-century novel, have much to recommend them beyond that one scene. The story of the Rake's Progress—the growth and development of the bad boy—is a classic, and this one is very funny.

Secondary Sources

There are a great many books that will help you become a better reader and interpreter of literature. These suggestions are brief, arbitrary, and highly incomplete.

M. H. Abrams, *A Glossary of Literary Terms* (1957). As the name suggests, this is not a book to read but one to refer to. Abrams covers hundreds of literary terms, movements, and concepts, and the book has been a standard for decades.

John Ciardi, *How Does a Poem Mean?* (1961). Since it first appeared, Ciardi's book has taught tens of thousands of us how to think about the special way poems convey what they have to say. As a poet himself and a translator of Dante, he knew something about the subject.

E. M. Forster, *Aspects of the Novel.* Although it was published in 1927, this book remains a great discussion of the novel and its constituent elements by one of its outstanding practitioners.

Northrop Frye, *Anatomy of Criticism* (1957). You've been getting watered-down Frye throughout this book. You might find the original interesting. Frye is one of the first critics to conceive of literature as a single, organically related whole, with an overarching framework by which we can understand it. Even when you don't agree with him, he's a fascinating, humane thinker.

William H. Gass, *Fiction and the Figures of Life* (1970). Another primarily theoretical work, this book discusses how we work on fiction and how it works on us. Gass introduces the term "metafiction" here.

Edward Hirsch, *How to Read a Poem and Fall in Love with Poetry* (2000). The former American poet laureate can make you want to fall in love with poetry even if you didn't know you wanted to. He also provides valuable insights into understanding poetry.

David Lodge, *The Art of Fiction* (1992). Lodge, an important postmodern British novelist and critic, wrote the essays in this collection in a newspaper column. They're fascinating, brief, easy to comprehend, and filled with really fine illustrative examples.

Princeton Encyclopedia of Poetry and Poetics. Another important reference book. If you want to know something about poetry, look in here.

Francine Prose, *Reading Like a Writer* (2006). Excellent recommendations on what and how to read for aspiring writers—and readers who would understand them.

Master Class

If you want to put together the total reading experience, here you go. These works will give you a chance to use all your newfound skills and come up with inventive and insightful ways of seeing them. Once you learn what these four novels can teach you, you won't need more advice. There's nothing exclusive to these four, by the way. Any of perhaps a hundred novels, long poems, and plays could let you apply the whole panoply of newly acquired skills. I just happen to love these.

Charles Dickens, *Great Expectations* (1861). Life, death, love, hate, dashed hopes, revenge, bitterness, redemption, suffering, graveyards, fens, scary lawyers, criminals, crazy old women, cadaverous wedding cakes. This book has everything except spontaneous human combustion (that's in *Bleak House*—really). Now, how can you not read it?

James Joyce, *Ulysses* (1922). Don't get me started. First, the obvious: *Ulysses* is not for beginners. When you feel you've become a graduate reader, go there. My undergraduates get through it, but they struggle, even with a good deal of help. Hey, it's difficult. On the other hand, I feel, as do a lot of folks, that it's the most rewarding read there is.

Gabriel García Márquez, *One Hundred Years of Solitude* (1970). This novel should have a label: "Warning: Symbolism spoken here." One character survives both the firing squad and a suicide attempt, and he fathers seventeen sons by seventeen women, all the sons bearing his name and all killed by his enemies on a single night. Do you think that means something?

Toni Morrison, *Song of Solomon* (1977). I've said so much throughout this book, there's really nothing left, except read it.

Acknowledgments

I t is impossible to thank individually all the students who have had a hand in creating this book, and yet it couldn't have come into being without them. Their constant prompting, doubting, questioning, answering, suggesting, and responding drove me to figure out most of the ideas and observations that have gone into these essays. Their patience with my wacky notions is often astonishing, their willingness to try on difficult ideas and perplexing works gratifying. For every routine comment or piercing query, every bright idea or dull-eyed stare, every wisecrack of theirs or groan at one of mine, every laugh or snarl, every statement praising or dismissing a literary work, I am profoundly grateful. They never let me rest or become complacent. Several students in particular have had a hand in the development of this book, and I wish to single them out for special thanks. Monica Mann's smart-aleck comment pointed out to me that I have quite a number of little aphorisms about literature, although even then it took several years for me to see the possibilities in the "Quotations of Chairman Tom," as she called them. Mary Ann Halboth has listened to and commented on much of what became the material of this study, often pushing my ideas well beyond my initial conceptions. Kelly Tobeler and Diane Saylor agreed to be guinea pigs for certain experiments and offered insightful, amazing interpretations of the Katherine Mansfield story; their contributions made my final chapter immeasurably better.

I am deeply indebted to numerous colleagues for their assistance, insight, encouragement, and patience. I especially wish to thank Professors Frederic Svoboda, Stephen Bernstein, Mary Jo Kietzman, and Jan Furman, who read drafts, provided ideas and information, listened to my complaints and obsessions, and offered support and wisdom. Their intelligence, good humor, and generosity have made my efforts lighter and the product greatly improved. To have such brilliant and dedicated colleagues is a genuine gift. They make me sound much smarter than I am. The errors, however, are purely my own.

To my agent, Faith Hamlin, and my editor at HarperCollins throughout this revision, Michael Signorelli, many thanks for their belief in the work, as well as for their many constructive criticisms and suggestions.

As ever, I wish to thank my family for their support, patience, and love. My sons Robert and Nathan read chapters, contributed interpretations, and gave me firsthand insights into the student mind. My wife, Brenda, took care of worldly and mundane tasks and made it possible for me to lose myself in the writing. To all three I offer my immense gratitude and love.

And finally I wish to thank my muse. After all these years of reading and writing, I still don't understand where inspiration comes from, but I am profoundly grateful that it keeps coming.